Grammar and Writing 5

Teacher Guide

Answer Keys and Tests

Second Edition

Christie Curtis

Mary Hake

Houghton Mifflin Harcourt Publishers, Inc.

Grammar and Writing 5

Second Edition

Teacher Guide
Answer Keys and Tests

Copyright © 2014 by Houghton Mifflin Harcourt Publishing Company and Mary E. Hake and Christie Curtis

All rights reserved. No part of this work may be reproduced or transmitted in any form or by any means, electronic or mechanical, including photocopying or recording, or by any information storage and retrieval system, without the prior written permission of the copyright owner unless such copying is expressly permitted by federal copyright law. Requests for permission to make copies of any part of the work should be addressed to Houghton Mifflin Harcourt Publishing Company, Attn: Contracts, Copyrights, and Licensing, 9400 Southpark Center Loop, Orlando, Florida 32819-8647.

This edition is based on the work titled *Grammar and Writing 5* © 2006 by Mary E. Hake and Christie Curtis and originally published by Hake Publishing.

Printed in the U.S.A.

ISBN 978-0-5440-4425-8

1 2 3 4 5 6 7 8 9 10 XXXX 22 21 20 19 18 17 16 15 14 13

4500000000   B C D E F G

If you have received these materials as examination copies free of charge, Houghton Mifflin Harcourt Publishing Company retains title to the materials and they may not be resold. Resale of examination copies is strictly prohibited.

Possession of this publication in print format does not entitle users to convert this publication, or any portion of it, into electronic format.

Contents

Fifth Grade Grammar and Writing Schedule   v
Textbook Topical Table of Contents   vii
Student Workbook Writing Lessons Answer Key   1
Student Edition Practice and Review Set Answer Key   6
Tests Answer Key   113
Student Workbook More Practice Answer Key
    Lesson 4   157
    Lesson 8   158
    Lesson 12   159
    Corny Chronicle #1   160
    Lesson 15   161
    Lesson 25   162
    Lesson 26   163
    Lesson 38   164
    Corny Chronicle #2   165
    Lesson 40   166
    Lesson 43   167
    Lesson 47   168
    Lesson 49   169
    Lesson 50   170
    Corny Chronicle #3   171
    Lesson 57   172
    Lesson 59   173
    Lesson 60   174
    Lesson 67   175
    Lesson 73   176
    Lesson 74   177
    Lesson 76   178
    Lesson 80   179
    Lesson 81   180
    Lesson 84   181
    Lesson 85   182
    Lesson 86   184
    Lesson 87   186
    Lesson 101   188
    Lesson 103   189
    Lesson 109   190
Tests   191

Fifth Grade Grammar & Writing Schedule

School Day	Grammar Lesson	Writing Lesson	School Day	Grammar Lesson	Writing Lesson	School Day	Grammar Lesson	Writing Lesson
1	1		49	test 7	9	97		22
2	2		50	41		98		23
3	3		51	42		99	76	
4	4		52	43		100	77	
5	5		53	44		101	78	
6	6		54	45		102	79	
7	7		55	test 8	10	103	80	
8	8		56	46		104	test 15	24
9	9		57	47		105		25
10	10		58	48		106		26
11	test 1	1	59	49		107		
12	11		60	50		108	81	
13	12		61	test 9	11	109	82	
14	13		62		12	110	83	
15	14		63	51		111	84	
16	15		64	52		112	85	
17	test 2	2	65	53		113	test 16	27
18		3	66	54		114	86	
19		4	67	55		115	87	
20	16		68	test 10	13	116	88	
21	17		69	56		117	89	
22	18		70	57		118	90	
23	19		71	58		119	test 17	28
24	20		72	59		120		29
25	test 3	5	73	60		121		30
26	21		74	test 11	14	122	91	
27	22		75		15	123	92	
28	23		76		16	124	93	
29	24		77	61		125	94	
30	25		78	62		126	95	
31	test 4	6	79	63		127	test 18	31
32	26		80	64		128	96	
33	27		81	65		129	97	
34	28		82	test 12	17	130	98	
35	29		83	66		131	99	
36	30		84	67		132	100	
37	test 5	7	85	68		133	test 19	32
38	31		86	69		134	101	
39	32		87	70		135	102	
40	33		88	test 13	18	136	103	
41	34		89		19	137	104	
42	35		90		20	138	105	
43	test 6	8	91	71		139	test 20	33
44	36		92	72		140	106	
45	37		93	73		141	107	
46	38		94	74		142	108	
47	39		95	75		143	109	
48	40		96	test 14	21	144	110...	

Writing Lessons 34–38 may be completed on the remainder of your school days.

Grammar and Writing 5   **Teacher Guide** Grammar and Writing Schedule

Topical Table of Contents

Lesson Number

Capitalization

Proper Nouns	8
First Word of a Sentence	15
The Pronoun *I*	15
First Word in a Line of Poetry	15
Titles	25
Outlines	26
Direct Quotations	26
People Titles	38
Family Words	38
School Subjects	38
Areas of the Country	41
Religions, Bible, Deity	41
Greeting and Closing of a Letter	41
No Capital Letter	43

Punctuation

The Period	47, 50
The Comma	57, 59, 60, 63, 67, 68, 74, 76
Quotation Marks	80, 81
Italics or Underline	84
The Exclamation Mark	88
The Question Mark	88
The Hyphen	94, 97, 99
The Semicolon	103
The Colon	105
The Apostrophe	108, 109

Lesson Number

Sentence Structure

Two Parts	1
Four Types of Sentences	2
Complete Sentences, Fragments, Run-on Sentences	5, 6, 23, 24
Simple Subject/Simple Predicate	3, 4
Compound Subjects and Predicates	49
Direct Objects	37
Phrases and Clauses	36
The Prepositional Phrase	44, 45, 106
Indirect Objects	46
The Predicate Nominative	51
The Predicate Adjective	54
Appositives	58
The Compound Sentence	75
Dependent and Independent Clauses	73
The Complex Sentence	110
The Compound-Complex Sentence	110

Eight Parts of Speech

Verbs

Action Verbs	7
Helping Verbs	12
Linking Verbs	31
Past, Present, and Future Tenses	9, 10, 14
Four Principal Parts	19
Irregular Verbs	18, 65, 85, 86, 87

Nouns

Common/Proper	8
Concrete/Abstract, Collective	11
Singular, Plural	13, 16, 17, 22
Compound	13
Possessive	13
Case	52, 53

Lesson Number

Pronouns

Pronouns and Antecedents	62
Personal Pronouns	64
Nominative Case	66, 70
Objective Case	69, 70
Possessive Case	70, 72
Case Chart	70
Relative Pronouns	77
Interrogative Pronouns	79
Demonstrative Pronouns	82
Indefinite Pronouns	83

Adjectives

Descriptive Adjectives	39
Proper Adjectives	42
Limiting Adjectives	40
Comparison Adjectives	55
Irregular Comparison Adjectives	56

Prepositions   20, 21

Adverbs

Adverbs That Tell "How"	95
Adverbs That Tell "Where"	98
Adverbs That Tell "When"	100
Adverbs That Tell "How Much"	101
Comparison Adverbs	102

Conjunctions

Coordinating	48
Subordinating	73

Interjections   112

Lesson Number

Usage

Pronouns	78
Subject-Verb Agreement	89, 90, 91, 92
Negatives	93
Adverbs	102, 104
Prepositions	107
Overused Adjectives	61
Active or Passive Voice	111

Spelling Rules

Silent Letters *k, g, w, t, d,* and *c*	28
Silent Letters *p, b, l, u, h, n,* and *gh*	29
Suffixes	33, 34
ie or *ei*	35
Dictionary Information About a Word	27, 30

Diagramming

Subject–Verb–Direct Object	32, 37
Complements	51, 54
Modifiers	40, 98
Appositives	58
Indirect Objects	46
Word Groups as Modifiers	45, 106
Compound Constructions	49, 75

Student Workbook Writing Lessons Answer Key

WRITING LESSON 1   The Sentence

a. My neighbor Jalana has a vegetable garden.

b. She grows squash, tomatoes, and beans.

c. That ripe tomato will taste delicious.

d. The question confused them.

e. The loud noise had startled Max.

f. A dump truck made the loud noise.

WRITING LESSON 2   The Paragraph

a. <u>Peter is an artist!</u>

b. <u>People call Michigan the Great Lake State for good reasons.</u>

c. <u>Last night's windstorm made a big mess.</u>

d. ~~My cousin rides horses.~~

e. ~~My friend Jenny used to live on an island.~~

f. ~~Lemons and oranges are citrus fruits.~~

g. That bright star is far away.

h. We can identify stars and planets.

i. Saturn's rings fascinated Jo.

j. Most people appreciate Sergio's humor.

WRITING LESSON 3   The Paragraph, Part 2

a. 3, 4, 1, 2

b. *Each student will write his or her paragraph on the lines provided or on a separate sheet of paper that can be turned in to the teacher.*

c. <u>The Gem State is a fitting nickname for Idaho.</u>

d. ~~Nancy's house is yellow with white trim.~~

e. June has short, curly hair. (or) June's hair is short and curly.

f. Eagles soar and land in high places.

g. Rufus's barking distracted Debby.

h. All the tourists can see the magnificent statue.

WRITING LESSON 4   The Paragraph, Part 3

a. 3, 5, 1, 4, 2

b. *Students' questions will vary. Each student will write his or her paragraph on the lines provided or on a separate sheet of paper that can be turned in to the teacher.*

c. <u>Andrew collects seashells.</u>

d. ~~Elle has a hamster named Trina.~~

e. Elle has a neat, clean desk.

f. We drove through Colorado, Kansas, and Missouri.

g. The gift surprised me.

h. Rufus might frighten Max's cat.

Additional Practice: *Each student will write his or her paragraph on a sheet of paper.*

WRITING LESSON 5   The Essay: Three Main Parts

a. 1, 4, 3, 2

b. *Students' paragraphs will vary.*

c. <u>The Austrian Franz Schubert became a famous music composer.</u>

d. ~~Ting has a bird and two fish.~~

e. Juan has a huge, long-haired cat.

f. Ms. Hoo has lived in North Dakota, Minnesota, and New York.

g. The dog's barking might have startled the horse.

h. Schubert composed that waltz.

i. Introductory Paragraph
Body Paragraph
Body Paragraph
Body Paragraph
Concluding Paragraph

WRITING LESSON 6 — The Essay: Introductory Paragraph

a. Three of the most famous German composers are Johann Sebastian Bach, Felix Mendelssohn, and Robert Schumann.

b. 1, 3, 4, 2

c. *Students' paragraphs will vary.*

d. This spring I shall plant a vegetable garden.

e. ~~Mr. Shade wears red tennis shoes.~~

f. The Komodo dragon has a long, forked tongue.

g. My classmate Juan plays the violin and the cello.

h. Aunt Steph baked that apple pie.

i. Introductory Paragraph
   1. Introductory sentence
   2. Thesis statement
Body Paragraph
Body Paragraph
Body Paragraph
Concluding Paragraph

WRITING LESSON 7 — The Essay: Body Paragraph

a. *Students may use the lines provided or a separate sheet of paper to be handed to the teacher.*

b. *See student work.*

c. I like the desert's creatures, the wide-open space, and the hot temperatures.

d. 2, 1, 4, 3

e. Alaska is the source of many products that people in other states enjoy.

f. ~~Daniela collects postage stamps.~~

g. The hens laid six big brown eggs.

h. My cousin John plays the guitar.

i. Ron and Susan peel the potatoes.

j. *See chart showing structure of typical five-paragraph essay on page 26 in the Student Workbook.*

WRITING LESSON 8 — The Essay: Concluding Paragraph

a. *Students may use the lines provided or a separate sheet of paper.*

b. I would like to improve my study skills, my nutrition, and my sleeping habits.

c. 2, 4, 1, 3

d. Norman feels irritable today.

e. ~~Pigeons come in many colors.~~

f. Dr. Ledfoot drives a small red truck.

g. Lucy has straight brown hair.

h. Machines assemble these toys.

i. Introductory Paragraph
   1. Introductory sentence
   2. Thesis statement
Body Paragraph
   Topic sentence
   1. Supporting sentence
   2. Supporting sentence
   3. Supporting sentence
Body Paragraph
   Topic sentence
   1. Supporting sentence
   2. Supporting sentence
   3. Supporting sentence
Body Paragraph
   Topic sentence
   1. Supporting sentence
   2. Supporting sentence
   3. Supporting sentence
Concluding Paragraph
   1. Restatement of thesis
   2. Reference to each topic sentence
   3. Clincher sentence

WRITING LESSON 9 — The Essay: Transitions

a. <u>also</u>
b. <u>Besides that</u>
c. <u>therefore</u>
d. <u>I believe that we should keep the pigeons because of their beauty, their friendliness, and their pleasant cooing sounds.</u>
e. 2, 1, 3, 4
f. <u>James loves to photograph wildlife.</u>
g. ~~Denver is the capital of Colorado.~~
h. Ted wrote a long, funny essay.
i. Gia has a turtle named Oliver.
j. Moths destroyed my wool coat.
k. *See chart showing structure of typical five-paragraph essay in the Student Workbook.*

WRITING LESSON 10 — Brainstorming for Ideas

Students may use the lines provided or a separate sheet of paper to be handed to the teacher.

a. <u>Furthermore</u>
b. <u>on the other hand</u>
c. <u>similarly</u>
d. <u>Kurt is learning to sketch animals.</u>
e. ~~Corn grows in Iowa.~~
f. The finch had a red head and a black beak.
g. Ms. Hoo is wearing large, round sunglasses.
h. The young artist sketched various reptiles.
i. *See chart showing structure of typical five-paragraph essay.*

WRITING LESSON 11 — Writing a Complete Essay

See student work.

WRITING LESSON 12 — Evaluating Your Essay

See student work.

Note: Some teachers will prefer that their students use a 1-5 number scale instead of yes/no on the evaluation forms.

Example:
5 = excellent
4 = good
3 = satisfactory
2 = needs improvement
1 = poor

When the student can write a 4 or 5 on each blank, then his or her essay is complete.

WRITING LESSON 13 — Supporting a Topic Sentence with Experiences, Examples, Facts, and Opinions

a. *Students may use the lines provided or a separate sheet of paper to be handed to the teacher.*
b. <u>First</u>
c. <u>as a result</u>
d. <u>Therefore</u>
e. <u>Nels captures the attention of many creatures at the lake.</u>
f. ~~Caribou roam the plains of Alaska.~~
g. Tyrell wrote me a long, newsy letter.
h. The hungry black bears eat fish and wild berries.
i. Nels fed the turtles.
j. *See chart showing structure of typical five-paragraph essay.*

WRITING LESSON 17 Writing a Strong Thesis Statement
Developing an Outline

Outlines will vary. Sample outline is provided.

Sports

    I.   Basketball
         A. Forward
         B. Hoop
         C. Traveling
         D. Layup
         E. Dribble
         F. Free throw
    II. Volleyball
         A. Jump serve
         B. Dig
         C. Set
         D. Spike
         E. Bump pass
         F. Server
    III. Baseball
         A. Pitcher
         B. Diamond
         C. Mitt
         D. Bat
         E. Shortstop
         F. Home run
         G. Catcher
         H. Bunt

WRITING LESSON 32 Writing in Response to Literature

1. The author writes the selection to entertain.
2. The effect of beginning the selection with a storm is to establish a mood of suspense.
3. The descriptions appeal to the sense of hearing. The author uses words such as *groan, crack, splitting sound, tearing*, and *crashing*.
4. Answers will vary. Suggested: The theme of the selection is that animals possess an understanding that humans lack.
5. The next time the master is caught in a storm with Beauty, he will probably trust Beauty's instincts.

WRITING LESSON 33 — Writing in Response to Informational Text

1. Newton and Halley were both scientists.
2. *Verify* means "confirm" in this selection.
3. The comet was named after Halley because he correctly predicted the comet would return in 1758.
4. Answers will vary. Suggested: Halley's Comet is named after Edmund Halley, who used scientific theories to predict the comet's appearance every 76 years.

WRITING LESSON 38 — Idioms and Proverbs

Answers for idioms and proverbs will vary. Accept all reasonable answers.

Idioms:
1. lose your sanity
2. new person in a social group
3. give your opinion or contribution to conversation
4. cause laughter
5. encounter
6. in a habit

Proverbs:
1. People who are similar gather in groups.
2. Things cannot change their very nature.
3. Work done now may save time later.
4. Good-looking things may not be valuable.
5. Physical beauty does not compare with inner beauty, which is more lasting.
6. Every bad situation has something good in it.

Student Edition Practice and Review Set Answer Key

LESSON 1 — The Sentence: Two Parts

Practice 1

a. The United States

b. The city of Montgomery

c. measures 52,432 square miles

d. comprises 50,750 square miles

e. Water | covers 1673 square miles in Alabama.

f. Tyrell and Marisol | live in Alabama.

g. essential

h. nonessential

Review Set 1

1. essential
2. Nonessential
3. essential
4. two
5. subject
6. predicate
7. sentence
8. predicate
9. Farmers
10. Poultry and eggs
11. Lumber and wood products
12. Alabama's flag
13. resembles a Confederate Battle Flag
14. is the yellowhammer
15. belongs to the woodpecker family
16. border Alabama
17. Booker T. Washington | founded a school in Tuskegee, Alabama.
18. Boll weevils | destroyed a cotton crop!
19. George Washington Carver | experimented with peanuts and other crops.
20. Julian | made a peanut butter pie.
21. Sweet potato pie | is my favorite.
22. Tyrone's chickens | laid two dozen eggs!
23. His rooster | crows too early.
24. Miss Snoot | complains.
25. She | wakes in a bad mood.

LESSON 2 — Four Types of Sentences

Practice 2

a. interrogative

b. exclamatory

c. declarative

d. imperative

e. synonyms

f. antonyms

Review Set 2

1. Essential
2. antonym
3. declarative
4. interrogative
5. imperative
6. exclamatory
7. period
8. subject
9. predicate
10. capital
11. question mark
12. exclamation point
13. declarative
14. exclamatory
15. interrogative

16. declarative
17. imperative
18. The willow ptarmigan
19. seafood
20. Moose and brown bears
21. The economy
22. Petroleum and natural gas
23. adopted a state flag in 1959
24. represents the sky, the sea, the lakes, and the wildflowers
25. contains seven stars
26. connect Juneau to the rest of the world
27. The salmon swam upstream.
28. Where is Mount McKinley?
29. Alaska's motto | is "North to the Future."
30. People | rushed to the goldfields.

LESSON 3 Simple Subjects • Simple Predicates

Practice 3

a. caves
b. states
c. roadrunner
d. raise
e. displays
f. formed
g. scarce
h. abundant

Review Set 3

1. subject
2. subject
3. predicate
4. verb
5. subject
6. Nonessential
7. plentiful
8. synonyms
9. antonyms
10. Antonyms
11. Mount McKinley
12. United States
13. Mount Katmai
14. glacier
15. live
16. lies
17. are blooming
18. has been following
19. Prospectors discovered gold.
20. Why is Wyatt Earp famous?
21. Look out for the snake!
22. Watch where you step.
23. imperative
24. interrogative
25. declarative
26. exclamatory
27. The river | eroded the soil.
28. Many tourists | have walked through this ghost town.
29. Coyotes | are howling at the moon.
30. Spanish explorers | were searching for "Cities of Gold."

LESSON 4 Reversed Subject and Predicate Split Predicate

Practice 4

a. pessimism
b. optimism

c. ladybugs
d. gopher
e. Have migrated
f. Did Hear

More Practice 4   *See answers on page 157. Teachers: "More Practice" is optional. Some students will need it; others will not.*

Review Set 4

1. predicate
2. subject
3. verb
4. action
5. sentence
6. essential
7. Scarce
8. antonyms
9. synonyms
10. Synonyms
11. Arkansans
12. mockingbird
13. blossoms
14. William J. Clinton
15. agriculture
16. turkeys
17. Do grow
18. wandered
19. Did catch
20. balances
21. will arrive
22. chugged
23. imperative
24. interrogative
25. declarative
26. exclamatory
27. Can turkeys fly?
28. My uncle | found a diamond in Arkansas.
29. Laborers | are harvesting cotton and rice.
30. The Mississippi River | divides Arkansas and Mississippi.

LESSON 5   **Complete Sentence or Sentence Fragment?**

Practice 5

a. complete sentence
b. sentence fragment
c. sentence fragment
d. complete sentence
e. There
f. Their
g. homophones

More Practice 5   *(optional)*

1. sentence fragment
2. complete sentence
3. complete sentence
4. sentence fragment
5. sentence fragment
6. sentence fragment

Review Set 5

1. predicate
2. fragment
3. predicate
4. subject
5. predicate
6. homophones
7. there
8. pessimism

9. abundant
10. synonyms
11. complete sentence
12. sentence fragment
13. complete sentence
14. sentence fragment
15. sentence fragment
16. sentence fragment
17. complete sentence
18. complete sentence
19. California
20. forty-niners
21. you
22. Does have
23. came
24. Have climbed
25. exclamatory
26. declarative
27. imperative
28. interrogative
29. Who burned the toast?
30. California | has the tallest and oldest trees in the world.

LESSON 6 Correcting a Sentence Fragment

Practice 6

a. I found a big silver nugget.
b. An enormous dinosaur once lived here.
c. My best friend laughs at my jokes.
d. The tiger was sharpening its claws.
e. It's
f. its

More Practice 6

1. A mean-looking, bearded pirate guards the treasure.
2. A box of gold coins lies in a cave.
3. I would like to find the coins.
4. My friend and I searched the cave.
5. A bear makes its home in the cave.

Review Set 6

1. their
2. optimism
3. scarce
4. antonyms
5. Essential
6. it's
7. interrogative
8. predicate
9. action
10. exclamatory
11. sentence fragment
12. complete sentence
13. sentence fragment
14. complete sentence
15. We plan to hike to Pike's Peak.
16. My favorite place in the whole world is Rocky Mountain National Park in Colorado.
17. Cattle are grazing in the meadow.
18. Two bald eagles landed on the mountaintop.
19. snow
20. falcon
21. miners
22. fell
23. sits

24. Did find
25. declarative
26. interrogative
27. imperative
28. exclamatory
29. Ranchers irrigate their fields.
30. Bighorn sheep | dot Colorado's slopes.

LESSON 7 Action Verbs

Practice 7

a. influenced
b. spotted, admired
c. named
d. conceal
e. disclose

Review Set 7

1. disclose
2. its
3. their
4. Pessimism
5. abundant
6. visited
7. manufacture
8. included
9. clucked, scratched
10. breached, blew
11. sentence fragment
12. sentence fragment
13. complete sentence
14. complete sentence
15. A noisy helicopter landed on the beach.
16. I hope to see the Statue of Liberty.
17. A delicious snack food is an apple.
18. Dad was photographing Niagara Falls.
19. products
20. roses
21. lobster
22. contribute
23. Are blooming
24. is
25. exclamatory
26. interrogative
27. declarative
28. imperative
29. The lobster pinched me!
30. Lobster | flourishes off the coast of Connecticut.

LESSON 8 Capitalizing Proper Nouns

Practice 8

a. The Dutch formed a whaling colony in 1631.
b. They named the colony Lewes.
c. Let's read the book *Hans Brinker or the Silver Skates*.
d. The capital city of Delaware is Dover.
e. In 1609, Henry Hudson sailed into Delaware Bay.
f. geo-
g. geography
h. Geology

More Practice 8 *See answers on page 158.*

Review Set 8

1. Earth
2. conceal

3. it's
4. their
5. scarce
6. Noxingtown Pond
7. Lynne Reid Banks, *The Indian in the Cupboard*
8. French, Delaware
9. tiptoes, makes
10. Have nibbled
11. sentence fragment
12. complete sentence
13. sentence fragment
14. complete sentence
15. Migrating ducks and geese are quacking and honking.
16. The peach blossoms smell heavenly.
17. Katy learned to play the trombone.
18. A blue hen from Delaware laid an egg.
19. cabins
20. salamander
21. geese
22. were built
23. swam
24. Are resting
25. imperative
26. declarative
27. interrogative
28. exclamatory
29. Do oranges grow in Delaware?
30. Delaware | was the first state in the union.

LESSON 9 Present Tense of Verbs

Practice 9

a. archipelago
b. estuary
c. washes
d. wishes
e. replies
f. tries

Review Set 9

1. river
2. geography
3. uncover
4. it's
5. Their
6. Friday, Kennedy Space Center
7. catches
8. flies
9. flock
10. opens, snaps
11. sentence fragment
12. sentence fragment
13. complete sentence
14. sentence fragment
15. A crocodile in the Everglades chased a turtle.
16. Laborers were picking bushels of juicy oranges.
17. Would you like to vacation in the Sunshine State?
18. An aggressive, grayish-brown mockingbird attacked a cat!
19. Juan Ponce de León
20. panthers
21. crocodile
22. claimed

23. Do live
24. crawled
25. imperative
26. exclamatory
27. interrogative
28. declarative
29. Drink plenty of water.
30. My friend from Michigan | enjoys Florida's warm winters.

LESSON 10 — Past Tense of Regular Verbs

Practice 10

a. fauna
b. flora
c. clapped
d. buried
e. dropped
f. raced
g. dried
h. hiked
i. dipped
j. stepped
k. escaped
l. swallowed

Review Set 10

1. bird
2. archipelago
3. geology
4. hide
5. its
6. Florida's, Tallahassee, Maclay Gardens
7. hisses
8. fries
9. putt, chip, drive
10. squeezed, drank
11. sentence fragment
12. sentence fragment
13. complete sentence
14. complete sentence
15. Bumper-to-bumper traffic on the highway slowed our progress.
16. Someone is growing large, delicious peaches.
17. My dog Rover is the friendliest animal of all.
18. Would you like to become the President of the United States?
19. gin
20. otter
21. parade
22. Does separate
23. dove
24. comes
25. chatted
26. picked
27. a. clipped
    b. tried
    c. chatted
    d. denied
28. declarative
29. Jimmy Carter came from Georgia
30. Mills in Georgia | make paper from trees.

LESSON 11 — Concrete, Abstract, and Collective Nouns

Practice 11

a. isthmus

b. peninsula

c. concrete

d. abstract

e. abstract

f. concrete

g. bushel

h. colony

More Practice 11

1. abstract
2. concrete
3. concrete
4. abstract
5. concrete
6. abstract
7. abstract
8. concrete
9. concrete
10. concrete
11. concrete
12. abstract
13. class, collection
14. school, fleet
15. swarm, assortment

Review Set 11

1. weed
2. estuary
3. Earth
4. antonyms
5. it's
6. Gulf of Mexico, Hurricane Rita
7. kisses
8. flies
9. depicts
10. lived, worked
11. sentence fragment
12. complete sentence
13. sentence fragment
14. complete sentence
15. An aggressive alligator in the Okefenokee swamp opens its mouth.
16. We need to protect endangered animals.
17. a. concrete
    b. abstract
    c. concrete
    d. abstract
18. gaggle
19. Daniel Boone
20. stallion
21. Secretariat
22. led
23. Did race
24. goes
25. named
26. baked
27. a. chopped
    b. fried
    c. pitted
    d. replied
28. exclamatory
29. That cave is deep!
30. Georgia's nickname, the Empire State of the South,| refers to its size and wealth.

LESSON 12   Helping Verbs

Practice 12

a. is, am, are, was, were, be, being, been, has, have, had, may, might, must, can, could, do, does, did, shall, will, should, would

b. (must)(have)(been) harvesting

c. (should)(have) called

d. (could)(have) helped

e. (shall) volunteer

f. strait

g. lagoon

More Practice 12 *See answers on page 159.*

Review Set 12

1. peninsula
2. flora
3. islands
4. geo-
5. disclose
6. tapped
7. turned
8. Rosalba, University, Hawaii, Manoa
9. tries
10. misses
11. paddled
12. exports, imports
13. is, am, are, was, were, be, being, been, has, have, had, may, might, must, can, could, do, does, did, shall, will, should, would
14. (will)(be) surfing
15. (should)(have) seen
16. sentence fragment
17. complete sentence
18. complete sentence
19. sentence fragment
20. My favorite summertime activities are swimming and reading.

21. a. concrete
    b. abstract
    c. abstract
    d. concrete
22. pod, team
23. volcano
24. goose
25. is
26. flew
27. a. jogged
    b. relied
    c. mopped
    d. dried
28. exclamatory
29. The Hawaiian alphabet has twelve letters.
30. My cousin on Maui | has planted a macadamia nut tree.

LESSON 13 Singular, Plural, Compound, and Possessive Nouns

Practice 13

a. plural
b. singular
c. singular
d. plural
e. son-in-law, check mark, doorknob
f. Idaho's
g. collectors'
h. delta
i. tributary

More Practice 13 *See "Corny Chronicle #1" on page 160. Answers will vary.*

Review Set 13

1. water
2. water

3. fauna
4. estuary
5. Nonessential
6. rubbed
7. walked
8. plural
9. Shoshone, Sacagawea, Lewis, Clark, Bitterroot Range
10. hurries
11. brushes
12. leaps, digs, chases
13. is, am, are, was, were, be, being, been, has, have, had, may, might, must, can, could, do, does, did, shall, will, should, would
14. (was) built
15. (might) ride
16. complete sentence
17. sentence fragment
18. warm-up, trailblazer, pathfinder,
19. Idaho's
20. I would like to pick bing cherries near Boise, Idaho.
21. a. concrete
    b. abstract
    c. abstract
    d. concrete
22. crop
23. mountains
24. Ms. Galindo
25. are
26. Has been skiing
27. a. slipped
    b. hurried
    c. scrubbed
    d. replied
28. interrogative
29. Eat your green vegetables
30. A band of mountain men | have been telling tall tales.

LESSON 14 — Future Tense

Practice 14

a. present
b. future
c. future
d. past
e. telephoned
f. will prove
g. talks
h. will
i. shall
j. will
k. shall
l. meridian
m. hemisphere

Review Set 14

1. tributary
2. lagoon
3. land
4. Fauna
5. Earth's
6. carried
7. shall
8. singular
9. Florida, Atlantic Ocean, Gulf of Mexico
10. worries
11. rushes
12. shuffles, dart

13. is, am, are, was, were, be, being, been, has, have, had, may, might, must, can, could, do, does, did, shall, will, should, would
14. (had) perfected
15. past tense
16. sentence fragment
17. complete sentence
18. place mat, cookbook
19. state's
20. We should be eating more fresh fruits and vegetables.
21. a. concrete
    b. abstract
    c. concrete
    d. abstract
22. crew
23. hero
24. shall pull
25. can buy
26. May borrow
27. a. dipped
    b. married
    c. rubbed
    d. buried
28. declarative
29. Shall we plow the field?
30. The Great Chicago Fire | destroyed much of the city in 1871.

LESSON 15 Capitalization: Sentence, Pronoun *I*, Poetry

Practice 15

a. In, March, I, Indianapolis, Indiana
b. Listen, Of, Paul Revere, On, April, Hardly, Who
c. The, Ohio River, Indiana
d. longitude
e. latitude

More Practice 15 *See answers on page 161.*

Review Set 15

1. meridian
2. stream
3. pond
4. isthmus
5. antonym
6. worked, their
7. shall, there
8. plural
9. The Isthmus of Panama connects North America with South America.
10. carries
11. polishes
12. sailed, crossed
13. where
14. (has) (been) playing
15. future tense
16. sentence fragment
17. complete sentence
18. playground, footprint
19. Longfellow's, Paul Revere's
20. I would love to ride a galloping horse.
21. a. abstract
    b. concrete
    c. concrete
    d. abstract
22. drove
23. residents
24. shall bake
25. work

26. Birds of a feather flock together,
    And so will pigs and swine;
    Rats and mice will have their choice,
    And so will I have mine.

27. a. hugged
    b. skipped
    c. hopped
    d. bullied

28. imperative

29. Abe Lincoln's log cabin is in Indiana.

30. John Chapman | planted apple trees from Pennsylvania to Illinois.

LESSON 16 Irregular Plural Nouns, Part 1

Practice 16

a. atoll
b. arroyo
c. mosses
d. lakes
e. donkeys
f. brushes
g. Burgesses
h. boundaries
i. deltas
j. wrenches
k. days
l. taxes
m. turkeys
n. toys
o. berries
p. puppies

Review Set 16

1. latitude
2. meridian
3. triangle
4. lagoon
5. Optimism
6. trimmed, their
7. shall, there
8. never
9. Yes, I think Julia lives near the Mississippi River, in Memphis, Tennessee.
10. fries
11. waxes
12. believes, expects
13. munch
14. (was) born
15. future tense
16. complete sentence
17. sentence fragment
18. toothbrush, mailbox
19. Daniel Boone's
20. Example: A strong thoroughbred racehorse speeds around the track.
21. a. abstract
    b. abstract
    c. concrete
    d. concrete
22. cast
23. daughter
24. shall answer
25. Did survive
26. Mary had a little lamb.
    Its fleece was white as snow.
    And everywhere that Mary went
    The lamb was sure to go.
27. tried
28. interrogative
29. a. keys
    b. babies

    c. lunches
    d. cherries
30. Colorful American goldfinches | peck at thistle seeds.

LESSON 17   Irregular Plural Nouns, part 2

Practice 17

  a. cliffs
  b. tomatoes
  c. chiefs
  d. knives
  e. salmon
  f. teeth
  g. geese
  h. cellos
  i. zoos
  j. Tropic of Capricorn
  k. Tropic of Cancer

More Practice 17

1. crosses
2. bunches
3. boys
4. lunches
5. bushes
6. bosses
7. cherries
8. bays
9. sheep
10. men
11. ladies
12. women
13. people
14. mice
15. geese
16. cliffs
17. leaves
18. loaves
19. altos
20. potatoes

Review Set 17

1. lagoon
2. longitude
3. hemispheres
4. delta
5. its
6. sipped, their
7. It's
8. plural
9. Every Sunday, Juan jogs down Myrtle Street in Monrovia, California.
10. replies
11. wishes
12. believes, expects
13. dip
14. (Have) tasted
15. past tense
16. complete sentence
17. sentence fragment
18. railroad, spaceship
19. pelican's
20. A brown pelican with its long gray bill caught a dozen fish.
21. a. abstract
    b. concrete
    c. abstract
    d. concrete
22. colony

23. Mardi Gras
24. shall paint
25. May taste
26. Twinkle, twinkle, little star.
    How I wonder what you are,
    Up above the world so high,
    Like a diamond in the sky.
27. clapped
28. declarative
29. a. pianos
    b. benches
    c. lives
    d. children
30. The people of Louisiana | listen to Cajun music.

LESSON 18 Irregular Verbs, Part 1: *Be, Have, Do*

Practice 18

a. are
b. has
c. does
d. had
e. were
f. did
g. timberline
h. Torrid Zone

More Practice 18

1. a. am
   b. are
   c. is
   d. are
2. a. have
   b. have
   c. has
   d. have
3. a. do
   b. do
   c. does
   d. do
4. a. was
   b. were
   c. was
   d. were
5. does
6. has
7. was
8. Are
9. were
10. are
11. Were
12. Was
13. has
14. Does
15. am
16. did

Review Set 18

1. equator
2. coral reef
3. Longitude
4. hemispheres
5. isthmus
6. were, called
7. It's, there
8. are, their
9. This February, I would like to sail to Catalina Island.
10. dries
11. washes
12. feeds, visits
13. bill

14. (might) (have) painted
15. present tense
16. complete sentence
17. sentence fragment
18. baseball, earthworm
19. Maine's
20. An active little chickadee with a black cap calls to the other chickadees.
21. a. abstract
    b. concrete
    c. abstract
    d. concrete
22. herd
23. Leif Erickson
24. were
25. Was built
26. A diller, a dollar, a ten o'clock scholar!
    What makes you come so soon?
    You used to come at ten o'clock;
    Now you come at noon.
27. dropped
28. exclamatory
29. a. sheep
    b. churches
    c. thieves
    d. potatoes
30. Maine | has a jagged coastline with rocky cliffs.

LESSON 19 Four Principal Parts of Verbs

Practice 19

a. (is) acting, acted, (has) acted
b. (is) wanting, wanted, (has) wanted
c. (is) walking, walked, (has) walked
d. (is) viewing, viewed, (has) viewed
e. (is) working, worked, (has) worked
f. tundra
g. savanna

Review Set 19

1. timberline
2. tropic
3. atoll
4. Latitude
5. water
6. does
7. It's, there
8. has
9. present
10. Is Salem, Oregon, in the Willamette Valley?
11. applies
12. mows, sweeps
13. far
14. (Does) have
15. present tense
16. sentence fragment
17. complete sentence
18. sunflower, moonlight
19. country's
20. My ancestors were brave to sail across the Atlantic Ocean.
21. a. concrete
    b. abstract
    c. abstract
    d. concrete
22. family
23. Clarissa
24. has
25. Has been jousting

26. I scream,
    You scream,
    We all scream
    For ice cream!

27. a. (is) mixing
    b. mixed
    c. (has) mixed

28. declarative

29. a. berries
    b. monkeys
    c. halves
    d. tomatoes

30. A long bridge | stretches across the Chesapeake Bay.

LESSON 20   Simple Prepositions, Part 1

Practice 20

a. aboard, about, above, across, after, against, along, alongside, amid, among, around, at, before, behind, below, beneath

b. beside, besides, between, beyond, but, by, concerning, considering, despite, down, during, except, excepting, for, from, in

c. *See preposition list.*

d. At, for

e. from, to

f. near, off, of

g. chasm

h. mesas

More Practice 20

1. above, after, around, before, below
2. between, but, down, excepting, from
3. for, over, through
4. along, at
5. to, around
6. Opposite
7. During, with
8. without, on

Review Set 20

1. tropical
2. Trees
3. Capricorn
4. atoll
5. disclose
6. am
7. its, there
8. does
9. past
10. At the store, I bought Washington apples, Idaho potatoes, and Wisconsin cheese.
11. mixes
12. gathers, milks, drives
13. mad
14. (has)(been) harvesting
15. past tense
16. sentence fragment
17. of, into
18. across, after, alongside, among, below
19. eyewitness's
20. I will be wearing a warm, woolen sweater on a cold, winter morning.
21. a. concrete
    b. abstract
    c. concrete
    d. abstract
22. shipment
23. Kelloggs
24. had
25. Did make
26. The bee is not afraid of me,
    I know the butterfly;

The pretty people in the woods
Receive me cordially.

27. a. (is) answering
    b. answered
    c. (has) answered

28. declarative

29. a. foxes
    b. discoveries
    c. butterflies
    d. ostriches

30. Both tart and sweet cherries | grow in Michigan.

LESSON 21 Simple Prepositions, Part 2

Practice 21

a. inside, into, like, near, of, off, on, onto, opposite, out, outside, over, past, regarding, round, save

b. since, through, throughout, till, to, toward, under, underneath, until, unto, up, upon, via, with, within, without

c. *See preposition lists.*

d. During, of

e. Underneath, with

f. Since, in, from

g. fissure

h. plateau

More Practice 21

1. near, off, out, past, round
2. throughout, to, underneath, unto, with
3. V
4. N
5. P
6, V
7. P
8. N
9. V
10. P
11. N
12. P
13. V
14. N
15. P
16. V
17. P
18. P
19. N
20. P
21. N
22. V

Review Set 21

1. table
2. plain
3. timberline
4. Cancer
5. homophones
6. has
7. It's, there
8. does
9. past
10. In July, I shall visit the Smithsonian Institution in Washington, D.C.
11. copies
12. repairs, fills, sings
13. rust
14. (can) cultivate
15. present tense
16. sentence fragment

17. On, with, up, down
18. into, off, out, outside, round
19. factbook's
20. A Mississippi steamboat with two smokestacks and a paddle wheel cruises up the river.
21. a. concrete
    b. abstract
    c. abstract
    d. concrete
22. flock
23. Jefferson Davis
24. were
25. Did grow
26. If all the world were paper,
    And all the sea were ink,
    If all the trees
    Were bread and cheese,
    What should we have to drink?
27. a. (is) laughing
    b. laughed
    c. (has) laughed
28. exclamatory
29. a. inches
    b. photocopies
    c. blue jays
    d. wolves
30. Grover and Annie Mae | raise catfish in their pond.

LESSON 22 — Irregular Plural Nouns, Part 3

Practice 22

a. mothers-in-law
b. chiefs of staff
c. mouthfuls
d. pailfuls
e. placid
f. placare
g. placate
h. implacable

Review Set 22

1. crack
2. crack
3. tundra
4. equator
5. conceal
6. are
7. their, its
8. does
9. present
10. In our solar system, Mercury and Venus are the only planets without moons.
11. cashes
12. water, feed, left
13. wood
14. (may) follow
15. past tense
16. complete sentence
17. About, of, from
18. asked
19. storybook's
20. People are tapping their feet to country music.
21. a. concrete
    b. abstract
    c. abstract
    d. concrete
22. pack
23. fiddler
24. has
25. came

26. Red sky at night,
    Sailor's delight;
    Red sky at morning,
    Sailor's warning.

27. a. (is) sailing
    b. sailed
    c. (has) sailed

28. declarative

29. a. calves
    b. attorneys at law
    c. spoonfuls
    d. sheep

30. A white-haired fiddler in a plaid shirt | fiddled faster and faster.

LESSON 23 Complete Sentence or Run-on Sentence?

Practice 23

a. run-on sentence

b. complete sentence

c. complete sentence

d. run-on sentence

e. talk

f. elocution

g. ventriloquist

More Practice 23

1. run-on sentence
2. complete sentence
3. run-on sentence
4. complete sentence (subject, *you*, understood)
5. run-on sentence
6. complete sentence (subject, *you*, understood)

Review Set 23

1. calmed

2. chasm
3. chasm
4. cold
5. Earth's
6. were
7. it's, there
8. Does
9. past
10. One of Montana's richest gold deposits is in Virginia City.
11. mashes
12. made, signed, mailed
13. (have) (been) thriving
14. (Can) survive
15. future tense
16. Sentence fragment (missing predicate)
17. In, with
18. buy
19. gentleman's
20. Example: Someday I would like to canoe down the river through Montana's wild lands.
21. a. concrete
    b. concrete
    c. abstract
    d. abstract
22. herd
23. climbers
24. does
25. Have reached
26. I've been working on the railroad
    All the livelong day,
    I've been working on the railroad
    Just to pass the time away

27. a. (is) disclosing
    b. disclosed
    c. (has) disclosed

28. interrogative

29. a. shelves
    b. justices of the peace
    c. cupfuls
    d. deer

30. Two huge bison with thick brown coats | were minding their own business.

LESSON 24 Correcting a Run-on Sentence

Practice 24

a. My friends in Nebraska grow corn, and they also raise pigs.

b. Some ranchers felt lonely, so they had cornhusking parties with neighbors.

c. Corn grows well in Nebraska. Some of it is fed to livestock.

d. On the prairie, wood was scarce, so people built homes of sod.

e. strength

f. valor

g. valiant

More Practice 24

1. It's too dark. I can't see.
2. I have a map. Let's find the cave.
3. Please come with me. I need your help.
4. Bats live here. They sleep during the day.
5. Bats wake. They startle me!

Review Set 24

1. speaking
2. Implacable
3. fissure
4. mesa
5. arroyo
6. are
7. their, its
8. Have
9. present
10. Nebraska's capital, Lincoln, is named after President Abraham Lincoln.
11. magnifies
12. struts, pecks, calls
13. (Shall) follow
14. (have) (been) roping
15. present tense
16. run-on sentence
17. In, of, with
18. lake
19. Mr. Blue's
20. This is Arbor Day. We shall plant trees.
21. a. abstract
    b. abstract
    c. concrete
    d. concrete
22. committee
23. mammoths
24. shall be
25. were
26. O beautiful for spacious skies,
    For amber waves of grain,
    For purple mountain majesties
    Above the fruited plain!
27. a. (is) concealing
    b. concealed
    c. (has) concealed
28. imperative
29. a. estuaries
    b. sisters-in-law

c. fistfuls
d. countries

30. Cattle, corn, pigs, and oil | provide economic stability for Nebraska.

LESSON 25 Capitalization: Titles

Practice 25

a. *Winnie the Pooh*
b. *The Call of the Wild*
c. *The House at Pooh Corner*
d. "Home on the Range"
e. igneous rocks
f. ignis
g. ignite

More Practice 25 *See answers on page 162.*

Review Set 25

1. valiant
2. ventriloquist
3. calm
4. flat
5. Tundra
6. predicate
7. There, its
8. does
9. past
10. One of the world's biggest dams is Hoover Dam in Nevada.
11. flies
12. fell, tumbled, rolled
13. (Has) broken
14. *The Cat in the Hat*
15. future tense
16. complete sentence
17. In, around, under
18. tool
19. Nevada's
20. Prospectors went to Virginia City. There they found silver and gold.
21. a. concrete
    b. concrete
    c. abstract
    d. abstract
22. team
23. you
24. were
25. Have visited
26. I left you in the morning,
    And in the morning glow
    You walked a way beside me
    To make me sad to go.
27. a. (is) igniting
    b. ignited
    c. (has) ignited
28. exclamatory
29. a. skies
    b. lords of England
    c. tubfuls
    d. prefixes
30. The state of Nevada | mines silver, copper, and turquoise.

LESSON 26 Capitalization: Outlines and Quotations

Practice 26

a. I. Types of trees
   A. Deciduous trees
   B. Evergreen trees

b. Andrew Angles said, "Your grandmother and I came from Scotland."

c. Then he explained, "It was difficult leaving our families."

d. metamorphosis

e. metamorphic rocks

f. metamorphosis

More Practice 26 *See answers on page 163.*

Review Set 26

1. rocks
2. brave
3. Elocution
4. peaceful
5. warm
6. abstract
7. it's, their
8. has
9. present
10. Joseph said, "The honeybee is New Jersey's state bug."
11. hisses
12. drives
13. (should)(have) offered
14. "I've Been Working on the Railroad"
15. past tense
16. sentence fragment
17. During, alongside, without
18. understand
19. Alabama's
20. New Jersey has beautiful beaches. People like to come to the shore.
21. I don't want to swim in the ocean with jellyfish, sharks, and eels.
22. lighthouse, landmark
23. New Jersey
24. are
25. lies
26. I. The globe
    A. Continents
    B. Oceans
    II. Locating places
    A. Hemispheres
    B. Latitude and longitude
27. a. (is) playing
    b. played
    c. (has) played
28. interrogative
29. a. ladies
    b. brothers-in-law
    c. shovelfuls
    d. men
30. The state of New Jersey | protects plants and animals in the Pine Barrens.

LESSON 27 Dictionary Information About a Word, Part 1

Practice 27

a. 1. a fight between forces
   2. to struggle or fight

b. noun

c. brothers, brethren

d. per·pen·dic·u·lar

e. dis klōz′

f. Sediment

g. Sedimentary rocks

Review Set 27

1. Metamorphic
2. molten
3. Valor
4. talks
5. Placid
6. concrete
7. its, there

8. does
9. past
10. Besly said, "Next Tuesday I shall take the train to Santa Fe, New Mexico."
11. fizzes
12. yawns, rubs
13. (might) (have) built
14. "The Hunting of the Great Bear"
15. future tense
16. run-on sentence
17. In, with, at
18. a. noun
    b. at´ ol
19. roadrunners'
20. Ilbea ate a chili pepper. Tears came to her eyes.
21. An unidentified flying object in the night sky disappeared quickly.
22. grove
23. roadrunner
24. has
25. runs
26. I. Products of New Mexico
       A. Agricultural products
       B. Industrial products
27. a. (is) crying
    b. cried
    c. (has) cried
28. declarative
29. a. echoes
    b. editors in chief
    c. knives
    d. cities
31. Migrants from the East | headed west by wagon train.

LESSON 28 — Spelling Rules: Silent Letters *k, g, w, t, d,* and *c*

Practice 28

a. (w)restle
b. (w)hose
c. (g)nome
d. lis(t)en
e. (k)not
f. (k)nees
g. s(c)enery
h. whis(t)le
i. magma
j. caldera

Review Set 28

1. layers
2. changed
3. burn
4. courage
5. essential
6. plural
7. It's, their
8. were
9. present
10. Rosa said, "My family and I saw two plays in New York City."
11. fishes
12. thinks, speaks
13. (must) (have) entered
14. "Ali Baba and the Forty Thieves"
15. past tense
16. sentence fragment

17. Despite, along, over, around, into
18. a. transitive verb
    b. ig zôlt´
19. a. (k)nead
    b. si(g)n
    c. wa(t)ch
20. The Niagara River has magnificent waterfalls. Have you seen them?
21. Someday I shall take the elevator to the eighty-sixth floor of the Empire State Building.
22. gateway
23. glaciers
24. were
25. Did create
26. An apple a day
    Keeps the doctor away.
27. a. (is) drying
    b. dried
    c. (has) dried
28. exclamatory
29. a. logos
    b. bookshelves
    c. pailfuls
    d. counties
30. The Erie Canal | links the Atlantic and the Great Lakes.

LESSON 29 Spelling Rules: Silent Letters *p, b, l, u, h, n,* and *gh*

Practice 29
a. g(u)ess
b. althou(gh)
c. (ch)orus
d. r(h)yme
e. cou(l)d
f. ca(l)f
g. si(gh)t
h. cor(ps)
i. (p)neumonia
j. de(b)t
k. tom(b)
l. yo(l)k
m. meteor
n. meteorite

Review Set 29
1. rock
2. rocks
3. metamorphosis
4. ignite
5. synonym
6. concrete
7. There, its
8. did
9. past
10. The ship's captain said, "While out at sea, I spotted Cape Hatteras Lighthouse, warning me of hazardous waters ahead."
11. applies
12. warns, lights
13. (might)(have) crashed
14. "The Arrow and the Song"
15. future tense
16. complete sentence
17. After, through, around, into, for
18. a. adjective
    b. plas´ id

19. a. ⓚnow
    b. liⓖht
    c. limⓑ

20. Orville and Wilbur Wright successfully flew for the first time in 1903. They departed from Kitty Hawk, North Carolina.

21. The notorious pirate Blackbeard terrorized the high seas.

22. shipment

23. furniture

24. has

25. Was crafted

26. I. Florida's wetlands
    A. The world's largest swamp
    B. Endangered species

27. a. (is) doing
    b. did
    c. (has) done

28. imperative

29. a. trout
    b. children of the King
    c. axes
    d. industries

30. Many ships | have sunk off the coast of North Carolina.

LESSON 30 Dictionary Information About a Word, Part 2

Practice 30

a. Latin

b. Anatomy

c. permit or allow

d. vertebrate

e. invertebrate

Review Set 30

1. meteorite

2. magma

3. Sediment

4. change

5. scarce

6. possessive

7. etymology

8. similar

9. skipped

10. Lilah asked, "Have you ever experienced a North Dakota blizzard?"

11. qualifies

12. stings, bites, whistles

13. ⓒan teach

14. *Why the Chicken Crossed the Road*

15. past tense

16. run-on sentence

17. At, on, through, for, of, with, in

18. a. noun
    b. pla tō´
    c. French

19. a. briⓓge
    b. ⓗour
    c. taⓛk

20. Little ground squirrels flick their tails. Then they dive back into their burrows on the prairie.

21. I dream of growing sunflowers over ten feet tall.

22. waterfowl

23. insects

24. shall harvest

25. came

26. a. (is) trying
    b. tried
    c. (has) tried

27. interrogative

28. Twelve pairs hanging high,
    Twelve knights riding by,
    Each knight took a pear,
    And yet left a dozen there.

29. a. wives
    b. spoonfuls
    c. keys
    d. countries

30. All the giant golden sunflowers | turn their faces to the sunshine.

LESSON 31   Linking Verbs

Practice 31

a. is, am, are, was, were, be, being, been, look, feel, taste, smell, sound, seem, appear, grow, become, remain, stay

b. *See list above.*

c. became

d. was

e. appears

f. remains

g. seems

h. sounds

i. no linking verb

j. smells

k. liability

l. asset

More Practice 31

1. seems
2. remains
3. stayed
4. felt
5. appeared
6. tastes
7. grew
8. smells
9. become
10. sounded
11. action
12. linking
13. action
14. linking
15. action
16. linking

Review Set 31

1. invertebrate
2. meteor
3. Magma
4. liquid
5. pessimism
6. abstract
7. verb
8. opposite
9. hopped
10. Mr. Chen said, "The famous ballerina Maria Tallchief was a Native American from Fairfax, Oklahoma.
11. cashes
12. counted, considered
13. (might) (have) counted
14. "America the Beautiful"
15. grew
16. complete sentence
17. of, during, to
18. a. adjective
    b. liv´ id
    c. French (from Latin)

19. a. whose (w, h circled)
    b. sigh (g circled)
    c. folk (l circled)

20. Pam lives in Oklahoma City. Her husband works in the oil fields.

21. Example: We ran to escape the tornado.

22. spray

23. Sooners

24. fries

25. claimed

26. a. (is) worrying
    b. worried
    c. (has) worried

27. exclamatory

28. I. Resources of Oklahoma
    A. Oil
    B. Cattle
    C. Wheat

29. a. sheep
    b. sisters-in-law
    c. donkeys
    d. liabilities

30. Oklahoma's twisters | must have surprised the settlers.

LESSON 32 — Diagramming Simple Subjects and Simple Predicates

Practice 32

a. trees | cover

b. hazelnuts | taste

c. owls | hoot

d. you | Do fish

e. Pan American

f. Pan

g. panacea

Review Set 32

1. antonyms
2. invertebrate
3. meteor
4. depression
5. There
6. plural
7. left
8. right
9. mopped
10. Jamaica King said, "The people of Oregon care about their environment."
11. mashes
12. blast, create
13. (have)(been) banned
14. "Chased by the Trail"
15. feels
16. sentence fragment
17. Since, within, of
18. a. adjective
    b. sə rēn´
    c. Latin
19. a. who (w circled)
    b. high (g, h circled)
    c. guard (g, u circled)
20. Oregon's Columbia River has a strong current. It powers plants that provide electricity.
21. is, am, are, was, were, be, being, been, look, feel, taste, smell, sound, seem, appear, grow, become, remain, stay
22. lighthouse
23. fried

24. a. (is) carrying
    b. carried
    c. (has) carried

25. imperative

26. Elizabeth, Elspeth, Betsy, and Bess,
    They all went together to see a bird's nest;

27. a. boxes
    b. mugfuls
    c. Tuesdays
    d. abilities

28. pirates | go

29. hoodlum | looks

30. pirate | Has boarded

LESSON 33 Spelling Rules: Suffixes, Part 1

Practice 33

a. beautiful
b. gloominess
c. merriest
d. cheerily
e. plateful
f. biting
g. lively
h. driver
i. knowledgeable
j. rating
k. clueless
l. indispensable
m. dispensable

Review Set 33

1. pan
2. disadvantage
3. backbone
4. sky
5. It's
6. abstract
7. a. reliable
   b. playing
8. a. loving
   b. careful
9. denied
10. Miss Fortune said, "I lost my purse in Pennsylvania."
11. brushes
12. sits, binds
13. (must) (have) misplaced
14. "The Merchant of Venice"
15. remains
16. run-on sentence
17. Without, of
18. a. noun
    b. bō kā´
    c. French
19. a. wa(l)k
    b. desi(g)n
    c. (k)not
20. On February 2, Punxsutawney Phil saw his shadow. He predicts six more weeks of winter.
21. is, am, are, was, were, be, being, been, look, feel, taste, smell, sound, seem, appear, grow, become, remain, stay
22. colony
23. grinned
24. a. (is) marrying
    b. married
    c. (has) married
25. interrogative

26. I. Pennsylvania's agriculture
    A. Dairy products
    B. Fresh vegetables
    C. Eggs

27. a. faxes
    b. men
    c. piccolos
    d. duties

28. friends | come

29. player | seems

30. team | Did win

LESSON 34   Spelling Rules: Suffixes, Part 2

Practice 34

a. tapped
b. stopping
c. gladly
d. benefited
e. flatness
f. proclamation
g. clamor
h. Clamare

Review Set 34

1. synonyms
2. Pan
3. liability
4. backbone
5. archipelago
6. possessive
7. a. glorious
    b. scary
8. a. winning
    b. gladly
9. clapped
10. "No," said Miss Fortune, "I did not leave my purse at a bus station in Philadelphia."
11. rushes
12. left, started
13. (has)(been) fishing
14. *Gone with the Wind*
15. looks
16. sentence fragment
17. near, of
18. a. noun
    b. en´ klāv
    c. French (from Latin)
19. a. (w)rote
    b. e(d)ge
    c. hym(n)
20. Example: The state of Rhode Island is the smallest in area.
21. is, am, are, was, were, be, being, been, look, feel, taste, smell, sound, seem, appear, grow, become, remain, stay
22. Tugboats
23. grins
24. a. (is) hurrying
    b. hurried
    c. (has) hurried
25. declarative
26. A wise old owl sat in an oak;
    The more he heard, the less he spoke;
    The less he spoke, the more he heard;
    Why aren't we all like that wise old bird?
27. a. taxes
    b. women
    c. letters of reference
    d. duties
28. cow | leaps

29. cow | appears

30. cow | Will return

LESSON 35 Spelling Rules: *ie* or *ei*

Practice 35

a. achieve
b. piece
c. receive
d. conceit
e. freight
f. feign
g. kin
h. Akin

Review Set 35

1. proclamation
2. indispensable
3. all
4. asset
5. Flora
6. concrete
7. a. flier
   b. coming
8. a. shopped
   b. warmest
9. a. believe
   b. receive
10. Miss Fortune asked, "Have you seen my purse?"
11. expresses
12. clucked, laid
13. (have)(been) weaving
14. "King Arthur and the Round Table"
15. proved
16. complete sentence
17. After, through
18. a. verb
    b. dik´ tāt
    c. Latin
19. a. com(b)
    b. glis(t)en
    c. (p)salm
20. Example: South Carolina is the Palmetto State. Its capital is Columbia.
21. far
22. flock
23. will smile
24. a. (is) moving
    b. moved
    c. (has) moved
25. declarative
26. Use *i* before *e*
    Except after *c*
    Or when sounded like *ay*
    As in *neighbor* and *weigh*
27. a. inches
    b. deer
    c. sons-in-law
    d. dairies
28. cow | comes
29. laugh | sounds
30. dish | Does run

LESSON 36 Phrases and Clauses

Practice 36

a. clause
b. phrase

c. clause
d. phrase
e. concert | began
f. they | sang
g. David Crockett | remains
h. avaricious
i. avarice

Review Set 36

1. family
2. announcement
3. Dispensable
4. all
5. There
6. plural
7. a. readily
   b. player
8. a. biggest
   b. wishful
9. a. chief
   b. ceiling
10. The docent at Graceland said, "Here is Mr. Presley's study."
11. presses
12. clause
13. (might)(have) impressed
14. "The Hawaiian Wedding Song"
15. became
16. run-on sentence
17. around, under, through
18. a. noun
    b. diˊ graf
    c. Greek
19. a. (k)nee
    b. (s)cent
    c. (h)onor
20. Some people like to explore deep, dark caves.
21. pound
22. sunglasses
23. shall smile
24. a. (is) studying
    b. studied
    c. (has) studied
25. interrogative
26. I. Animal husbandry in Tennessee
    A. Poultry
    B. Pigs
    C. Horses
27. a. ranches
    b. cattle
    c. church mice
    d. diaries
28. Van | will sing   you | will play
29. dish | runs
30. (you) | Catch

LESSON 37   Diagramming a Direct Object

Practice 37

a. chili
b. (none)
c. lasso
d. Texans | eat | chili
e. rancher | is twirling | lasso
f. encumbrance

g. encumber

Review Set 37

1. Avarice
2. akin
3. clamare
4. unessential
5. peninsula
6. abstract
7. a. modifier
   b. sensible
8. a. funny
   b. madness
9. a. brief
   b. deceive
10. A newscaster reported, "Oil production increased in Texas this year."
11. munches
12. phrase
13. (could)(have) lassoed
14. "The Children's Hour"
15. grew
16. complete sentence
17. on, with
18. a. noun
    b. kup´ lit
    c. French
19. a. ba(d)ge
    b. recei(p)t
    c. thou(gh)t
20. Example: The frog leaped from the water. It landed on my shoe.
21. disappear
22. herd
23. ripped
24. a. (is) ripping
    b. ripped
    c. (has) ripped
25. exclamatory
26. Grammar rules are fun to learn, But an *A* is hard to earn.
27. a. roaches
    b. solos
    c. teaspoonfuls
    d. libraries
28. Van | has been singing
    Jan | has been playing
29. Robert | is reading | novel
30. Christie | Has found | accordian

LESSON 38 Capitalization: People Titles, Family Words, School Subjects

Practice 38

a. Are, Spanish
b. I, Grandpa
c. Have, Dr. U. B. Straight
d. I
e. exalt
f. humiliate

More Practice 38 *See answers on page 164.*

Review Set 38

1. encumber
2. synonyms
3. Akin
4. clamor
5. strait
6. possessive

7. a. sunnier
   b. admiration

8. a. beginning
   b. sadness

9. a. shield
   b. perceive

10. Ms. Lim asked, "Have you tried the Texas cheese bread?"

11. pacifies

12. clause

13. (should) (have) seen

14. Yes, Mom is taking a Spanish class from Professor Reyna.

15. looks

16. sentence fragment

17. along, of

18. a. adjective
    b. d ī dak´ tik
    c. Greek

19. a. com(b)
    b. ha(lf)
    c. rei(gn)

20. Example: People were fishing for marlin near Padre Island.

21. where

22. raincoat

23. snipped

24. a. (is) snipping
    b. snipped
    c. (has) snipped

25. imperative

26. I. Produce from Texas
       A. Bunches of carrots
       B. Bags of peanuts

27. a. anniversaries
    b. birthdays
    c. queens of England

28. Pac | was trimming

    Jud | was examining

29. Tyler | Has polished | shoes

30. Florinda | might have left | trumpet

LESSON 39   Descriptive Adjectives

Practice 39

   a. old, rusty

   b. Healthful, delicious

   c. ripe, juicy

   d. lively, friendly (*answers will vary*)

   e. deep, loud (*answers will vary*)

   f. warm, fuzzy (*answers will vary*)

   g. dogma

   h. dogmatic

More Practice 39   *See Corny Chronicle #2 on page 165. Answers will vary.*

Review Set 39

1. shame
2. burden
3. avaricious
4. similar
5. It's
6. abstract
7. a. pitiful
   b. said
8. a. dropping
   b. warmer
9. a. view
   b. neighbor

10. enormous, salty
11. reaches
12. phrase
13. (Has)(been) floating
14. *The Swiss Family Robinson*
15. remains
16. run-on sentence
17. On, down, until
18. a. adjective
    b. dij´ i tāt
    c. Latin
19. a. (k)neel
    b. t(w)o
    c. g(u)ard
20. Example: In Utah's Great Salt Lake, floating is easy, but swimming underwater is difficult.
21. paste
22. cluster
23. shall sing
24. a. (is) snapping
    b. snapped
    c. (has) snapped
25. heavy, holey, black, stylish, new, large, small, old, curious, empty, etc.
26. I have a hunch
    It's time for lunch.
27. a. dictionaries
    b. avocados
    c. rulers of Spain
28. teacher | asks   Perlina | scratches
29. Perlina | has been counting | freckles
30. Perlina | is rubbing | eyes

LESSON 40   The Limiting Adjective • Diagramming Adjectives

Practice 40

a. tangible
b. intangible
c. Juan's, several
d. Some, the
e. This, two
f. That, my
g. Amir | plays | bells
           \these \golden

More Practice 40   See answers on page 166.

Review Set 40

1. dogmatic
2. embarrass
3. encumber
4. greed
5. placare
6. plural
7. a. craziness
   b. paid
8. a. mopped
   b. raining
9. a. priest
   b. receipt
10. Lush, colorful, appreciative
11. relies
12. clause
13. (Should)(have) stuck
14. Sergeant Smug asked Mom if she passed her fourth grade English class.
15. seems

16. complete sentence
17. underneath, near
18. a. noun
    b. ra pôr´
    c. French (going back to Latin)
19. a. si(g)n
    b. lis(t)en
    c. (h)onesty
20. Example: Luey is pouring maple syrup on the pancakes.
21. blow
22. This, Max's, two, several, his
23. emptied
24. a. (is) emptying
    b. emptied
    c. (has) emptied
25. weary, young, happy, old, frantic, energetic, sleepy, serious, suspicious, sneaky, etc.
26. Addicus said, "There is a copy of *The Wizard of Oz* on Ms. Blue's bookshelf."
27. a. Mondays
    b. brushes
    c. private investigators
28. others | are taking   Perlina | is chewing
29. Mr. Hake | can wiggle | ears \ his
30. you | Can wiggle | ears \ your

c. Look
d. Dear Dad,
      I am having fun at camp.
         Your son,
         Alex
e. cognizant
f. cognizance

Review Set 41

1. intangible
2. authoritative
3. praise
4. encumbrance
5. Mesa
6. possessive
7. a. laziness
   b. daily
8. a. committed
   b. cloudless
9. a. niece
   b. deceit
10. Fertile, tasty
11. Nancy attends a Lutheran church in the Northeast.
12. phrase
13. (Has)(been) hiking
14. "A Bicycle Built for Two"
15. appears
16. sentence fragment
17. in, near, beneath
18. a. noun
    b. durth
    c. Middle English
19. a. desi(g)n
    b. lam(b)
    c. (h)ourly

LESSON 41   Capitalization: Areas, Religions, Greetings

Practice 41

a. These passages are from the King James Bible.
b. When I…East, I….

20. Crossing the Connecticut River is a covered bridge. It is one of the longest in the world.

21. declarative

22. Max's, many, his, two, that

23. empties

24. a. (is) spying
    b. spied
    c. (has) spied

25. red, messy, black, curly, long, shiny, short, blonde, straight, gray

26. Mortimer asked, "How many copies of *Robinson Crusoe* does Mr. Garza have?"

27. a. copies
    b. axes
    c. secret agents

28. Perlina | was solving

    classmates | were sleeping

29. Perlina | is taking | test
    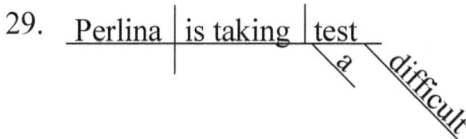

30. Perlina | Will pass | test
    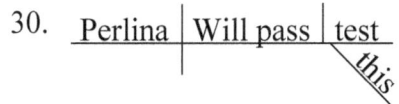

LESSON 42 Proper Adjectives

Practice 42

a. Italian sausage

b. Renaissance fair

c. Scottish bagpipes

d. Chinese martial arts

e. Bob | wore | shirt

f. Frugal

g. Extravagant

Review Set 42

1. antonyms

2. Tangible

3. Dogma

4. exalt

5. *loqui*

6. concrete

7. a. readily
   b. coming

8. a. winning
   b. rained

9. a. relieve
   b. freight

10. French, Canadian

11. Dear Quan,
    Please don't eat all of the Canadian bacon.
    Your brother,
    Sheung

12. clause

13. (might) (have) heard

14. Next semester, Dad will take Mr. Castro's Spanish class.

15. sound

16. run-on sentence

17. throughout, about, beyond

18. a. noun
    b. dis´ taf
    c. Old English

19. a. (k)not
    b. (w)ritten
    c. clim(b)

20. Example: Would you like to taste cheese from Wisconsin?

21. flea
22. her, three, the, Harts', that
23. shall feed
24. a. (is) wrapping
    b. wrapped
    c. has wrapped
25. sweaty, tired, energetic, happy, tall, skinny, short, muscular, friendly, elderly
26. It's raining, it's pouring,
    The old man is snoring…
27. a. branches
    b. calves
    c. sons-in-law
28. bell | rang   Ms. Hoo | stood
    class | applauded

29.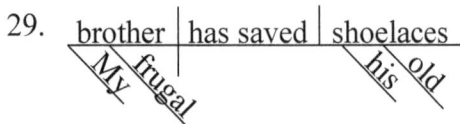

30.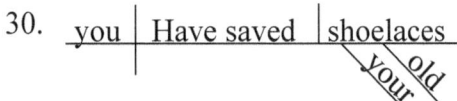

LESSON 43 No Capital Letter

Practice 43

a. maternal
b. paternal
c. no additional capital letter
d. no additional capital letter
e. Chinese
f. We
g. Twenty-four

More Practice 43 *See answers on page 167.*

Review Set 43

1. Frugal
2. Cognizance
3. touch
4. belief
5. talk
6. collective
7. a. steadily
   b. peaceful
8. a. sipping
   b. broadest
9. a. weigh
   b. achieve
10. Russian, Australian
11. My Jewish friend Lenny won the chess championship in the Western division.
12. phrase
13. (May) sample
14. "The Race for the South Pole"
15. remains
16. complete sentence
17. alongside, through
18. a. noun
    b. pōl´ tis
    c. Latin
19. a. (p)neumonia
    b. wou(l)d
    c. pi(t)ch
20. Example: Please bring some cheese. I am baking bread.
21. declarative
22. my, the, those, two, Ms. Hoo's
23. hushes
24. a. (is) denying
    b. denied
    c. (has) denied
25. rusty, old, shiny, new, compact, sporty, gigantic, powerful, classy, expensive

26. Ms. Hoo said, "My car was made in France, not in Japan."

27. a. leaves
    b. bison
    c. mouthfuls

28. Ms. Hoo | drove   I | walked

    friends | rode

29. ancestors | built | cabins
    \My \maternal   \some \rustic

30. ancestors | Did build | teepees
    \Dan's \paternal

LESSON 44   Object of the Preposition • The Prepositional Phrase

Practice 44

a. around (us)
   in (some)
   of (us)

b. to (us)
   from (Washington)
   by (truck) and (train)

c. of the (Cascade Mountains)
   like a (desert)

d. Beyond the (shoreline)
   off (rocks)
   into the (ocean)

e. Prudent

f. Imprudent

More Practice 44

1. At (sunrise)
   at her (clock)
   about her (students)
   into her (car)

2. past a (house)
   with (daffodils)
   in the (yard)

3. Along the (way)
   at a (cow)
   in the (middle)
   of the (road)

4. to the (left)
   on the (right)

5. Near the (school)
   for (pedestrians)

6. Without (doubt)
   on (time)
   for (class)

Review Set 44

1. Paternal

2. waste

3. knowledge

4. touched

5. strength

6. plural

7. a. buried
   b. beautiful

8. a. topped
   b. referred

9. a. reign
   b. yield

10. Washington, American

11. Dear James,
    Please join me for dinner on Saturday. I shall serve Boston baked beans.
    Love,
    Ima

12. clause

13. (will) (be) flying

14. I believe Dr. Rhombus was Mother's geometry professor.

15. seemed
16. run-on sentence
17. With (ease)
    through the (door)
    down the (stairs)
    into the (basement)
18. a. intransitive verb
    b. ri sēd´
    c. Latin
19. a. e(dg)e
    b. g(ue)st
    c. hi(gh)
20. Example: Washington, D.C., is our nation's capital.
21. throughout
22. a, few, Jasmin's, my, two, her
23. tried
24. a. (is) stopping
    b. stopped
    c. (has) stopped
25. rare, poisonous, slithery, slender, gigantic, strong, dangerous, hungry, harmless, friendly
26. I. Gopher snakes
       A. Where they live
       B. What they eat
27. a. waltzes
    b. pennies
    c. autos
28. trouble | starts   Ann | opens

    Rufus | escapes
29. cousin | eats | vegetables
      \My \prudent \many \green
30. you | Have been eating | vegetables
                                 \your

LESSON 45 The Prepositional Phrase as an Adjective • Diagramming

Practice 45

a. picture
b. flag
c. friendship
d. *for you* describes "surprise"
e. *through the forest* describes "road"
f. malicious
g. Malice
h.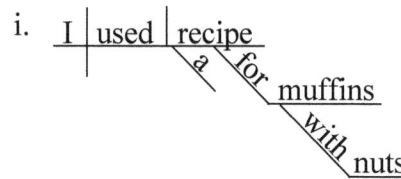
   Wally | likes | stories
                    \about
                      \spies
i. I | used | recipe
            \a \for
                \muffins
                  \with
                    \nuts

Review Set 45

1. Prudent
2. Maternal
3. economical
4. synonyms
5. fire
6. abstract
7. a. fried
   b. sleepiness
8. a. matted
   b. preferred
9. a. belief
   b. weight
10. Scottish
11. Out in the wild West, a Baptist preacher read from the Holy Bible.
12. phrase

13. (should) (have) brought

14. "Adrift on an Ice Pan"

15. smell

16. complete sentence

17. For (fun)
    to my (friend)
    into a (bottle)
    into the (sea)

18. a. adjective
    b. rō tund´
    c. Latin

19. a. (wrist)
    b. (rh)ombus
    c. si(gh)

20. Example: We toured the White House, and then we saw the Jefferson and Lincoln Memorials.

21. imperative

22. her, Jasmin's, my, two

23. hisses

24. a. (is) multiplying
    b. multiplied
    c. (has) multiplied

25. delicious, buttery, dry, crumbly, sweet, sticky, gooey, vanilla-flavored, over-cooked, inedible

26. Jasmin asks, "Where are my Jerusalem crickets?"

27. a. public libraries
    b. apologies
    c. Tuesdays

28. Ms. Hoo | is shouting

    students | are searching

    pet | has disappeared

29.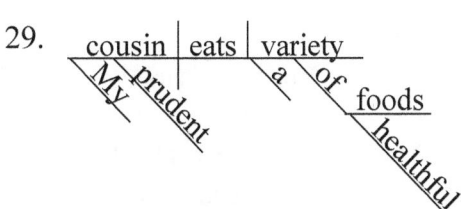

30. search | has begun
    A frantic for Rufus

LESSON 46   Indirect Objects

Practice 46

a. Illiterate

b. Literate

c. him

d. owner

e. teams

f. no indirect object

g. Ms. Hoo | read | poem
                      (x) us

Review Set 46

1. Malice

2. prudent

3. father

4. wasteful

5. *ignis*

6. compound

7. a. gripping
   b. creepiest

8. Vivian

9. a. grief
   b. sleigh

10. Jerusalem

11. Dear Ms. Hoo,
    I am sorry about Rufus's disappearance. We shall continue the search.
                    Respectfully,
                    Ann

12. clause

13. (Could)(have) jumped

14. Did Deputy Jesse learn to fix flat tires in Dr. Funk's Latin class?

15. remains

16. complete sentence

17. under the (seat) of William's (bicycle)

18. a. adjective
    b. ar´ id
    c. Latin

19. a. door(k)nob
    b. s(c)ience
    c. a(dj)ective

20. Example: Are we hearing the song of a meadowlark?

21. beware

22. three, the, their, this

23. will find

24. a. (is) glorifying
    b. glorified
    c. (has) glorified

25. ridiculous, tall, magnificent, fuzzy, small, round, crazy, crooked, funny, square

26. A cat came fiddling out of a barn
    With a pair of bagpipes under her arm.

27. a. mothers-in-law
    b. peaches
    c. Wednesdays

28. Moses | empties   Rosa | moves
        students | squeal

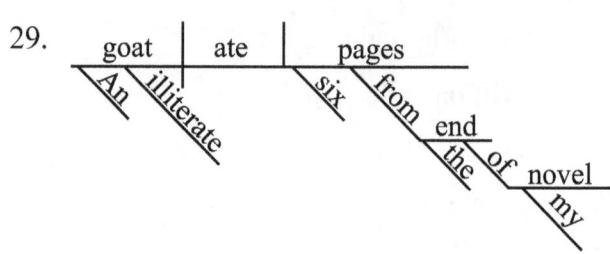

29. (diagram: An illiterate goat ate six pages from the end of my novel)

30. (diagram: Quan handed remains me (x) the of the novel)

LESSON 47   The Period, Part 1

Practice 47

a. I. Rodeo competitions
   A. Riding broncos
   B. Roping steer

b. J.B. Hoven wrote a novel called *The Bucking Bronco.*

c. Don't be ridiculous.

d. Eagles soar among the clouds.

e. momentary

f. momentous

More Practice 47   *See answers on page 168.*

Review Set 47

1. Literate
2. Malicious
3. unwise
4. mother
5. *Val-*
6. possessive
7. a. drying
   b. bigger
8. me
9. a. believing
   b. deceiving

10. Swiss, Russian
11. Black-collared lizards live in deserts of the Southwest.
12. phrase
13. (can) broaden
14. "On the Sunny Side of the Street"
15. grew
16. sentence fragment
17. at the (school)
    except the (principal)
    about this missing (pet)
18. a. noun
    b. bā′ lif
    c. Old French
19. a. wa(l)king
    b. s(c)ent
    c. ba(d)ge
20. I believe A. J. Gallo plays the violin.
21. interrogative
22. The, his, Ms. Hoo's, many
23. catches
24. a. (is) simplifying
    b. simplified
    c. (has) simplified
25. long, silly, serious, true, mysterious, imaginative, fictitious, humorous, dark, scary
26. The principal says, "A bearded dragon belongs in central Australia, not in a classroom."
27. a. fistfuls
    b. cherries
    c. trays
28. principal | scowls   Ms. Hoo | snaps
          students | take

29.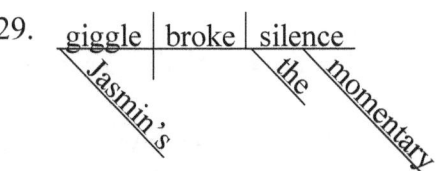
30.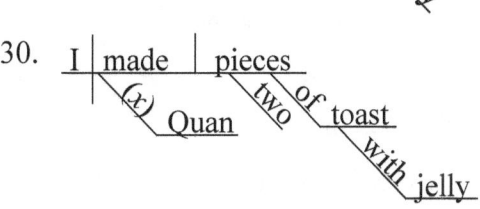

LESSON 48 Coordinating Conjunctions

Practice 48

a. and, or, for, so
b. but, nor, yet
c. *listed above*
d. and, but, and
e. or, nor
f. for, yet
g. so
h. plausible
i. implausible

Review Set 48

1. Momentary
2. read
3. evil
4. Prudent
5. strength
6. abstract
7. a. laid
   b. spinning
8. Dolly
9. a. briefcase
   b. their
10. and, but

11. Dear Ann,
    Perhaps I shall retire and move to North Dakota.
    Sincerely,
    Ms. Hoo

12. clause

13. (might) (be) passing

14. I think Officer Ambush has issued more speeding tickets than any other officer in the West.

15. sounds

16. complete sentence

17. Beside William's (chair)
    of (bread)
    amid (pieces)
    of torn (paper)

18. a. noun
    b. bi kwest´
    c. Old English

19. a. han(d)some
    b. cha(l)k
    c. s(c)ene

20. Give my regards to Paul R. Flores.

21. hook

22. This, some, Florida, six

23. hummed

24. a. (is) humming
    b. hummed
    c. (has) hummed

25. malicious, sneaky, shy, timid, friendly, exuberant, generous, vivacious, quiet, serene

26. I. Thomas's hobbies
    A. Reading mysteries
    B. Riding bikes
    C. Playing the trumpet

27. a. children of the king
    b. hobbies
    c. trout

28. Jasmin | snorts   face | turns
    everyone | looks

29. principal | Does fear | reptiles
    \the   \long \slender

30. Ms. Hoo | gives | explanation
    \(x)   \a \plausible \for \crickets
    \principal   \the   \in \classroom
    \the   \her

LESSON 49 Diagramming Compound Subjects and Predicates

Practice 49

a. tolerable

b. intolerable

c.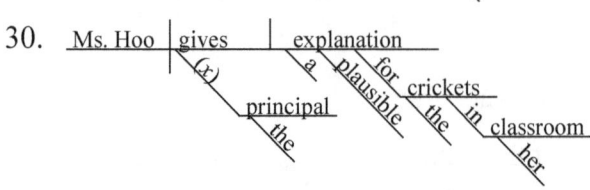
Drummers ──┐
           and ├── practice
guitarists ──┘

d.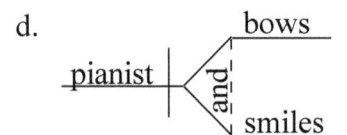
          bows
pianist ─┬── and
          smiles

e.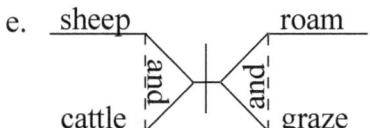
sheep ──┐   ┌── roam
        and   and
cattle ──┘   └── graze

More Practice 49 *See answers on page 169.*

Review Set 49

1. true

2. Momentous

3. read

4. harm

5. metamorphosis

6. collective

7. a. driest
   b. hopped
8. Sarah
9. a. piece
   b. beige
10. and, but, or, for, nor, yet, so
11. In October we enjoy fall colors in the Northeast.
12. phrase
13. (could)(have) run
14. *The Tales of Uncle Remus*
15. felt
16. run-on sentence
17. throughout the (classroom)
    around (books)
    under (desks)
    behind (cabinets)
18. a. adjective
    b. skant
    c. Middle English
19. a. (g)naw
    b. (w)rench
    c. solem(n)
20. Jack B. Nimble burned his toes.
21. interrogative
22. Those, Labrador, the, several
23. identifies
24. a. (is) identifying
    b. identified
    c. (has) identified
25. large, empty, small, dirty, clean, comfortable, spacious, elegant, expansive, sturdy
26. The principal complains, "This chaos is intolerable."
27. a. Labrador retrievers
    b. feet
    c. capfuls

28. Crickets | hop   Ms. Hoo | steps
    dog | sniffs

29.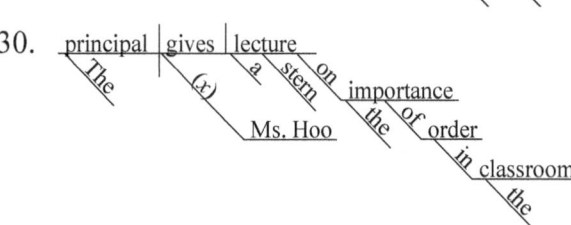

30. principal | gives | lecture ...

LESSON 50 — The Period, Part 2: Abbreviations, Decimals

Practice 50

a. Mr. and Mrs. Hatti drove south on Baldwin Avenue. (3 periods)

b. School begins at 8 a.m. each weekday. (3 periods)

c. Ms. Lim winked at Ms. Hoo. (3 periods)

d. Rev. Freddy Rivas performed the marriage ceremony. (2 periods)

e. Capt. H. R. Montgomery commands the troops. (4 periods)

f. "Gimme Toy Co." was the name on the box. (2 periods)

g. Prof. Werks wrote, "Hike to Mt. Whitney in Aug." (3 periods)

h. We had driven 7.2 (seven and two tenths) miles. (2 periods)

i. benevolence

j. benevolent

More Practice 50 *See answers on page 170.*

Review Set 50

1. Tolerable
2. believable
3. short
4. Illiterate
5. transformation
6. possessive
7. a. patted
   b. cried
8. Aaron
9. a. receiver
   b. neighborly
10. or, so
11. Dear Ms. Hoo,
    The noise from your room disturbs my students.
    Respectfully,
    Mr. Annoyd
12. clause
13. (must) warn
14. Is Rufus attending Professor Speek's French class with Uncle Noah?
15. grew
16. sentence fragment
17. After (lunch)
    at the (clock)
    on her (desk)
    for thirty (minutes)
18. a. adjective
    b. lim´ pid
    c. French (from Latin)
19. a. cas(t)le
    b. s(c)ent
    c. shou(l)d
20. An ambulance rushed Mr. Jack B. Nimble to the Joan C. Giddy Hospital at seven p.m.
21. swell
22. One, Labrador, a, Perlina's
23. swatted
24. a. (is) swatting
    b. swatted
    c. (has) swatted
25. kind, helpful, patient, benevolent, compassionate, caring, strict, stern, friendly, passionate
26. Little Miss Muffet
    Sat on a tuffet…
27. a. men of God
    b. geese
    c. matches
28.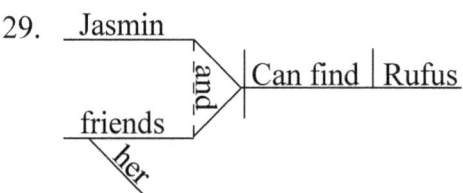
29.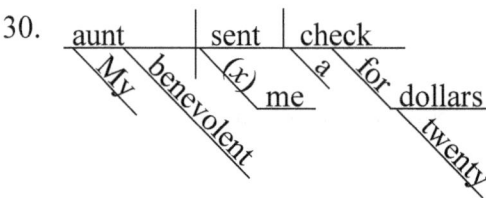
30. aunt | sent | check
    My \ benevolent \ (x) me \ a \ for \ dollars \ twenty

LESSON 51 The Predicate Nominative

Practice 51

a. canine
b. feline
c. Lake Placid | became \ resort
d. Uncle Sam | was \ person
e. Jimmy Carter | became \ President

f. father | is \ Virginian

More Practice 51 *See "Corny Chronicle #3" on page 171. Answers will vary.*

Review Set 51

1. generous
2. intolerable
3. unlikely
4. important
5. delta
6. abstract
7. a. happiest
   b. bigger
8. Isabel
9. a. friend
   b. weighing
10. and, but, or, for, nor, yet, so
11. Mr. Annoyd would send the bearded dragon back to Central Australia.
12. phrase
13. (have)(been) picking
14. "There's a Hole in the Bucket"
15. character
16. complete sentence
17. During the (blizzard)
    into the (wind)
    toward (home)
18. a. noun
    b. nut´ hach
    c. Middle English
19. a. (k)nowing
    b. ac(h)e
    c. bri(gh)t
20. Dr. Payne will mail the bill to Mr. Jack B. Nimble, 531 Candlestick Rd.
21. smelled
22. A, Russian, the, Jasmin's
23. cherishes
24. a. (is) verifying
    b. verified
    c. (has) verified
25. worried, fretful, angry, resentful, sour, unfriendly, serious, no-nonsense, grouchy, unhappy, jolly, gracious, mischievous, sneaky
26. Mr. Annoyd says, "Please be quiet."
27. a. glasses of milk
    b. children
    c. glassfuls
28. principal | has gone
    secretary | will handle   she | is
29.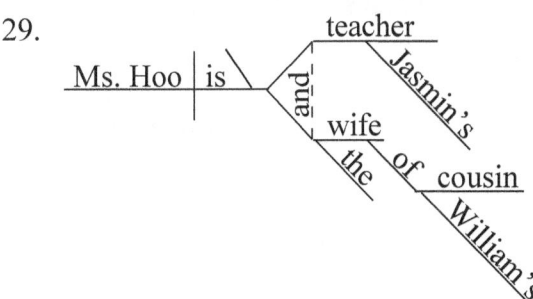
30. friends | are giving | headache
    Our canine (x) Mr. Annoyd a

LESSON 52 Noun Case, Part 1: Nominative, Possessive

Practice 52

a. nominative case; subject
b. nominative case; predicate nominative
c. possessive case
d. nominative case; subject
e. nominative case; predicate nominative
f. equine

g. bovine

Review Set 52

1. feline
2. Benevolent
3. bearable
4. antonyms
5. tributary
6. collective
7. a. merrily
   b. admitted
8. Esperanza
9. a. relief
   b. weighty
10. and, yet
11. Dear Mr. Annoyd,
       Please believe me. I am trying to keep my class quiet.
                     Seriously,
                     Ms. Hoo
12. clause
13. (might) (have) given
14. Does Aunt Rosa believe that Officer Ambush has an invisible car?
15. gift
16. sentence fragment
17. of (love) for the (land)
18. a. adjective
    b. mān´ jē
    c. Middle English
19. a. colum(n)
    b. ma(t)ch
    c. (w)ho
20. Ms. Hatti will begin teaching on Sept. 9.
21. interrogative
22. A, helpful, the, clear, glass
23. stirred
24. a. (is) stirring
    b. stirred
    c. (has) stirred
25. nominative case
26. I. Bovine animals
       A. Oxen
       B. Antelope
       C. Cows
27. a. science teachers
    b. oxen
    c. thieves
28. he | returns

    Mr. Stoneman | will visit

    she | has gone

29.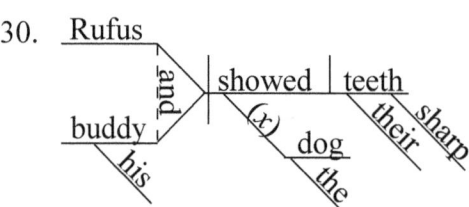

30. Rufus (and) buddy | showed | teeth / their \ sharp ... dog / the

LESSON 53   Noun Case, Part 2: Objective

Practice 53

  a. O.P.
  b. I.O.
  c. D.O.
  d. O.P.
  e. D.O.
  f. I.O.
  g. nominative case

h. objective case
i. possessive case
j. objective case
k. auditory
l. olfactory

Review Set 53

1. horses
2. canine
3. good
4. Intolerable
5. hemisphere
6. plural
7. a. cries
   b. topping
8. fiddler
9. a. field
   b. conceit
10. and, but, or, for, nor, yet, so
11. In the Midwest, people attend rodeos for entertainment.
12. phrase
13. (will) (have) completed
14. *Little House on the Prairie*
15. waterfall
16. run-on sentence
17. From the (city)
    of (Hershey)
    in (Pennsylvania)
    of the world's (chocolate)
18. a. noun
    b. mal′ is
    c. Old French (from Latin)
19. a. (k)nock
    b. lam(b)
    c. (g)uess

20. Dr. Jo B. Ngo will see you at two p.m. tomorrow.
21. wart
22. A, glorious, the, smooth, glacial
23. shall paint
24. a. (is) dipping
    b. dipped
    c. (has) dipped
25. objective case
26. Mr. Stoneman said, "Perhaps I shall cancel school until Friday."
27. a. birds of prey
    b. Fridays
    c. centuries
28. chaos | continues

    Mr. Stoneman | will cancel

    Ms. Hoo | captures

29.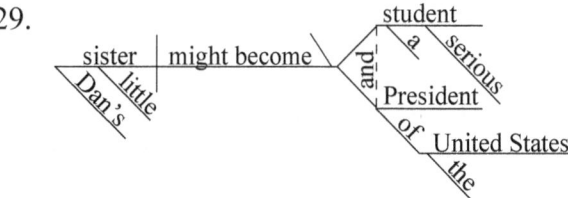

30. Adam
    and
    Eva | sent | address
         | (x) me | their \ new

LESSON 54 The Predicate Adjective

Practice 54

a. Bison | are \ plentiful

b. Beets
   and
   hay | have been \ profitable

c.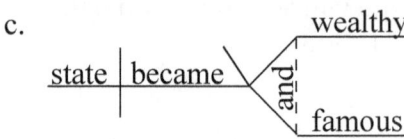
state | became \\ wealthy and famous

d. Designers | were \ creative

e. Aboreal

f. amphibian

Review Set 54

1. olfactory
2. bovine
3. cat
4. Benevolent
5. Latitude
6. concrete
7. tried
8. neighbor, believes
9. Erik
10. and, but
11. Dear Officer Ambush,
    Please stop those who speed on Fourth Street.
                        Respectfully,
                        Josef Habib
12. clause
13. (must) (have) seen
14. Esperanza desperately wants Grandma to join her.
15. hopeful
16. sentence fragment
17. From (dawn)
    until (dusk)
    in (baskets)
18. a. noun
    b. māz
    c. Spanish

19. a. (w)reath
    b. a(d)just
    c. ca(l)f
20. I. Cities in Delaware
       A. Wilmington—capital
       B. Lewes—whaling colony
21. interrogative
22. this, delicious, ripe, fertile
23. pries
24. a. (is) prying
    b. pried
    c. (has) pried
25. nominative case
26. No one can say
    What will happen today.
27. a. lunch breaks
    b. calves
    c. stories
28. Ms. Hoo | finds \ she | will scold
    he | has caused

29.
    My cousin | has been feeling \ joyful and optimistic

30.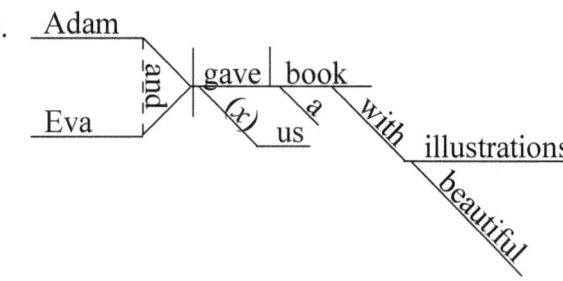
    Adam and Eva | gave | book (with beautiful illustrations) (x) us a

LESSON 55 Comparison Adjectives

Practice 55

a. bigger, comparative

b. youngest, superlative

c. most, superlative

d. sleepier, comparative

e. cutest; superlative

f. faster; comparative

g. louder, loudest

h. more (or less) plausible
most (or least) plausible

i. gentility

j. genteel

Review Set 55

1. land
2. auditory
3. cow
4. canine
5. longitude
6. collective
7. famous, funny
8. thieves, received, their
9. smaller
10. and, but, or, for, nor, yet, so
11. Many Quakers settled in the Northeast.
12. phrase
13. Tanner
14. *A New Dictionary of Quotations*
15. delicious
16. complete sentence
17. Throughout the (year) of (exercisers) on the (path) around the (park)
18. a. noun
    b. lin′ gwist
    c. Latin

19. a. cou(ld)
    b. g(u)ide
    c. (w)hose

20. Mario M. DeSurra provided these instructions: on Mon., Feb. 2, go west to Arrival St. to see the groundhog.

21. swell

22. The, frigid, blustery, watery, red

23. dried

24. a. (is) drying
    b. dried
    c. (has) dried

25. nominative case

26. Ms. Hoo said, "Please take your seats."

27. a. flower boxes
    b. shovelfuls
    c. bunches

28. Ms. Hoo | smiled   students | cheered

    Jasmin | found

29.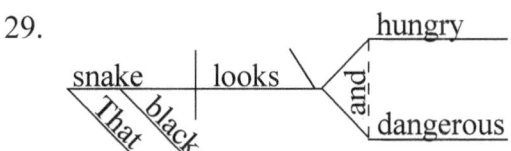

30. Adam and Eva (x) | baked | loaf (a) of bread / Ms. Hoo

LESSON 56 Irregular Comparison Adjectives

Practice 56

a. Many
b. much
c. worst
d. More
e. Little

Grammar and Writing 5

f. more scary

g. Indolent

h. Industrious

More Practice 56

1. Less
2. better
3. worst
4. better
5. more reliable
6. more
7. most benevolent
8. wiser

Review Set 56

1. polite
2. trees
3. smell
4. cattle
5. arroyo
6. plural
7. beginning, sadder
8. niece, beige
9. tallest
10. redder
11. Dear Mr. Stoneman,
    We have found one of the lost critters, but I do not know where the others are.
    Regretfully,
    Ms. Hoo
12. clause
13. nor, but, and
14. Professor U.R. Thair teaches history and Spanish.
15. spaghetti
16. run-on sentence
17. across the (United States) of (wheat) of (cattle)
18. a. noun
    b. links
    c. Middle English
19. a. (w)hole
    b. sket(c)h
    c. (h)our
20. Ms. Hoo wrote, "All assignments are due Fri., Apr. 21."
21. exclamatory
22. The, white, fluffy, small, long
23. polishes
24. a. (is) hopping
    b. hopped
    c. (has) hopped
25. objective case
26. I. Common pets
       A. Dogs
       B. Cats
       C. Birds
27. a. dog dishes
    b. handfuls
    c. sheep
28. Dogs | are sniffing

    students | are searching

    Rufus | is resting

29. students | appear \ calmer and braver (with "Ms. Hoo's" and "thirty" on diagonals)

30.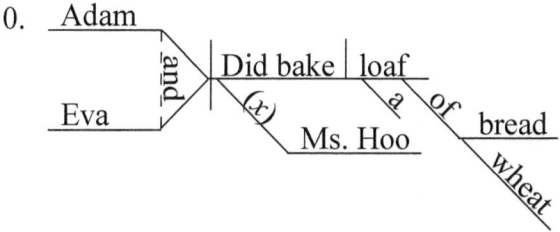

LESSON 57 The Comma, Part 1: Dates, Addresses, Series

Practice 57

a. providential

b. providence

c. Lily ran fast and broke the school record in the mile on Wednesday, December 7, 2005.

d. no comma needed

e. Christmas fell on Sunday, December 25, in the year 2005.

f. The post office has moved to 612 W. Duarte Road, Arcadia, California 91007.

g. Boise, Idaho, was Mr. Spud's birthplace.

h. Are you talking about Salem, Massachusetts, or Salem, Oregon?

i. The eight parts of speech include nouns, pronouns, verbs, adverbs, adjectives, prepositions, conjunctions, and interjections.

j. Lucy saw two gray squirrels, a blue jay, and three robins in the park.

More Practice 57 *See answers on page 172.*

Review Set 57

1. Industrious
2. gentility
3. amphibian
4. hearing
5. Capricorn
6. abstract
7. flies, biggest
8. believe, ceiling
9. taller
10. fewer
11. Dear Katy,
    Shall we play Chinese checkers after school?
                                    Your friend,
                                    Marta
12. phrase
13. Chris
14. "Bicycle Built for Two"
15. glorious
16. complete sentence
17. Inside a coal (mine)
    of (coal)
    on a (track)
18. a. adjective
    b. kyōō′ boid
    c. Greek
19. a. ta(l)k
    b. li(gh)t
    c. (g)nat
20. Dr. Ngo's office has moved to 54 W. Main Street.
21. play
22. A, huge, brown, the, red
23. Lana was born on Sunday, November 4, 1973, in Detroit, Michigan.
24. a. (is) slamming
    b. slammed
    c. (has) slammed
25. possessive case
26. Nora asked, "May I help you?"

27. a. dog leashes
    b. babies
    c. wolves

28. Ms. Hoo | thinks
    Jasmin | should take
    he | has caused

29. [diagram: lizard | seems \ sorry and regretful, with Jasmin's, shy]

30. [diagram: Adam and Eva | Did offer | slices \ two of bread \ rye, Mr. Stoneman (x)]

LESSON 58 Appositives

Practice 58

a. Superfluous
b. supersonic
c. super
d. the capital of Georgia
e. cinnamon
f. Ben Chu (artist) | draws | cartoons \ an
g. Ms. Hoo, my teacher, wants me to succeed.
h. Mr. Stoneman, principal of Giggly School, encourages students to try hard.

Review Set 58

1. providence
2. indolent
3. Genteel
4. tree
5. Torrid
6. compound
7. tries, matted
8. received, neighbor
9. wiser
10. fewer
11. Dear Ms. Hoo,
       Pets are not allowed at Mudvalley Middle School.
                 Regards,
                 Mr. Stoneman
12. clause
13. and, but, or, for, nor, yet, so
14. Did you, Auntie, call Dr. Rizkalla?
15. teacher
16. sentence fragment
17. Despite our (fatigue) against the strong (current) toward the distant (shore)
18. a. adjective
    b. krip´ tic
    c. Greek
19. the site of the first World Series
20. The bridge on First Ave. will be closed Dec. and Jan.
21. declarative
22. Two, gooey, the, their
23. Nancy raises cattle, sheep, chickens, and horses.
24. a. (is) replying
    b. replied
    c. (has) replied
25. objective case
26. Smile at your troubles
    And pop them like bubbles.
27. a. watch dogs
    b. earfuls
    c. candies

28.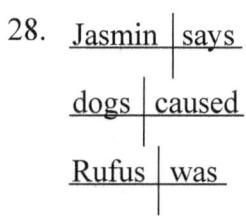

29.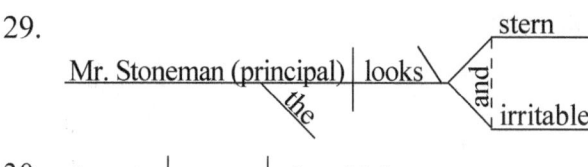

30.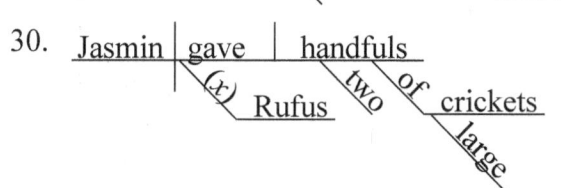

LESSON 59 The Comma, Part 2: Direct Address and Academic Degrees

Practice 59

a. Baukien, we learned a new song yesterday.

b. Please remember, my dear friends, that I shall return soon.

c. Carrie Prince, R.N., cares for newborn babies.

d. My cat's health is very important to Carla Wheat, D.V.M.

e. *lumen*

f. illuminate

g. Luminous

More Practice 59 *See answers on page 173.*

Review Set 59

1. super
2. fortunate
3. hardworking
4. polite
5. savanna
6. plural
7. winner, famous
8. chief, receive
9. friendliest
10. fewer
11. On a humid afternoon in the South, my cousins gather at the northeast corner of the park to play checkers.
12. phrase
13. Chris
14. "When Icicles Hang by the Wall."
15. energetic
16. run-on sentence
17. For this (assignment) of the (states) on the (walls) around the (room)
18. a. (w)rinkle
    b. ca(l)m
19. Nevada, the "silver state," borders five other states.
20. On Thurs. at nine a.m., I shall attend a lecture on the life of Dr. Martin L. King.
21. fleeing
22. a, generous, the, ugly
23. Ms. Hoo, have you seen my lunch, my backpack, or my history book?
24. a. (is) smiling
    b. smiled
    c. (has) smiled
25. objective case
26. Mr. Stoneman replied, "No, Jasmin, I have not fired your teacher."
27. a. topic sentences
    b. rosebushes
    c. Jennys

28. Jasmin | is weeping

Mr. Stoneman | says

Rufus | must go

29.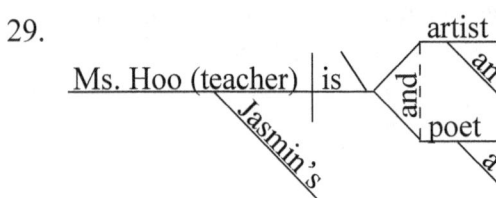

30.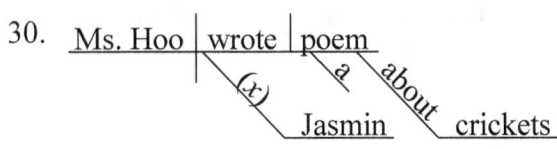

LESSON 60 The Comma, Part 3: Appositives

Practice 60

a. Chris—an essential appositive

b. "the girl with black silky hair"—a nonessential appositive

c. Hans Christian Andersen, author of "The Princess and the Pea," wrote many entertaining stories for children.

d. no commas needed, essential appositive

e. Dr. May, the town's only physician, is busy during flu season.

f. no commas needed, essential appositive

g. inopportune

h. opportune

More Practice 60 See answers on page 174.

Review Set 60

1. *lumen*
2. greater
3. Providence
4. *Indolent*
5. plateau
6. abstract
7. cries, biggest
8. friend, freight
9. quieter
10. many
11. Dear Cousin Anabel,
    Please meet me at Chop Sticks Palace on Tuesday.
              Love,
              Marta
12. clause
13. or, so
14. Why, Dr. Mejares, must I study a foreign language?
15. violinist
16. complete sentence
17. out the (door)
    down the (street)
    to the (post office)
18. a. noun or verb
    b. hej
    c. Old English
19. My father, Mr. Curtis, can repair your broken computer.
20. Were Mr. and Mrs. Hahn married on Mt. Wilson?
21. imperative
22. the, mature, gentle, the, white, my, two
23. I spoke with Ann Wong, R.N., on Monday, January 2, 2006.
24. a. (is) pitying
    b. pitied
    c. (has) pitied
25. nominative case
26. I. Crops in Iowa
        A. Corn
        B. Oats
        C. Soybeans

27. a. journal entries
    b. cans of corn
    c. truckfuls

28. Rufus | leaves

    critters | will miss

    he | is

29.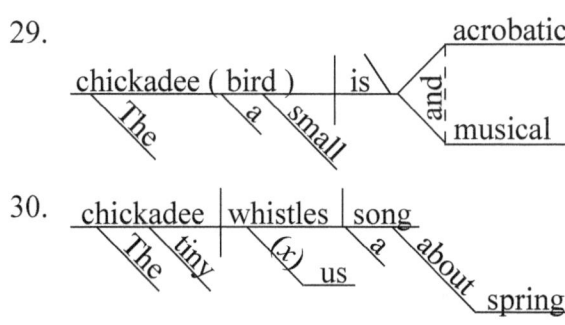

30.

LESSON 61 — Overused Adjectives • Unnecessary Articles

Practice 61 *Answers will vary.*

a. foul, stormy, dreary, foggy, miserable

b. interesting, thoughtful, entertaining

c. pretty, glamorous, lovely, stylish

d. old, sour, foul, spoiled

e. That sort of bug frightens me.

f. The babies were tired, so we put both of them to bed.

g. Intuition

h. Intuitive

Review Set 61

1. Opportune
2. light
3. Supersonic
4. care
5. Its
6. collective
7. gently, sadder
8. their, beliefs
9. quietest
10. fewer
11. Do citrus trees grow in the West?
12. phrase
13. Rosella
14. *The Heart of a Chief*
15. delightful and educational
16. B (unnecessary article "the" in sentence A)
17. Down the (hill;) across the (meadow)
18. a. s(c)issors
    b. (p)neumonia
    c. throu(gh)
19. Mr. Cabrera, my next-door neighbor, owns a Mexican restaurant in Los Angeles.
20. Dr. Y. I. Knap rests each day at two p.m.
21. cook
22. Ambitious, tiny, the, versatile, popular
23. Dr. Chu, you have an appointment with Thomas Curtis, M.B.A., on Tuesday, January 2, 2007.
24. a. (is) begging
    b. begged
    c. (has) begged
25. objective case
26. Miss Fortune asked, "Have you seen my purse?"
27. a. trenches
    b. human rights
    c. dishfuls
28. Rufus | cries

    nose | runs

    he | gets

Grammar and Writing 5

29.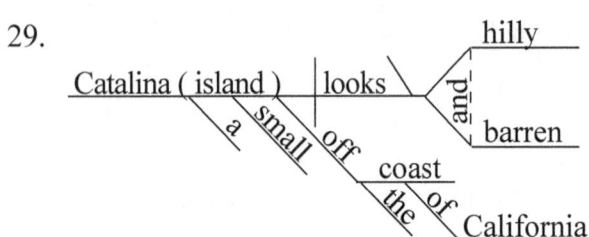

30.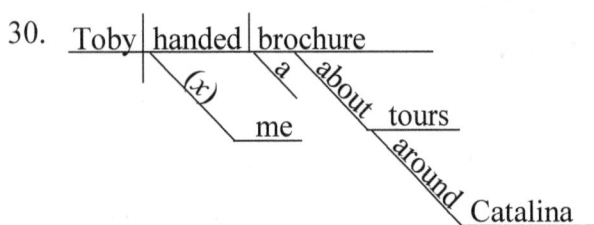

LESSON 62 Pronouns and Antecedents

Practice 62

a. Opal

b. Juan

c. Clem, Violet; llamas

d. umbrella

e. While Elle and Amelia were waiting, Elle wrote her essay.

f. The engine sputtered and coughed.

g. cowardice

h. intrepid

Review Set 62

1. Intuition
2. bad
3. shining
4. above
5. high
6. possessive
7. happiest, smiling
8. relieved, neighbor
9. quieter
10. quietest

11. Dear Mrs. Roper,
   I wish to commend your intrepid assistant for capturing the run-away cheetah last Wednesday.
        Gratefully,
        Mr. Ortiz

12. purse
13. and
14. May I keep this stray dog, Daddy?
15. electrician
16. B (unnecessary article "a" in A)
17. During the (storm;) around the (room;) under the (sofa)
18. a. adjective
    b. hek´ tik
    c. Greek
19. Rosa's youngest sister, Violeta, has chickenpox.
20. Mr. Dew now lives on S. Olive St. in Sacramento.
21. imperative
22. A, smelly, mangy, stray, the, her
23. Mora, we were on vacation in Oskaloosa, Iowa.
24. a. (is) steadying
    b. steadied
    c. (has) steadied
25. possessive case
26. Cut thistles in May,
    They'll grow in a day…
27. a. Gómezes
    b. waltzes
    c. women
28. horses | stomp

    cows | moo

    Olaf | delivers

29.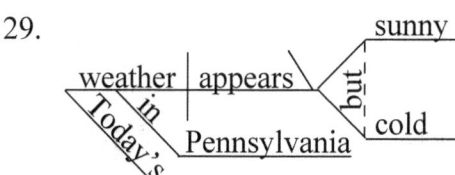

30.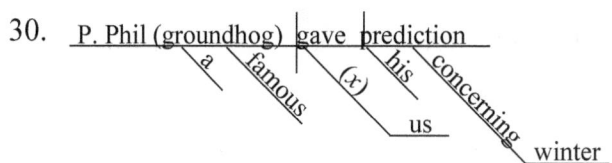

LESSON 63 — The Comma, Part 4: Greetings and Closings, Last Name First

Practice 63

a. Dear Tyrell,
   Thank you… "Abram, Peter."
   Gratefully,
   Hepzy

b. The index… "Carroll, Lewis" ….

c. Tenacity

d. Tenacious

Review Set 63

1. fearless
2. intuition
3. well-timed
4. Luminous
5. placate
6. abstract
7. funny, daily
8. deceive, chief
9. redder
10. reddest
11. Dear Mrs. Roper,
    I appreciate your tenacity in arguing my case in court on Thursday.
    Gratefully,
    Mr. Palma
12. phrase
13. Gertrude
14. *Because of Winn-Dixie*
15. clean, attractive
16. Examples: captivating, encouraging, inspiring
17. about (you;) since (Tuesday)
18. a. adjective
    b. si fal' ik
    c. Greek
19. Pewny, my youngest cousin, eats my broccoli for me.
20. The dog's collar costs $2.50 (two dollars and fifty cents).
21. is
22. a, shimmery, green
23. Luis, you may pick up your order on Monday, Wednesday, or Friday.
24. a. (is) tapping
    b. tapped
    c. (has) tapped
25. nominative case
26. Inez asked, "Who spilled the paint?"
27. a. sea serpents
    b. sheep
    c. thieves
28. Lily | made
    she | did
    she | has been studying
29.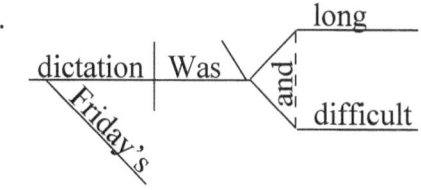

30.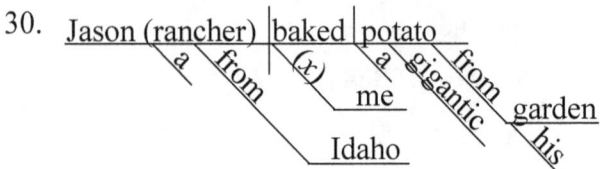

LESSON 64 Personal Pronouns

Practice 64

a. Unethical
b. Ethical
c. me, first person
d. He, third person
e. you, second person
f. us, plural
g. me, singular
h. subject
i. direct object
j. indirect object
k. possession

More Practice 64

1. we, first person plural; you, second person singular or plural
2. they, third person plural
3. him, third person singular
4. They, third person plural; their, third person plural; it, third person singular
5. you, second person singular or plural; my, first person singular
6. her, object
7. We, subject; our, possessive; them, object
8. I, subject; them, object; my, possessive
9. They, subject; me, object
10. She, subject; us, object

Review Set 64

1. Tenacious
2. Cowardice
3. knowledge
4. inopportune
5. calm
6. compound
7. mopped, dried
8. friend, field
9. many
10. first, singular
11. Dear Mr. Palma,
    I shall represent you in the Philadelphia courthouse as long as your behavior remains ethical.
                    Sincerely,
                    Mrs. Roper
12. Miss Fortune
13. or
14. My mother, Dr. Ting Lacy, studied Latin.
15. today
16. sentence fragment
17. in the (corner;) opposite (Harry;) for two (hours)
18. br(i)dge
19. Chester, the biggest cat on the farm, is disturbing the hens.
20. Mrs. Ross gave us these directions: Go north to Vista St. and turn right.
21. declarative
22. clause
23. Boise, Idaho, will be my destination, John.
24. a. (is) supplying
    b. supplied
    c. (has) supplied
25. object

26. I. New hospital staff
    A. Dr. Eric Koesno
    B. Ms. Cherry Clegg, R.N.

27. a. can openers
    b. wolves
    c. radios

28. Omar | made   he | did
    he | has been working

29.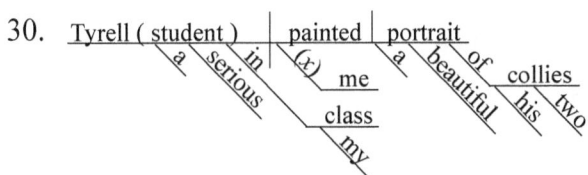

30. (diagram: Tyrell (student) | painted | portrait, with modifiers a, serious, in class, my, (x) me, a, beautiful, of, his, collies, two)

o. sang, sung
p. drank, drunk
q. chose, chosen
r. broke, broken
s. wore, worn
t. knew, known
u. blew, blown
v. began, begun
w. swore, sworn
x. spoke, spoken

LESSON 65 Irregular Verbs, Part 2

Practice 65

a. elation
b. elated
c. blew
d. worn
e. sang
f. spoken
g. tore
h. known
i. stole
j. rung
k. grew, grown
l. bore, borne
m. rang, rung
n. sank, sunk

Review Set 65

1. Ethical
2. tenacity
3. Intrepid
4. instinctive
5. bottom
6. plural
7. beginning, worrisome
8. perceives, achieved
9. better
10. first, plural
11. Dear Uncle Sergio,
    You can find her information in the directory under Blackly, Doris.
        Your niece,
        Daniela
12. boy
13. Lily
14. *The Sound of Music*
15. majestic
16. Examples: relaxing, exciting, fun
17. toward the ripest (tomato) on the (vine)
18. a. verb
    b. di lōōd´
    c. Middle English (from Latin)

19. Marigold, a spotted mare, likes to gallop through the mud.
20. At one a.m. Ms. Overwork tore up her essay and began again.
21. swell
22. phrase
23. I shall see you, John, on Tuesday, January 16, 2007.
24. a. (is) blowing
    b. blew
    c. (has) blown
25. subject
26. A man of words and not of deeds
    Is like a garden full of weeds.
27. a. eyelashes
    b. bagfuls
    c. sopranos
28. Miss Fortune | lost
    Hector | found
    thief | did

29.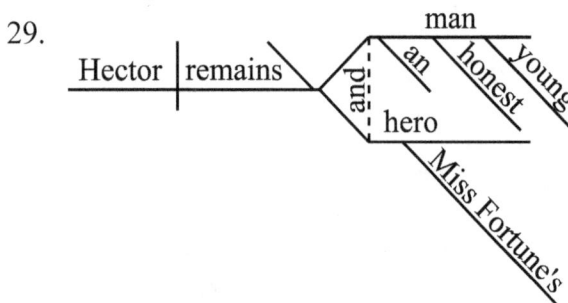

30.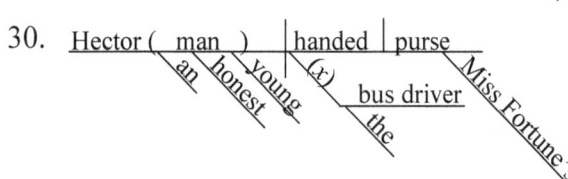

b. They are excellent writers.
c. The best writer was he.
d. Contrite
e. Contrition
f. She and I wore green
g. I, she, they, he, we
h. she
i. she
j. he
k. I

Review Set 66

1. Elated
2. unethical
3. tenacious
4. courage
5. Sedimentary
6. abstract
7. preferred, sunnier
8. weigh, piece
9. fewer
10. second
11. Dear Aunt Beki,
    Can you come to Mother's birthday party on Monday, May 5?
          Your niece,
          Daniela
12. purse
13. and, and, but
14. Leonard learned all about geology from his father, Dr. Trent, but nothing about English.
15. president
16. sentence fragment

LESSON 66 Nominative Pronoun Case

Practice 66

a. *Refer to the chart in Example 1.*

17. With Yosemite's (Half Dome) in the (background) of our long (hike) to the (falls)

18. g(u)ide

19. My littlest brother, Andrew, found a worm in his apple.

20. On Dec. 24, 1914, Mr. John Muir died at the age of seventy-six.

21. he

22. clause

23. Jacob, I would like you to meet Yin Yu, D.D.S.

24. a. (is) bearing
    b. bore
    c. (has) borne

25. object

26. Hector said, "This purse belongs to the woman who stepped off the bus at Oak Street."

27. a. cups of tea
    b. cupfuls
    c. altos

28.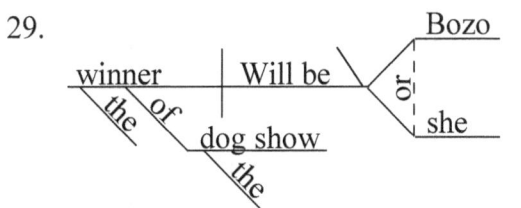

29.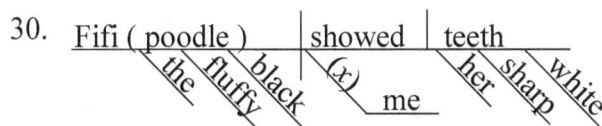

30. Fifi (poodle) | showed | teeth

LESSON 67 The Comma, Part 5: Introductory and Interrupting Elements, Afterthoughts

Practice 67

a. Yes, I speak English.

b. Of course, not everyone does.

c. His grandfather, I believe, came from Denmark.

d. The camel, it is said, has no sense of humor.

e. pertinent

f. irrelevant

More Practice 67 *See answers on page 175.*

Review Set 67

1. Contrite
2. high
3. Ethical
4. tenacious
5. caldera
6. possessive
7. fries, flattest
8. briefcase, conceited
9. worst
10. third, singular
11. Dear Daniela,
    Yes, I shall come to your mother's party on Monday, May 5.
    　　　　Love,
    　　　　Aunt Beki
12. Miss Fortune
12. us
14. *The Red Pony*
15. passionate
16. A (unnecessary article "The" in B)

17. With a (child) in a (backpack) to the (top) of (Sentinel Dome)

18. tw(o)

19. Ms. Hoo flew to Sacramento, the capital of California.

20. Dr. Kraning will lecture on Aug. 14.

21. I

22. phrase

23. If you have time, Mark, please bake two potatoes, some rolls, and a pie.

24. a. (is) beginning
    b. began
    c. (has) begun

25. subject

26. I. National parks
    A. Yosemite
    B. Yellowstone

27. a. pennies
    b. boxes of cereal
    c. trout

28.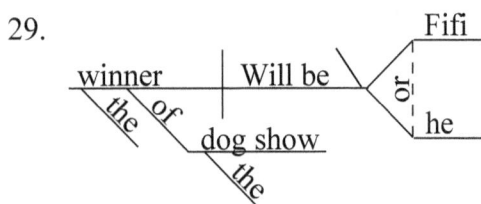

29.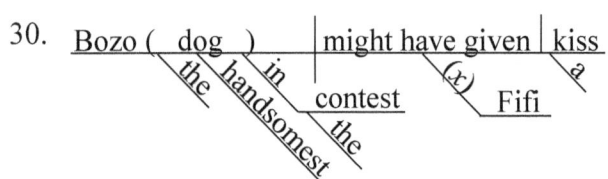

30. Bozo (dog) | might have given | kiss
    the handsomest in contest (x) a Fifi

LESSON 68 The Comma, Part 6: Clarity

Practice 68

a. To Karen, Joyce meant trouble.

b. While passing, the driver honked.

c. After John, Thomas will speak.

d. Ornithology

e. Meteorology

Review Set 68

1. Pertinent
2. regret
3. high
4. Unethical
5. volcano's
6. interrogative
7. shopping, beautiful
8. receive, priest's
9. worse
10. third, plural
11. Dear Aunt Beki,
    Please bring paper plates, cups, and napkins to Mom's party, all right?
        Many thanks,
        Daniela
12. bus driver
13. and, or
14. I'll ask Mother for the Spanish translation.
15. rich
16. complete sentence
17. To see that dog, Bozo would do anything.
18. a. noun
    b. dē′ toor
    c. French (from Latin)

19. Ms. Hoo, a middle-school teacher, needs a vacation.
20. At one p.m. Mrs. Sizzle arrived in Death Valley.
21. she
22. clause
23. When you come, Ms. Hoo, please plan to stay until Friday, August 12.
24. a. (is) choosing
    b. chose
    c. (has) chosen
25. object
26. Fuzzy Wuzzy was a bear,
    Fuzzy Wuzzy had no hair,
    So Fuzzy Wuzzy wasn't fuzzy,
    Was he?
27. a. Rufuses
    b. French fries
    c. leashes
28.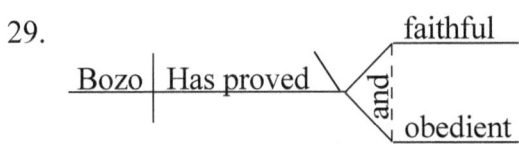
29.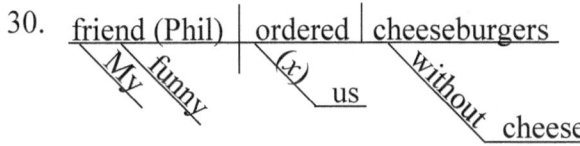
30.

LESSON 69 Objective Pronoun Case

Practice 69

a. *Refer to the chart in Example 1.*
b. The noise frightened her.
c. Jesse sang me a song.
d. He has sung to us. *(Also correct: To us he has sung.)*

e. unfeigned
f. feign
g. Don't forget him or me.
h. me, him, them, her, us
i. him
j. him
k. me

Review Set 69

1. Irrelevant
2. Meteorology
3. sorry
4. Elation
5. meteorite
6. plural
7. objective
8. thief, freight
9. fewer
10. third, singular
11. Dear Peter,
    As I remember, your maternal ancestors are listed under Hillborne, Winona.
        Warmly,
        Uncle Jakob
12. telephone
13. Dara
14. "The Velveteen Rabbit"
15. tree
16. A (unnecessary article "a" in B)
17. To Elle, Gabriel seems indispensable.
18. (k)nee
19. Puerto Rico, a U.S. territory, has beautiful rain forests.
20. Mr. Lee N. Chen sent us to 142 E. Ash Ave.
21. subject

22. phrase
23. On June 26, 2008, I shall be eighty-six, my dear.
24. a. (is) knowing
    b. knew
    c. (has) known
25. me
26. Jasmin said, "We shall miss Ms. Hoo."
27. a. butterflies
    b. dollar bills
    c. peaches
28.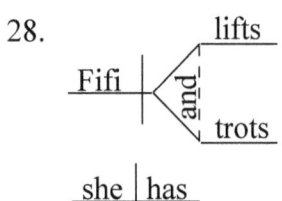
29.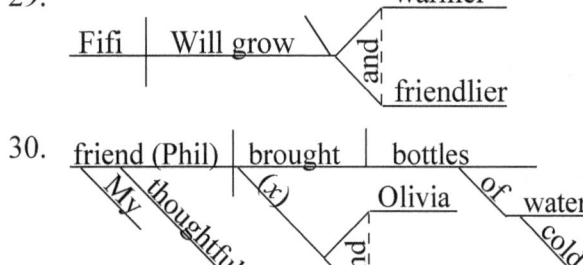
30.

LESSON 70 Personal Pronoun Case Forms

Practice 70

a. objective case
b. nominative case
c. possessive case
d. objective of preposition
e. subject
f. direct object
g. indirect object
h. possession
i. they

j. me
k. linguistics
l. linguist

Review Set 70

1. Ornithology
2. Unfeigned
3. relevant
4. Contrition
5. meteor
6. concrete
7. nominative
8. trotted, steadily
9. prettiest
10. first, singular
11. Dear Uncle Jakob,
       I found my maternal ancestors, my paternal ancestors, and my lost library card.
              With gratitude,
              Peter
12. Juan
13. or, but
14. Yes, Dad, you have an appointment with Dr. Payne on Monday.
15. up the (trail)
    over the (bridge)
    through the (woods)
16. sentence fragment
17. Soon after, Ben fell asleep.
18. a. noun
    b. sī′ klō n
    c. Greek
19. Colorado, the Centennial State, is known for its many high mountain peaks.
20. Col. Robert Andrews has moved to St. Louis, Missouri.
21. she

22. clause
23. Professor Luna, Ph.D., teaches English, French, and poetry.
24. a. (is) tearing
    b. tore
    c. (has) torn
25. B
26. I. The old railroad
    A. Steam trains
    B. Jenny railcars
27. a. solos
    b. sisters-in-law
    c. children
28.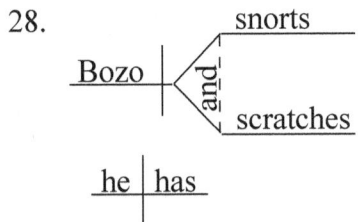
29.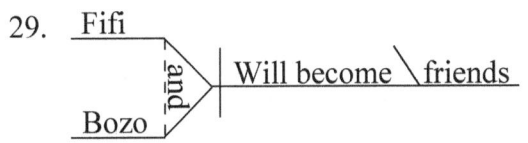
30.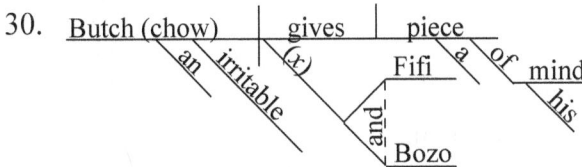

LESSON 71   Diagramming Pronouns

Practice 71

a. ardent
b. ardor
c.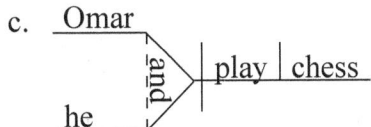

d.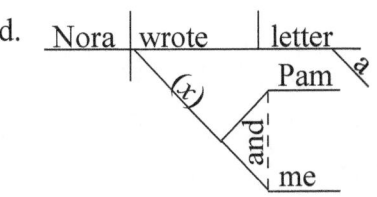

e.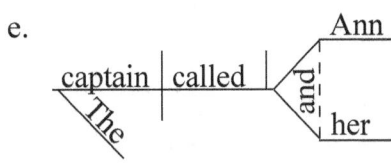

Review Set 71

1. Linguistics
2. feign
3. weather
4. relevant
5. Vertebrate
6. collective
7. objective
8. achieve, their
9. many
10. first, plural
11. Dear Quan,
        The deadline is Monday, May 10, 2010.
            Sincerely,
            Juan
12. bus
13. parks
14. "Look for the Silver Lining"
15. oak
16. Examples: faithful, reliable, cheerful
17. As you know, everything needs cleaning.
18. walk
19. Kansas, the Sunflower State, has prairies, farms, and rolling hills.
20. Mr. Thomas Cross, Jr., works for Barrons, Inc., in St. Louis.
21. subject

22. phrase
23. Egbert, my new address is 123 Fourth Avenue, Montgomery, Alabama.
24. a. (is) ringing
    b. rang
    c. (has) rung
25. her
26. Olivia said, "Thank you, Phil."
27. a. wrenches
    b. lawn mowers
    c. daisies
28.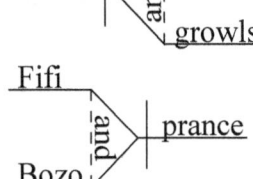
29.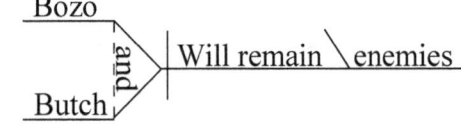
30. Butch (dog) | shows | side
    an unfriendly (x) the impolite of personality his everyone

LESSON 72 Possessive Pronouns and Possessive Adjectives

Practice 72

a. its
b. their
c. hers
d. your
e. ours
f. serene
g. serenity

More Practice 72

1. their
2. They're
3. its
4. ours
5. hers
6. yours
7. your
8. It's, its

Review Set 72

1. linguist
2. Ardor
3. sincere
4. birds
5. vertebrate
6. interrogative
7. possessive
8. Your
9. better
10. you
11. Dear Juan,
    I cannot do my schoolwork, clean my room, and meet your deadline.
                    Regretfully,
                    Quan
12. Juan
13. jay
14. Her classes include mathematics, Latin, biology, and English.
15. a. clapped
    b. glorious
16. run-on sentence
17. Because of Clark, Kent was late.

Grammar and Writing 5   72   Teacher Guide
                                Student Edition Answers

18. a. verb
    b. delv
    c. Middle English

19. Hawaii, the Aloha State, was formed by volcanic eruptions.

20. Ms. Hoo's note reads, "Homework due Fri., Feb. 3."

21. I

22. clause

23. No, Egbert, I did not move to Little Rock, Arkansas.

24. a. (is) freezing
    b. froze
    c. (has) frozen

25. A

26. Twinkle, twinkle, little star,
    How I wonder what you are…

27. a. patches
    b. dictionaries
    c. basketfuls

28.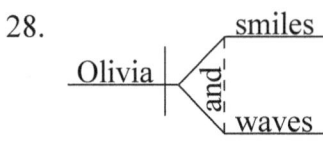

    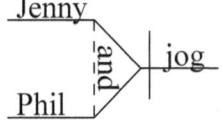

29.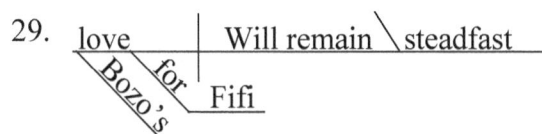

30.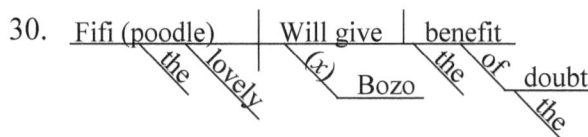

LESSON 73 Dependent and Independent Clauses • Subordinating Conjunctions

Practice 73

a. dependent

b. independent

c. independent

d. dependent

e. Unless

f. even though

g. When

h. sagacity

i. Sagacious

More Practice 73 *See answers on page 176.*

Review Set 73

1. Serene
2. passionate
3. linguistics
4. pretend
5. valuable
6. possessive
7. nominative
8. yours
9. best
10. third, singular
11. Dear Cousin Wassim,
       Please come to my piano recital on Monday, April 2, 2008, at Grandmother's house.
                   Your cousin,
                   Aleda
12. Ms. Hoo
13. around the campground
    for bear-proof lockers
    for our food
14. while
15. a. trapped
    b. cloudiness
16. A
17. The day after, I mopped the floor.

Grammar and Writing 5 — 73 — Teacher Guide Student Edition Answers

18. flight

19. Moe, the smallest boy on the team, won the cross-country race last Saturday.

20. Capt. Rice lives on E. Sunshine Blvd. in St. Petersburg.

21. object

22. dependent

23. Luey, you may speak with Professor Grin, Ph.D., tomorrow.

24. a. (is) throwing
    b. threw
    c. (has) thrown

25. me

26. Carl said, "You should paint the room mustard yellow."

27. a. lives
    b. Fridays
    c. parties

28.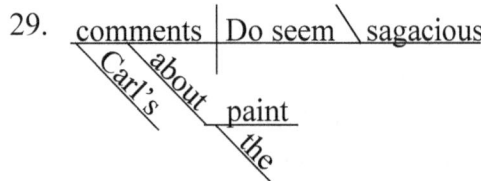

29.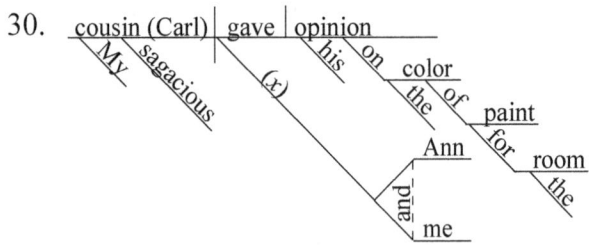

30.

LESSON 74 The Comma, Part 7: Descriptive Adjectives, Dependent Clauses

Practice 74

a. We could hardly see through the deep, dense fog.

b. I took my biggest, warmest jacket to Minnesota, but ….

c. When … store, get a few peaches.

d. If they look bruised, buy ….

e. As soon … home, we'll ….

f. Redundancy

g. redundant

More Practice 74 *See answers on page 177.*

Review Set 74

1. Sagacious
2. peace
3. passion
4. language
5. asset
6. abstract
7. objective
8. hers
9. fewer
10. third, singular
11. Dear Cousin Aleda,
    On Monday, April 2, I shall be in Montpelier, Vermont.
                Regretfully,
                Wassim
12. sock
13. and, but
14. After
15. a. tapping
    b. penniless
16. complete sentence
17. To Omar, Nicasio appears malicious.
18. a. noun
    b. plum´ it
    c. Middle English (from Middle French)

19. Wyoming, the Equality State, has rugged mountains and windy flatlands.

20. He works at the Wumpit Toy Co., 12 N. Main St., Alhambra, CA.

21. she

22. independent

23. If you go to Alaska, you might meet a huge, friendly moose.

24. a. (is) wearing
    b. wore
    c. (has) worn

25. her

26. I. Lakes
    A. Scenic views
    B. Water sports
    C. Houseboats

27. a. opportunities
    b. police chiefs
    c. knives

28.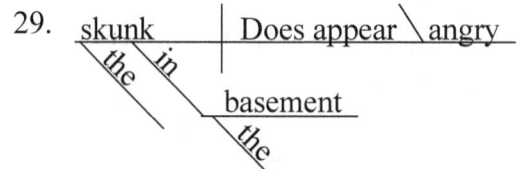

29.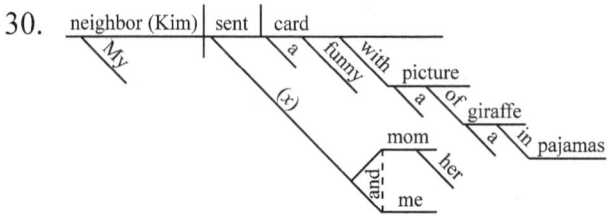

30.

LESSON 75 Compound Sentences • Coordinating Conjunctions

Practice 75

a. simple

b. compound; but

c. compound; and, so

d. simple

e. compound; for

f. You | should use
   or
   bugs | will bite

g. insatiable

h. satiable

Review Set 75

1. Redundant

2. Sagacity

3. peaceful

4. passionate

5. asset

6. collective

7. possessive

8. theirs

9. faster

10. third, plural

11. Dear Mrs. Cruz,
    My new address is 12 Sun Avenue, Frankfort, Kentucky.
            Sincerely,
            Mrs. Otto

12. compound

13. geyser

14. as

15. a. sleigh
    b. view

16. Examples: helpful, considerate, patient

17. With Dan, Smith can accomplish much.

18. bough

19. Tyrell, a tennis champion, is learning to play chess.

20. Dr. Norris's note reads, "Every 45 to 90 min., Old Faithful erupts."

19. Wyoming, the Equality State, has rugged mountains and windy flatlands.
20. He works at the Wumpit Toy Co., 12 N. Main St., Alhambra, CA.
21. she
22. independent
23. If you go to Alaska, you might meet a huge, friendly moose.
24. a. (is) wearing
    b. wore
    c. (has) worn
25. her
26. I. Lakes
    A. Scenic views
    B. Water sports
    C. Houseboats
27. a. opportunities
    b. police chiefs
    c. knives
28.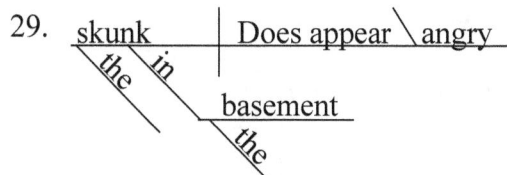
29.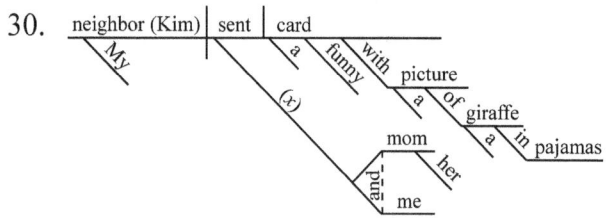
30.

d. simple
e. compound; for
f.
```
   you │ should use
 or
   bugs │ will bite
```
g. insatiable
h. satiable

Review Set 75

1. Redundant
2. Sagacity
3. peaceful
4. passionate
5. asset
6. collective
7. possessive
8. theirs
9. faster
10. third, plural
11. Dear Mrs. Cruz,
    My new address is 12 Sun Avenue, Frankfort, Kentucky.
        Sincerely,
        Mrs. Otto
12. compound
13. geyser
14. as
15. a. sleigh
    b. view
16. Examples: helpful, considerate, patient
17. With Dan, Smith can accomplish much.
18. bou(gh)
19. Tyrell, a tennis champion, is learning to play chess.
20. Dr. Norris's note reads, "Every 45 to 90 min., Old Faithful erupts."

LESSON 75 — Compound Sentences • Coordinating Conjunctions

Practice 75

a. simple
b. compound; but
c. compound; and, so

24. a. (is) speaking
    b. spoke
    c. (has) spoken

25. me

26. and, but, or, for, nor, yet, so

27. a. eyeteeth
    b. toothbrushes
    c. team captains

28. Egbert | is writing

    Ivy | is playing

29.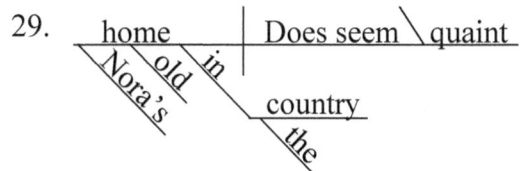

30.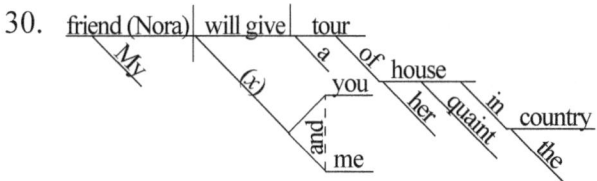

LESSON 77 Relative Pronouns

Practice 77

a. who
b. who
c. whomever
d. that
e. whom
f. who | is \ friend

g. ameliorate
h. amelioration

More Practice 77

1. who
2. who
3. whom
4. whom
5. whom
6. who

Review Set 77

1. old-fashioned
2. satisfied
3. wordy
4. wisdom
5. all
6. possessive
7. nominative
8. Your
9. fewer
10. first, plural
11. whom
12. simple
13. magnificent
14. because
15. a. pieces
    b. eight
16. B
17. Without Mia, Curtis is defenseless.
18. taught
19. Jerusalem crickets, scary-looking bugs, are not poisonous.
20. Mrs. Lowe's baby, James L. Ditter, Jr., weighs 27 lbs., 3 oz.
21. subject
22. phrase
23. As I stepped outside, I nearly squashed the biggest, ugliest bug on the planet.
24. a. (is) growing
    b. grew
    c. (has) grown

25. A

26. Ivy is playing games, for she has finished her essay.

27. Dear Anabel,
    Please call, write, or email me soon.
    Love,
    Uncle Rigo

28.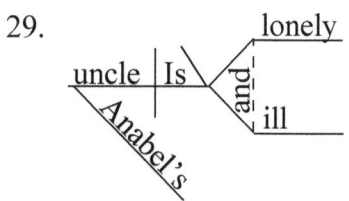

29.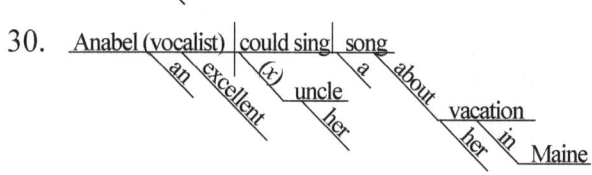

30. Anabel (vocalist) could sing song
    an excellent (x) uncle a about
    Anabel's her vacation
    her in Maine

LESSON 78   Pronoun Usage

Practice 78

a. We
b. us
c. us
d. I
e. we
f. salinity
g. saline

More Practice 78

1. he
2. We
3. us
4. she
5. her
6. he
7. she
8. they
9. We
10. us

Review Set 78

1. ameliorate
2. Quaintness
3. satisfied
4. words
5. dispensable
6. concrete
7. nominative
8. hers
9. curlier
10. third, plural
11. who
12. We
13. and, but, or, for, nor, yet, so
14. that
15. people
16. sentence fragment
17. From the sun, people were burned.
18. a. verb or noun
    b. di sper´
    c. Middle English (from Latin)
19. Missouri, the Show Me State, lies in the center of the continent.
20. The Atlas Tile Co. is located on S. Third St. in Rock City.
21. she
22. independent
23. As Olaf rode a white Arabian horse, Sven played a shiny, loud trumpet.

24. a. (is) swearing
    b. swore
    c. (has) sworn
25. her
26. Leo is playing games, but he hasn't won any.
27. *A Light in the Attic*
28. hair | has shrunk
    he | washed
29. we | shall call | Whom
30. Buzz (barber) | Did give | haircut
    the / (x) Alex / a \ short

LESSON 79 Interrogative Pronouns

Practice 79

a. what
b. none (*which* is an adjective)
c. Whose
d. Whom
e. Whose
f. Who
g. interrogative pronoun
h. adjective
i. daunt
j. dauntless

More Practice 79

1. Who's
2. Whose
3. Who
4. whom
5. Whom
6. Who's
7. Whose
8. whom
9. Who
10. Whom

Review Set 79

1. Saline
2. better
3. old
4. satisfied
5. essential
6. compound
7. objective
8. Their
9. curliest
10. second
11. whom
12. us
13. Whom
14. until
15. compound sentence
16. Who
17. This, Walter can do.
18. unfeigned
19. Arizona, the Grand Canyon State, gets very little rain.
20. They took water, fruit, cheese, etc., on their hike up Mt. Wilson.
21. object
22. except (Joe)
    alongside the (stream)
23. When Ms. Hoo retires, she will move to a quaint, small town.

24. a. (is) singing
    b. sang
    c. (has) sung

25. B

26. Yoli said, "I was born on Sunday, November 4, 1973, so how old am I?"

27. Dear Uncle Rigo,
       If you would like, I could bring you some bread, cheese, and grapes.
                Love,
                Anabel

28. Amy | planted
    ants | must have harvested

29. teacher | is \ who
    \The \new

30. Badchek (deceiver) | sold | ring
    \the (x) \a \with
    whom diamond \a \fake

LESSON 80   Quotation Marks, Part 1

Practice 80

a. none

b. none

c. "Inch by inch, … cinch," said Ms. Hoo.

d. "If … time," said the teacher, "you'll … work."

e. docent

f. curator

More Practice 80 *See answers on page 179.*

Review Set 80

1. daunt
2. saltiness
3. improvement
4. Quaint
5. Indispensable
6. declarative
7. possessive
8. Whose
9. fewer, he
10. first, singular
11. who
12. We
13. Who
14. Whenever
15. sheep
16. quaint
17. For that, Sven paid forty dollars.
18. a. noun
    b. īs´ burg
    c. Danish, or Norwegian
19. Minnesota, the Gopher State, borders Lake Superior.
20. The note says, "Come to the library on Sat., Feb. 12."
21. he
22. dependent
23. "I like my students," said Ms. Hoo, "but their animals can be difficult."
24. a. (is) breaking
    b. broke
    c. (has) broken
25. her
26. I. Bryce National Park
      A. Geology
      B. Paleontology
27. Dear Anabel,
       I do not like bread and cheese, nor do I like grapes.
               Thanks anyway,
               Uncle Rigo

28. sheep | has broken

    Miss BoPeep | must carry

29. Miss BoPeep | should notify | Whom

30.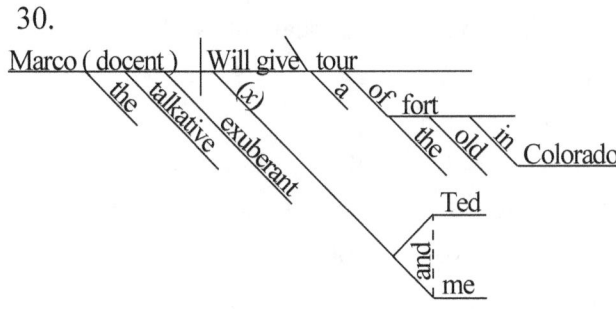

LESSON 81   Quotation Marks, Part 2

Practice 81

a. culprit

b. culpable

c. Have … "King Stork" by Howard Pyle?

d. Can … "Over the Rainbow" for me?

e. The … "Gone Is Gone" comes from Bohemia.

f. "Sit here, Molly, and tell me all about yourself. What are your hobbies?"
   "I like to catch butterflies and draw pictures," Molly said.

More Practice 81 *See answers on page 180.*

Review Set 81

1. docent
2. discouraged
3. salty
4. better
5. outcry
6. possessive
7. possessive
8. yours
9. fewest
10. first, plural
11. whom
12. we
13. whom
14. As soon as
15. simple sentence
16. Whom
17. That, Alba can take with her.
18. apologies
19. Badchek, the culprit, has fled to another country.
20. Mr. and Mrs. Tran live at 654 S. Alta Loma Dr. in Austin.
21. subject
22. Jenny replied, "No, I have not seen Badchek."
23. "If I see a suspicious, malicious person," said Jenny, "I shall call the police."
24. a. (is) drinking
    b. drank
    c. (has) drunk
25. Let us hum the song "The Old Gray Mare."
26. Fido eats my pizza, yet I forgive him.
27. Dear Officer Valiant,

    Your mean, avaricious culprit has lived in Iceland, Belgium, and Botswana.

    Respectfully,
    Mrs. Brite, P.I.

28. We | must locate

    he | will commit

29.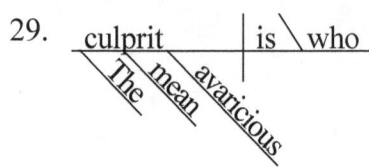

30.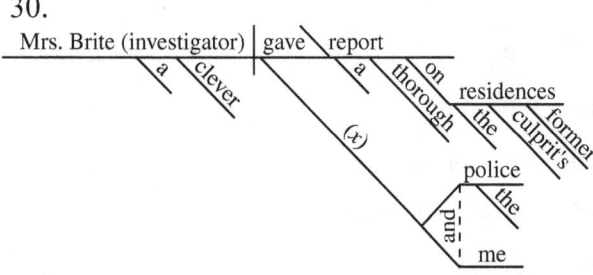

LESSON 82 Demonstrative Pronouns

Practice 82

a. Blissful

b. Bliss

c. This painting

d. Those colors

e. This relative

f. These reasons

g. This key

Review Set 82

1. Culpable
2. curator
3. heroic
4. saltiness
5. proclamation
6. abstract
7. possessive
8. Whose
9. better
10. third, singular
11. Whom
12. We
13. Those
14. Since
15. a. angriest
    b. winning
16. complete sentence
17. To Alba, Dunn appears blissful.
18. a. adjective, verb
    b. lav´ish
    c. Middle English, Old French
19. Boise, the capital of Idaho, lies at the foot of the Rocky Mountains.
20. Your appointment with Dr. Ramos is on Mon., Jan. 2.
21. he
22. over the (hill)
    around the (rocks)
23. Lulu said, "Although I was born in Cheyenne, Wyoming, I now live in Salem, Oregon."
24. a. (is) stealing
    b. stole
    c. (has) stolen
25. My aunt read me a short story called "Adrift on an Ice Pan."
26. Fido stole my pencil, so I didn't do my homework.
27. Dear Mrs. Brite, P.I.,
    The culprit, I believe, was last seen in Juneau, Alaska.
                    Respectfully,
                    Officer Valiant
28. Badchek | fled   we | shall find

    we | are

29. culprit | swindled | whom
    The mean avaricious

30.

Officer Valiant (assistant) | sent | message
    \ Mrs. Brite's   \(x) \a \about crimes
                          \me   \Badchek's \previous

LESSON 83 — Indefinite Pronouns

Practice 83

a. All; plural
b. Nobody; singular
c. are
d. are
e. is
f. has; its
g. wax, their
h. sells; it; is
i. subvert
j. subversion

More Practice 83

1. P
2. E
3. S
4. S
5. S
6. P
7. S
8. P
9. S
10. E
11. P
12. S
13. S
14. S
15. E
16. E
17. P
18. S
19. P
20. E

Review Set 83

1. Bliss
2. culprit
3. guide
4. Dauntless
5. similar
6. collective
7. nominative
8. theirs
9. fewer
10. third, singular
11. who
12. us
13. is
14. its
15. Wherever
16. plank
17. Looking up, Dana smiled.
18. grandchildren
19. The boll weevil, an insect with a long snout, ruined cotton crops in the South.
20. Both
21. subject
22. independent
23. Mrs. Brite, P.I., said, "Badchek cannot escape, for I have his name, address, and fingerprints."

24. a. (is) throwing
    b. threw
    c. (has) thrown

25. her

26. I. Fun at the ocean
       A. Fishing
       B. Surfing

27. Dear Mrs. Brite, P.I.,
    Obviously, Badchek does not live at 12 W. Palm Avenue, Juneau, Alaska. That place does not exist.
              Sincerely,
              Officer Valiant

28. canines | came   they | were
    plane | had left

29. Officer Valiant | should arrest | Whom
    (the) (intrepid)

30. Badchek (coward) | has written | checks
    (a) (culpable) (x) nephew (his) (seven) (bad)

LESSON 84   Italics or Underline

Practice 84

a. rapprochement

b. rapport

c. Time

d. is

e. Quercus

f. guapo

g. Betty Bee

More Practice 84 *See answers on page 181.*

Review Set 84

1. subvert
2. happy
3. blame
4. museum
5. kin
6. declarative
7. objective
8. Your
9. better
10. third, plural
11. whom
12. he
13. Is
14. Has, his or her
15. even though
16. What
17. Buenos días
18. palm
19. The island of Alcatraz, once a federal prison, lies in the middle of San Francisco Bay.
20. Neither
21. he
22. phrase
23. Officer Valiant replied, "Yes, as soon as we catch Badchek, we shall send him to Alcatraz."
24. a. (is) wearing
    b. wore
    c. (has) worn
25. B
26. No, I have not read a short story titled "Where the Sheep Went."

27. Dear Officer Valiant,
    On Friday, February 3, 2006, someone spotted Badchek in Columbus, Ohio.
    Sincerely,
    Mrs. Brite, P.I.

28.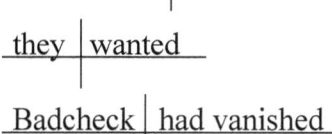

29.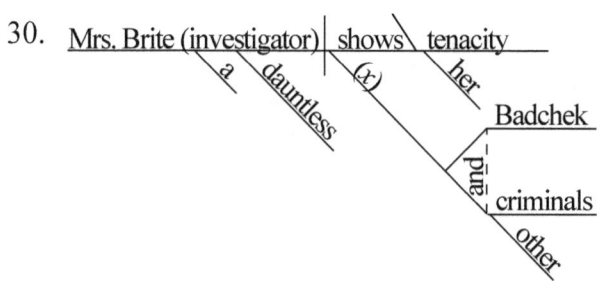

30. Mrs. Brite (investigator) shows tenacity...

LESSON 85   Irregular Verbs, Part 3

Practice 85

a. caught; (has) caught
b. came; (has) come
c. cost; (has) cost
d. dove or dived; (has) dived
e. dragged; (has) dragged
f. drew; (has) drawn
g. drowned; (has) drowned
h. drove; (has) driven
i. eaten
j. found
k. drove
l. cost
m. forgave
n. caught
o. flew
p. fell
q. grandiloquent
r. pretentious

More Practice 85 *See answers on pages 182–183.*

Review Set 85

1. Rapport
2. Subversion
3. happiness
4. guilty
5. Akin
6. plural
7. possessive
8. hers
9. best
10. third, plural
11. who
12. us
13. come
14. have, their
15. Until
16. Whose
17. Kim
18. houseflies
19. The Gila monster, Arizona's biggest lizard, is the only poisonous lizard in the United States.
20. compound sentence
21. subject
22. in California's (Humboldt Bay) by (H.D. Bendixsen)

23. Mrs. Brite, P.I., said, "We have not caught him, but we shall before summer."
24. a. (is) forgiving
    b. forgave
    c. (has) forgiven
25. me
26. Yes, I know the song "I've Been Working on the Railroad."
27. My dear Ms. Hoo,
       Get plenty of rest, exercise, and fresh air.
                Warm regards,
                Katy Diddit, R.N.
28. Badchek | bursts
    few | recognize
    he | has grown
29. Badchek | Has become \ caretaker (the, of riches, Mr. Knothead's)
30. billionaire (Mr. K.) | Did assign | task (x) (the, pretentious) a new of importance Badchek tremendous

LESSON 86 Irregular Verbs, Part 4

Practice 86

a. hid; (has) hidden or hid
b. held; (has) held
c. laid; (has) laid
d. led; (has) led
e. lent; (has) lent
f. mistook; (has) mistaken
g. put; (has) put
h. sold; (has) sold
i. hid
j. held
k. laid
l. led
m. colossal
n. colossus

More Practice 86 *See answers on pages 184–185.*

Review Set 86

1. Pretentious
2. Rapprochement
3. different
4. happiness
5. Kin
6. abstract
7. nominative
8. Whose
9. fewer
10. first, plural
11. Whom
12. I
13. gone
14. has, his or her
15. as if, that
16. optimistic
17. Seafoam Joy
18. a. noun or verb
    b. mīm
    c. Greek
19. Nashville, the capital of Tennessee, is famous for country music.
20. a. messiest
    b. thinner

21. they

22. phrase

23. Mrs. Brite, P.I., said, "Although a deceptive, malicious witness has given me false reports, I shall still find the culprit."

24. a. (is) driving
    b. drove
    c. (has) driven

25. me

26. In my opinion, the short story should be titled "Badchek on the Loose."

27. My dear Mrs. Hoo,
       You may see Dr. Rivas on Monday, February 6.
               Warm regards,
               Katy Diddit, R.N.

28.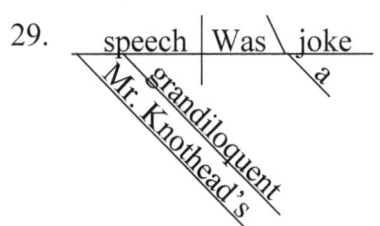

29.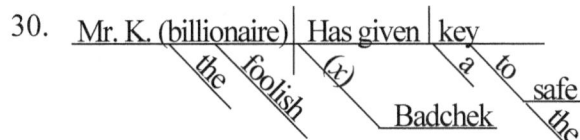

30. Mr. K. (billionaire) | Has given | key
       the   foolish   (x)   a   to   safe
               Badchek   the

LESSON 87   Irregular Verbs, Part 5

Practice 87

a. took; (has) taken

b. set; (has) set

c. taught; (has) taught

d. told; (has) told

e. woke; (has) woken

f. sprang or sprung; (has) sprung

g. strove; (has) striven

h. shut; (has) shut

i. written

j. slept

k. thought

l. taught

m. told

n. woken

o. sat

p. shut

q. coerce

r. coercion

More Practice 87 *See answers on pages 186–187.*

Review Set 87

1. colossus
2. pretentious
3. understanding
4. Avaricious
5. destruction
6. compound
7. objective
8. theirs
9. better
10. first, singular
11. whom
12. we
13. lay, slept
14. has, his or her
15. as, if
16. complete sentence
17. After the show, time stood still.
18. dropperfuls

19. South Dakota, the Mount Rushmore State, has a large area of forest called the Black Hills.
20. Bozo
21. object
22. Across the (field)
    under the (fence)
    over the (hill)
23. Katy Diddit, R.N., said, "I wrote to Ms. Hoo, but she has not written back."
24. a. (is) bringing
    b. brought
    c. (has) brought
25. B
26. That song, I believe, is called "Over the Waves."
27. Dear Grandmother,
       I have striven to do my best. Thank you for helping me.
                Love,
                Benito
28.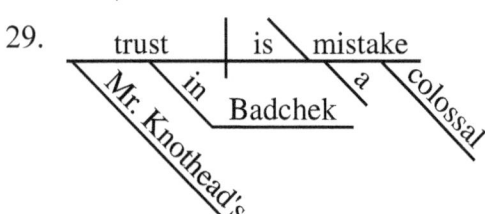
29.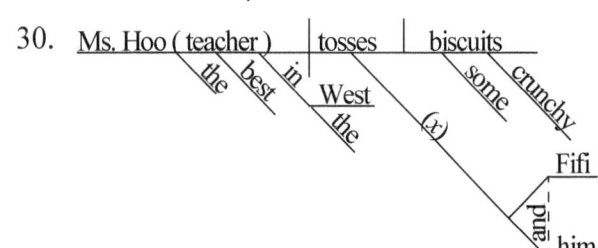
30. Ms. Hoo (teacher) tosses biscuits ...

LESSON 88 The Exclamation Mark • The Question Mark

Practice 88

a. Wow! That ... spectacular!
b. Do you understand Greek?
c. Who painted *Blue Boy*?
d. I know! It's Thomas Gainsborough!
e. complacency
f. complacent

Review Set 88

1. coerce
2. large
3. showy
4. reestablishment
5. greedy
6. imperative
7. objective
8. Who
9. better
10. third, singular
11. whom
12. she
13. taken, hung
14. have, their
15. While, so that
16. luminous
17. complacent
18. we(igh)
19. Dagny, a complacent player, seems unmotivated now.
20. compound sentence
21. she

22. phrase
23. Chloe asked, "Have you heard from Ms. Hoo, Katy?"
24. a. (is) buying
    b. bought
    c. (has) bought
25. me
26. What a silly story! It should be titled "Mr. Knothead's Colossal Mistake."
27. Dear Benito,
     Have you seen my old shoes? They are made out of string, straw, and wood.
                Love,
                Grandpa
28. Butch | has been growling
    Fifi | has been cowering
    Bozo | will save
29. Mr. Knothead | Has been \ imprudent
30.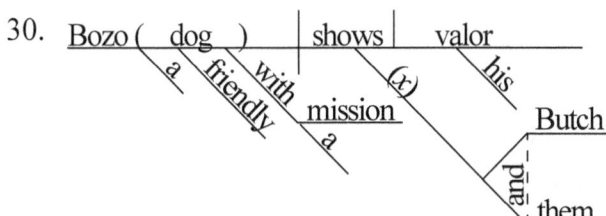

LESSON 89 Subject-Verb Agreement, Part 1

Practice 89

a. was
b. were
c. raise
d. makes
e. make
f. has
g. languid
h. languish

More Practice 89

1. sound
2. are
3. swim
4. are
5. has
6. were
7. have
8. sees

Review Set 89

1. Complacent
2. Coercion
3. large
4. reestablishment
5. Avarice
6. possessive
7. possessive
8. Their, yours
9. fewer
10. third, singular
11. who
12. us
13. kept, slain
14. has, his or her
15. likes
16. linguist
17. Pool of Waterlilies
18. paintbrushes
19. Tina, Butch's owner, spends three hours a day training her dog.
20. a. worrisome
    b. funnier

21. object
22. independent
23. Leo shouted, "Help! Since you are taller than I, can you reach that apple?"
24. a. (is) drawing
    b. drew
    c. (has) drawn
25. him
26. That song, I think, is called "Little Bunny Fufu."
27. Dear Tina,
       Why is your dog so crabby? Have you taught him no manners?
                    With concern,
                    Cousin Juan
28. Although, until
29. *(diagram: Mr. Knothead | Has become \ victim of behavior; modifiers: the, imprudent, a, Badchek's, criminal)*
30. *(diagram: Butch (dog) | Does give | snarl; modifiers: a, crabby, without manners, (x), a, rude, Fifi and him)*

LESSON 90 Subject-Verb Agreement, Part 2

Practice 90

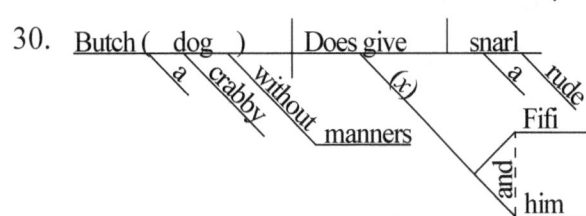

a. pictures | were   were
b. stations | were   were
c. kinds | are   are
d. leader | goes   goes
e. trucks | come   come

f. noxious
g. innocuous

More Practice 90

1. sits
2. weighs
3. is
4. go
5. are
6. breaks
7. makes
8. looks

Review Set 90

1. languish
2. contentment
3. force
4. large
5. burden
6. sells
7. concrete
8. Whose
9. fewest
10. first, plural
11. whom
12. they
13. risen, woken
14. has, its
15. like
16. sentence fragment
17. With this, Olga can repair the chair.
18. a. noun
    b. d ī′ kast
    c. Greek
19. Frankfort, the capital of Kentucky, lies along the Kentucky River.

20. biscuits
21. she
22. During the (night) toward my (muffins)
23. Lucy cries, "Watch out! A branch has broken, and it might fall on you."
24. a. (is) beating
    b. beat
    c. (has) beaten
25. her
26. As I remember, Ms. Hoo wrote an article titled "My Students' Lovable Pets."
27. Dear Juan,
       I have only had Butch for two months, three days, one hour, and five minutes. Please be patient with me.
                      Your cousin,
                      Tina
28. Though, wherever
29.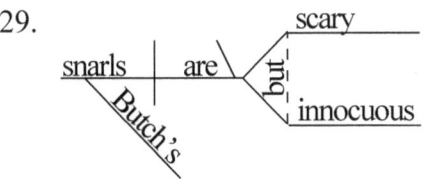
30.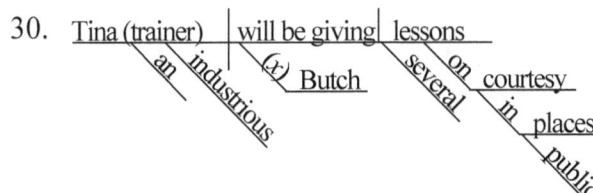

LESSON 91   Subject-Verb Agreement, Part 3

Practice 91

a. aren't
b. is
c. weren't
d. There are
e. has
f. obfuscation
g. obfuscate

More Practice 91

1. is
2. is
3. needs
4. wants
5. is
6. knows
7. has
8. understands
9. There are
10. There's
11. isn't
12. doesn't
13. don't
14. aren't
15. aren't

Review Set 91

1. Innocuous
2. Languid
3. content
4. force
5. encumbrance
6. were
7. collective
8. your
9. friendlier
10. second
11. Who
12. us
13. led, swam
14. have, their
15. knows

16. There are
17. <u>Skeedaddle</u>
18. fre(igh)t
19. Mount Whitney, California's tallest mountain, has more climbers than any other peak in the Sierra Nevada.
20. simple sentence
21. subject
22. dependent
23. Harold yells, "Don't go! Before you leave, I must warn you about the dangers."
24. a. (is) falling
    b. fell
    c. (has) fallen
25. A
26. I. Aesop's fables
    A. "The Tortoise and the Hare"
    B. "The Lion and the Mouse"
    C. "The Cat and the Bell"
27. Dear Tina,
    Please come to our family reunion in Jefferson City, Missouri, on Tuesday, January 2, 2007.
    Your cousin,
    Juan
28. As soon as, unless
29.

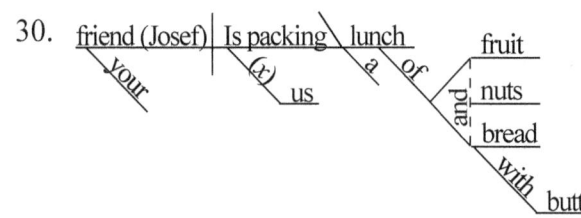

30.

LESSON 92 Subject-Verb Agreement, Part 4

Practice 92
a. covers
b. is
c. has
d. was
e. concise
f. conciseness

Review Set 92
1. obfuscate
2. antonyms
3. weak
4. satisfaction
5. exalt
6. come
7. exclamatory
8. whom
9. many
10. possessive
11. who
12. I
13. sat, ridden
14. has, his or her
15. hike
16. has
17. <u>Pytilia melba</u>
18. finches
19. The melba finch, an aggressive bird, eats seeds and insects.
20. a. penniless
    b. truly
21. he
22. clause
23. "May I please have more broccoli?" asked Mateo.

24. a. (is) finding
    b. found
    c. (has) found

25. me

26. Dad said, "I'm sorry, Luz, the broccoli is all gone."

27. Dear Juan,
    May I bring Butch? He is my friend, companion, and guard dog.
    Your cousin,
    Tina

28. After, because

29.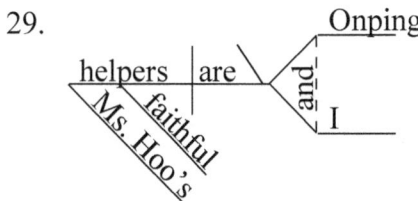

30.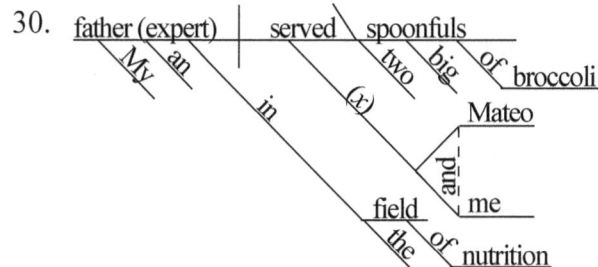

LESSON 93 — Negatives • Double Negatives

Practice 93

a. had
b. could
c. anything
d. ever
e. ever
f. minimum
g. optimum

More Practice 93

1. any, any
2. any
3. anybody
4. either
5. anyone
6. anywhere
7. any
8. ever
9. any
10. anything

Review Set 93

1. concise
2. unclear
3. harmless
4. energy
5. synonyms
6. go
7. possessive
8. can
9. bigger
10. first, singular
11. Who, hers
12. us
13. made, shaken
14. hasn't, her
15. plants
16. There are
17. For sewing, machines are helpful.
18. queens of Spain
19. The people of Olympia, the capital of Washington, are called "Olympians."
20. compound
21. subject

22. Aboard (ship)
    along the (coastline)
    amid a (pod)
    of (whales)

23. "That broccoli tastes delicious!" exclaims Mateo.

24. a. (is) building
    b. built
    c. (has) built

25. her

26. Luz said, "Please cook more broccoli, Dad."

27. Dear Tina,
    There is a dog hotel at 43 State Street, Jefferson City, Missouri.
    Your cousin,
    Juan

28. Whenever, where

29.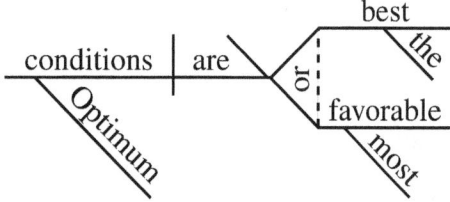

30.

LESSON 94 The Hyphen: Compound Nouns and Numbers

Practice 94

a. ostracize
b. ostracism
c. know-how
d. write-up
e. twenty-five
f. 13-20

More Practice 94

1. twenty-five
2. forty-seven
3. seventy-six
4. ninety-eight
5. twenty-first
6. thirty-second
7. forty-fifth
8. eighty-third
9. self-confidence
10. work-out
11. sister-in-law, go-getter
12. self-restraint

Review Set 94

1. Optimum
2. shortness
3. confuse
4. harmful
5. humiliate
6. sits
7. abstract
8. any
9. biggest
10. objective
11. Theirs, yours
12. I
13. woven, sold
14. haven't, their
15. wakes
16. was
17. patch
18. a. adjective
    b. di luks´
    c. French (going back to Latin)

19. Forty-two people attended the get-together.
20. ostrich
21. they
22. phrase
23. "If Butch howls, will you quiet him?" asked Tina.
24. a. (is) catching
    b. caught
    c. (has) caught
25. A
26. I shall title my essay "The Smooth, Enjoyable Voyage."
27. My dear cousin,
    Butch will stay with me, for he requires a soft bed, healthful food, and lots of attention.
    Love,
    Tina
28. than, when
29.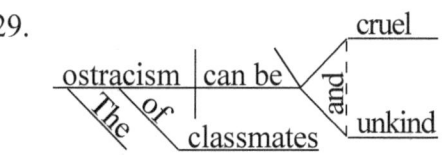
30.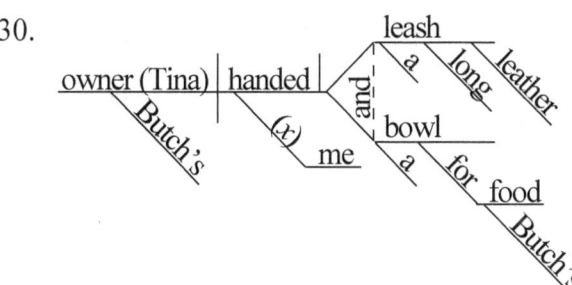

LESSON 95   Adverbs That Tell "How"

Practice 95

a. "proudly" modifies "sits"
b. "rapidly" modifies "burn"
c. "quickly" and "easily" modify "repaired"
d. adjective; modifies "lecture"
e. adverb; modifies "Did speak"
f. adjective; modifies "turn"
g. adverb; modifies "turned"
h. paltriness
i. Paltry

Review Set 95

1. ostracize
2. least
3. concise
4. confusion
5. antonyms
6. is
7. compound
8. any
9. fewer
10. first, plural
11. Whom
12. us
13. mistook, thought
14. haven't, their
15. wake
16. was
17. David
18. can openers
19. For exercise, we did seventy-five sit-ups.
20. compound
21. him
22. independent
23. Juan said, "I rented a large room for the party, but only a few people are coming."
24. a. (is) eating
    b. ate
    c. (has) eaten
25. "skillfully" modifies "write"

26. The scariest chapter was titled "Lost in the Jungle."
27. The colors of the rainbow, as I recall, are red, orange, yellow, green, blue, indigo, and violet.
28. as though, since
29.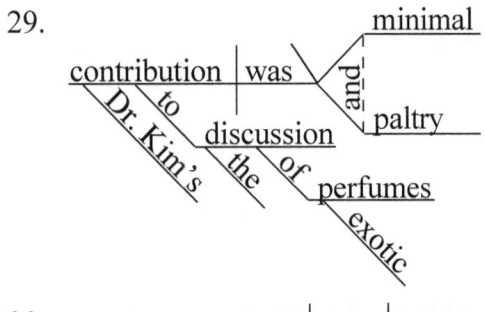
30. Dr. Kim (entomologist) shows enthusiasm for beetles and moths to us his an (x)

LESSON 96 Using the Adverb *Well*

Practice 96

a. well
b. good
c. well
d. good
e. well
f. perjure
g. Perjury

More Practice 96

1. well
2. well
3. well
4. good
5. good
6. good
7. well
8. good
9. well
10. good

Review Set 96

1. Paltry
2. ostracize
3. best
4. antonyms
5. true
6. are
7. well
8. has
9. tiredest
10. nominative
11. ours, theirs
12. he
13. lent, wrote
14. has, his
15. feeds
16. boards
17. Alice in Wonderland
18. lilac bushes
19. Thirty-three show-offs were trying to get attention.
20. bicycle
21. object
22. clause
23. My aunt asked if I would like any lemons, oranges, or avocados from her trees.
24. a. (is) biting
    b. bit
    c. (has) bitten
25. "blissfully" modifies "slept"
26. Jason wrote a poem and titled it "If I Were an Ant."

27. Please remember, I have moved to 960 Fox Lane, Frazzle Park, Oregon.

28. Before, so that, where

29.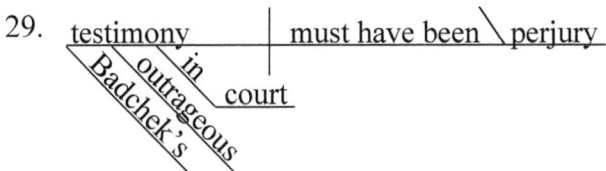

30.

Dr. Axle (herpetologist) | provided | information ... reptiles ... amphibians ... Lily ... me

LESSON 97 The Hyphen: Compound Adjectives

Practice 97

a. A-frame

b. none

c. re-cover

d. eight-ounce

e. Mud-coated

f. Plagiarism

g. plagiarize

Review Set 97

1. Perjury
2. Paltriness
3. exclude
4. lowest
5. Dogmatic
6. costs
7. well
8. any
9. fewer
10. first, plural
11. Who's
12. us
13. given, taught
14. has, his or her
15. sings
16. are
17. A Thatched Cottage by a Tree
18. a. verb
    b. en trap´
    c. French
19. I spent forty-five minutes scrubbing my paint-stained shirt.
20. simple
21. she
22. independent clause
23. Meg asks, "Would you like any lemons, oranges, or avocados?"
24. a. (is) feeling
    b. felt
    c. (has) felt
25. "concisely" modifies "writes"
26. An interesting article was titled "The Return of the Lynx."
27. Herbert, my oldest brother, graduated on June 16, 2006.
28. Even though, that
29.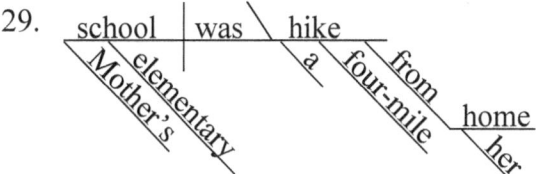
30.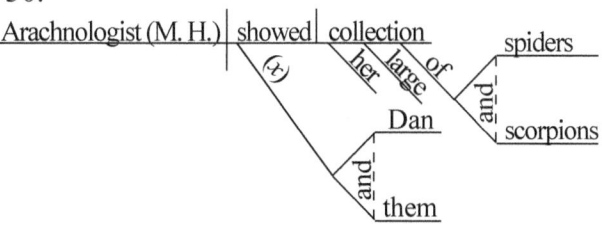

Grammar and Writing 5   97   Teacher Guide
                                            Student Edition Answers

LESSON 98 Adverbs That Tell "Where"

Practice 98

a. anywhere; can nap

b. home; have come

c. out; might have gone

d. around; wanders

e.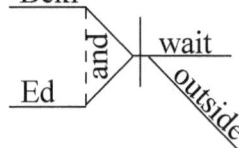

f.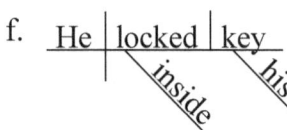

g. profusion

h. profuse

Review Set 98

1. plagiarize
2. lie
3. insignificant
4. excluding
5. Concrete
6. wears
7. good
8. have, any
9. more
10. possessive
11. their
12. they
13. lost, stood
14. There are
15. sing
16. are
17. were
18. car parts
19. James hammered twenty-four nails into two-by-four lumber.
20. a. jogging
    b. tried
21. subject
22. phrase
23. "I patted the goat's head, and it took a bite of my sleeve!" exclaimed Rondo.
24. a. (is) flying
    b. flew
    c. (has) flown
25. "suddenly" modifies "leap" (tells "how")
    "up" modifies "leap" (tells "where")
26. Riding home from Denver, Colorado, my sister sang "Old MacDonald Had a Farm" over and over again.
27. One the other hand, you could paint the table red, white, or blue.
28. Because, even though
29.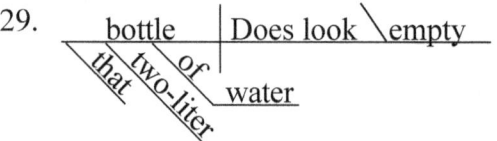
30. Arachnologist (Mari Hunt) | lifted | specimen
       up / carefully / each

LESSON 99 Word Division

Practice 99

a. no division
b. can- did
c. choco- late
d. no division
e. no division

f. forty- seven

g. prologue

h. epilogue

More Practice 99

1. no division
2. bliss- ful
3. anti- dote
4. no division
5. con- ceal
6. super- sonic
7. no division
8. con- trite
9. la- goon
10. no division
11. no division
12. pal- try
13. ig- nite
14. per- jure
15. pre- pare
16. no division
17. pad- dle
18. no division
19. hemi- sphere
20. pro- logue

Review Set 99

1. Profuse
2. Plagiarism
3. lying
4. little
5. Intangible
6. were
7. well
8. hasn't, any
9. most
10. third, plural
11. Whose
12. we
13. swung, run
14. there are
15. are
16. were
17. The White Horse
18. handfuls
19. Watching the penguin's egg hatch was a once-in-a-lifetime experience.
20. a. no division
    b. epi- logue
21. her
22. dependent clause
23. "Ms. Hoo, do goats normally eat sweaters?" asked Rondo.
24. a. (is) costing
    b. cost
    c. (has) cost
25. "gladly" modifies "sits" (tells "how")
    "nearby" modifies "sits" (tells "where")
26. I read an article titled "Russia's Giant Bears."
27. Lee B. Guo, R.N., has moved to 940 Fast Lane, Atlanta, Georgia.
28. When, if
29. Celly (horse) | Does look \ healthy
    the \ twenty-year-old
30. My cousin | mails | photographs
    in faithfully (x) me up-to-date of rabbits and her chickens
    Montana

LESSON 100 Adverbs That Tell "When"

Practice 100

a. Tonight; will build

b. later; can fish

c. ever; Have seen

d. yesterday; read

e.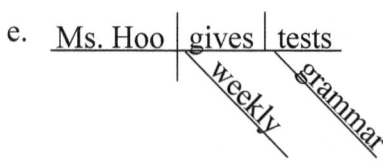

f.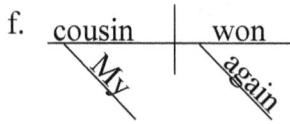

g. impropriety

h. propriety

Review Set 100

1. prologue
2. abundance
3. ideas
4. perjure
5. knowledge
6. was
7. well
8. has, any
9. fewer
10. objective
11. Your, ours
12. we
13. held, shut
14. contains
15. has
16. has
17. The Forbidden Door
18. pocket knives
19. Julio has completed fifty-four life-sized drawings.
20. a. no division
    b. un- feigned
21. he
22. clause
23. "Rondo, you have a hole in your shirt!" exclaims Ms. Hoo.
24. a. (is) fighting
    b. fought
    c. (has) fought
25. "quickly" modifies "tiptoes" (tells "how")
    "out" modifies "tiptoes" (tells "where")
26. Carl Sandburg wrote the poem "Buffalo Dusk."
27. This library book was due Friday, February 3, 2006, I believe.
28. never, again
29.
30.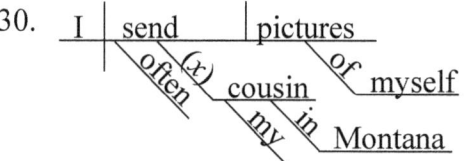

LESSON 101 Adverbs That Tell "How Much"

Practice 101

a. incredibly; talented

b. almost; missed

c. too; fast

d. n't; could understand

e. terribly; grumpy
f. enigma
g. enigmatic
h.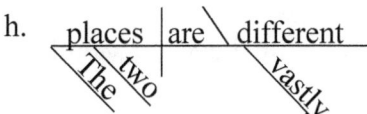
i.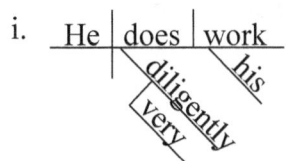

More Practice 101 *See answers on page 188.*

Review Set 101

1. Propriety
2. end
3. abundant
4. theft
5. Cognizant
6. were
7. good
8. is, any
9. fewest
10. first, plural
11. Whose
12. us
13. told, hid
14. pounces
15. has
16. has
17. For Amparo, Marco will do his best.
18. chiefs of staff
19. Forty-two English-speaking scientists have come from Japan.
20. a. no division
    b. silver- ware
21. him
22. independent clause
23. "Students," asks Ms. Hoo, "have you studied well?"
24. a. (is) forgetting
    b. forgot
    c. (has) forgotten
25. "timidly" modifies "glances" (tells "how")
    "around" modifies "glances" (tells "where")
26. The last chapter, "How They Caught the Culprit," is my favorite.
27. Yes, Neil B. Smart, Ph.D., teaches chemistry, physics, and Russian.
28. terribly (how much), late (when)
29.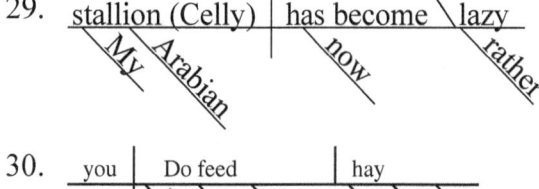
30.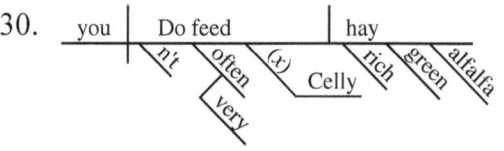

LESSON 102 Comparison Adverbs

Practice 102

a. more ferociously
b. most quickly
c. better
d. farthest
e. worse, worst
f. candid
g. candor

More Practice 102

1. better
2. best
3. farther

4. less
5. least
6. slower
7. longer
8. harder

Review Set 102

1. enigma
2. improper
3. introduction
4. profusion
5. aware
6. was
7. well
8. aren't, any
9. longest
10. objective
11. Who's
12. we
13. gotten, shined
14. are
15. have
16. was
17. <u>Enigma</u>, enigmatic
18. flu viruses
19. A color-blind painter used twenty-one different colors on the kitchen walls.
20. a. can- dor
    b. no division
21. he
22. phrase
23. "Catch those thieves!" cries Officer Valiant.
24. a. (is) fleeing
    b. fled
    c. (has) fled

25. "fearlessly" modifies "moves" (tells "how") "ahead" modifies "moves" (tells "where")
26. Omar titled his essay "Out of the Darkness."
27. Our essays are due, I believe, on Monday, February 26.
28. now (when), somewhat (how much)
29.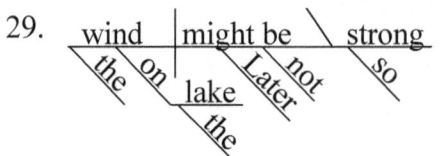
30.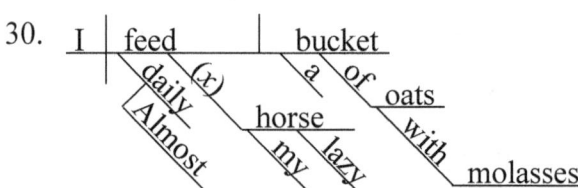

LESSON 103   The Semicolon

Practice 103

a. …blue, blew; hear, here; and no, know
b. …spring;
c. …home;
d. monarchy
e. anarchy

More Practice 103   *See answers on page 189.*

Review Set 103

1. Candor
2. Enigmatic
3. conformity
4. epilogue
5. Extravagant
6. come
7. good
8. has, any
9. longer

10. nominative
11. Your, ours
12. I
13. sprung, hanged
14. is
15. recycle
16. has
17. <u>Good Hope</u>
18. I remembered all the states and their capitals except for Madison, Wisconsin; Pierre, South Dakota; and Topeka, Kansas.
19. Their one-time offer was less desirable than a hand-me-down toothbrush.
20. a. dis- close
    b. no division
21. me
22. dependent clause
23. "Have you caught Badchek?" asked Ms. Hoo.
24. a. (is) bursting
    b. burst
    c. (has) burst
25. "profusely" modifies "grow" (tells "how")
    "here" modifies "grow" (tells "where")
26. Howard R. Garis, a newspaperman, wrote the short story "Uncle Wiggily and the Big Rat."
27. The culprits, it seems, are Badchek, Whipper, and Shadow.
28. Sometimes (when), too (how much)
29.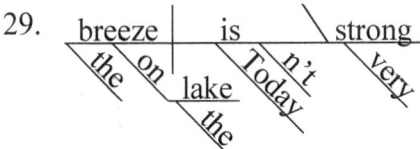
30. H. R. G. | would write | stories / Weekly / six / bedtime / about Uncle W. (hero) / a / rabbit

LESSON 104 Adverb Usage

Practice 104
a. parsimonious
b. parsimony
c. surely
d. really
e. really
f. badly
g. badly

More Practice 104
1. surely
2. certainly
3. really
4. really
5. really
6. badly
7. bad
8. badly

Review Set 104
1. Anarchy
2. honest
3. mystery
4. impropriety
5. antonyms
6. was, really
7. certainly, well

8. isn't, anybody
9. more
10. first, plural
11. Whom
12. We
13. wrung, hung
14. hears
15. recycles
16. is
17. <u>Frazzle Express</u>
18. He remembers her face; however, her name escapes him.
19. Mother has a curly, wash-and-wear hairdo.
20. a. tun- dra
    b. no division
21. she
22. clause
23. "There's smoke!" shouts Michael.
24. a. (is) diving
    b. dove or dived
    c. (has) dived
25. "intuitively" modifies "knew" (tells "how") "there" modifies "was" (tells "where")
26. Conrad, a camp counselor, played the guitar and sang "Kookaburra."
27. As we sat around the campfire, Conrad told us a long, scary story.
28. Afterward (when), terribly (how much)
29. [diagram: some of us | became \ sleepless / and \ homesick / rather ; Then]
30. [diagram: C. (counselor) | did tell | story ; our, camp, certainly, n't, (a), bedtime, about, us, Uncle W.]

LESSON 105   The Colon

Practice 105

a. 6:00 a.m.

b. I am taking the following classes: English, math, history, science, and P.E.

c. Dear Madam:
   Please send me your special recipe for the pea soup…

d. Abraham Lincoln spoke these words: "Most folks are about as happy as they make up their minds to be."

e. desecrate

f. consecrate

Review Set 105

1. Parsimony
2. ruler
3. honesty
4. mysterious
5. synonyms
6. itches, badly
7. surely, well
8. isn't, anything
9. most
10. possessive
11. Who
12. us
13. bought
14. hear
15. race
16. is
17. <u>The Japanese Bridge</u>
18. Rain fell; it beat on our tents.

19. All twenty-three campers wore water-repellent ponchos.

20. a. con- trite
    b. no division

21. me

22. Dear Teachers:

    By 2:00 p.m., I must have the following: your roll sheets, your grades, and your seating charts.

            Respectfully,
            Mr. Stoneman

23. Dr. Kim asks, "Is there a fire?"

24. Yes, she was born on Monday, May 10, 1948.

25. "generously" modifies "passes" (tells "how")
    "around" modifies "passes" (tells "where")

26. Erik, a young camper, prefers stories such as "Uncle Wiggily and the Watermelon."

27. If Conrad tells another dark, mysterious story, we shall turn on big, bright flashlights.

28. dreadfully (how much), later (when)

29.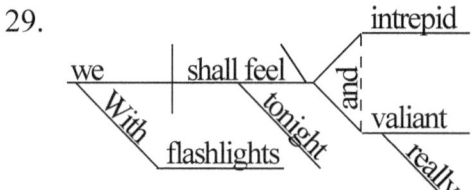

30.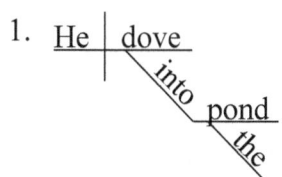

LESSON 106   The Prepositional Phrase as an Adverb • Diagramming

Practice 106

a. from hard work; come

b. in the city; lives

c. of prepositions; weary

d. for another lesson; ready

e. concerning grammar; wise

f.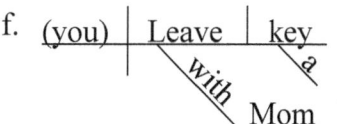

g.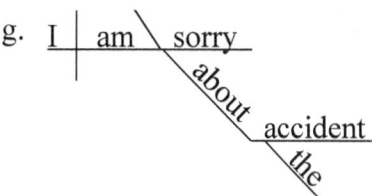

h. beguile

i. guile

More Practice 106

1.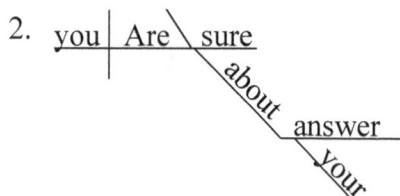

2.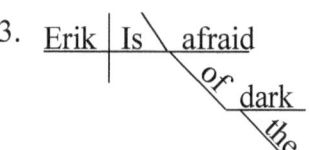

3.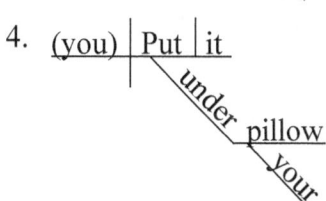

4.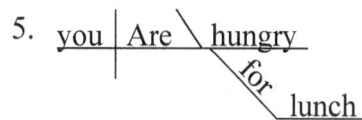

5. you | Are \ hungry
           \ for
             \ lunch

Review Set 106

1. consecrate

2. stingy

3. government

4. honest

5. father's
6. really, itch
7. certainly, badly
8. anything
9. farther
10. first, plural
11. Who's
12. we
13. saw
14. exercises
15. sweeps
16. is
17. Tribune
18. We saw the White House; however, we did not see the President.
19. I pushed the fast-forward button during the three-hour movie.
20. a. be- guile
    b. no division
21. she
22. Dear Council Members:
    From greatest to least, the problems are these: traffic, graffiti, and pollution.
        Sincerely,
        Ms. Hoo
23. Conrad exclaims, "Happy Friday, Erik!"
24. Obviously, Ms. Hoo dislikes traffic, graffiti, and pollution.
25. "carefully" modifies "searched" (tells "how"); "everywhere" modifies "searched" (tells "where")
26. Luz, a guitarist, ended with the song "Make New Friends."
27. While Conrad sleeps, Erik plans a clever, harmless prank.
28. Tomorrow (when); very (how much)

29.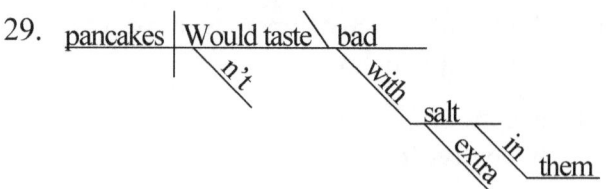
30.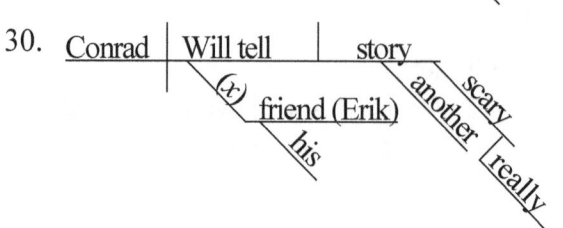

LESSON 107 Preposition or Adverb? • Preposition Usage

Practice 107

a. adverb
b. preposition
c. preposition
d. adverb
e. into
f. Between
g. besides
h. digressions
i. digress

Review Set 107

1. Guile
2. desecrate
3. stinginess
4. Monarchy
5. mother's
6. go, really
7. surely, well
8. any
9. farthest
10. into, among
11. Yours, theirs

12. us
13. seen
14. have
15. sweep
16. fits
17. <u>adios</u>
18. The bus will stop in Phoenix, Arizona; Santa Fe, New Mexico; and Oklahoma City, Oklahoma.
19. Twenty-eight singers performed a one-of-a-kind concert.
20. a. ar- dent
    b. no division
21. her
22. Dear Counselors:
    Please close the cabins as follows: sweep floors, take out trash, and lock doors.
    Sincerely,
    Mr. Vela
23. "Have Badchek and she fled to another country?" asked Ms. Hoo.
24. They have fled, I believe, to Ottawa, Canada.
25. adverb
26. I especially liked the last chapter, "A Warm Wind."
27. As the moon casts shadows, Erik imagines big, hungry beasts outside the tent.
28. Later (when); thoroughly (how much)
29. Pancakes | should taste | salty
       \n't   \so   \terribly

30.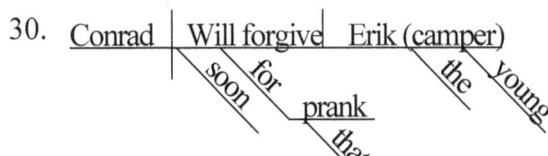

LESSON 108 — The Apostrophe: Possessives

Practice 108

a. futility
b. futile
c. sisters-in-law's
d. Rob's
e. kittens'
f. friends'
g. child's
h. bus's

More Practice 108

1. isthmus's
2. tributary's
3. delta's
4. estuary's
5. meteor's
6. kin's
7. story's
8. culprit's
9. deer's
10. days'
11. miners'
12. fish's
13. girls'
14. sheep's
15. stories'
16. men's

Review Set 108

1. digress
2. mislead
3. sacred

4. money
5. mother
6. writes, really
7. surely, well
8. was
9. cleaner
10. beside
11. Whose
12. We
13. saw
14. have
15. sweep
16. fits
17. <u>Waverly Bliss</u>
18. I remember Phoenix; however, I must have slept through our stop in Santa Fe.
19. From the third-story window, she could see moss-covered rocks.
20. a. fu- tile
    b. no division
21. she
22. Dear Mr. Vela:
    My cabin needs the following: paint, light bulbs, carpet.
        Sincerely,
        Conrad Dudd
23. Conrad shouts, "Look at that tarantula!"
24. a. boss's
    b. Chris's
    c. horses'
25. preposition
26. Erik will title his essay "A Long Week at Camp Woisme."
27. When Erik grows up, he might become a kind, thoughtful camp counselor.
28. Then (when); almost (how much)

29.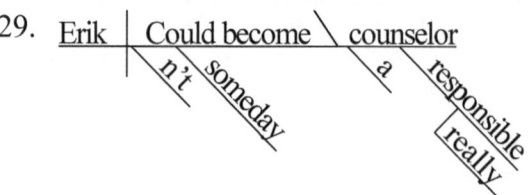

30.

LESSON 109 — The Apostrophe: Contractions, Omitting Digits and Letters

Practice 109

a. haven't
b. I've, workin'
c. '48, '02
d. shouldn't
e. they'd
f. dissent
g. dissension

More Practice 109 *See answers on page 190.*

Review Set 109

1. Futile
2. digression
3. deceit
4. destroy
5. Imprudent
6. writes, really
7. really badly
8. is
9. cleanest
10. besides
11. Who

12. I ("swim" omitted)
13. saw
14. has
15. You're
16. cuts well
17. <u>Charlotte's Web</u>
18. I am tired; nevertheless, I shall clean my room.
19. You can buy a five-pound melon for ninety-nine cents.
20. a. no division
    b. be- guile
21. a. wouldn't
    b. they're
22. Dear Sir or Madam:
    Why does my morning newspaper never arrive until 2:00 p.m. or later?
    Your customer,
    Ms. Hoo
23. Erik asked, "Have you seen my flashlight?"
24. a. artists'
    b. Melody's
    c. lady's
25. preposition
26. Melody, my niece, sang "Oklahoma."
27. If she sings it again, her sleepy, irritable friends might complain.
28. Tonight (when); terribly (how much)
29.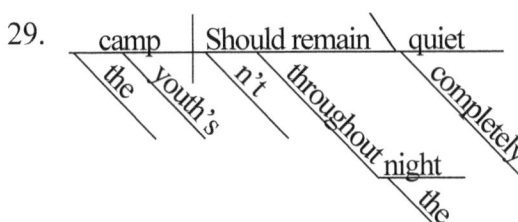

30.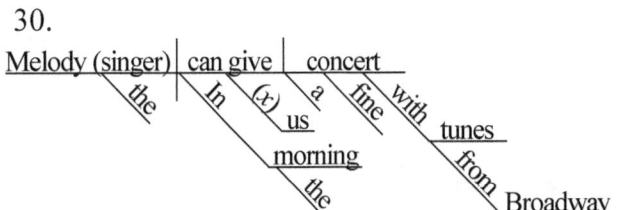

LESSON 110   The Complex Sentence • The Compound-Complex Sentence

Practice 110

a. simple
b. compound-complex
c. complex
d. compound
e. apathetic
f. apathy

More Practice 110

1. complex
2. compound
3. simple
4. compound-complex

Review Set 110

1. dissent
2. hopelessness
3. subject
4. beguile
5. wise
6. goes, really
7. surely, well
8. anybody
9. more
10. into
11. Who's
12. he ("is" omitted)

13. seen
14. has
15. They're
16. smells bad
17. <u>Apathy</u>, <u>apathetic</u>
18. My room is messy; therefore, I shall clean it.
19. My twenty-year-old sister took a five-day vacation in Arizona.
20. a. no division
    b. air- plane
21. a. you're
    b. can't
22. Dear Sir or Madam:
       I wish to cancel my subscription to the newspaper.
            A dissatisfied customer,
            Ms. Hoo
23. At Thursday's track meet, Grandpa yelled, "Run, Amelia!"
24. a. actors'
    b. Andy's
    c. James's
25. adverb
26. Kurt wrote the poem "If I Were You."
27. compound-complex
28. Soon (when); vastly (how much)
29.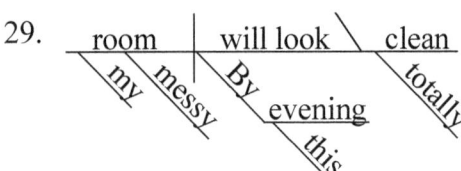
30.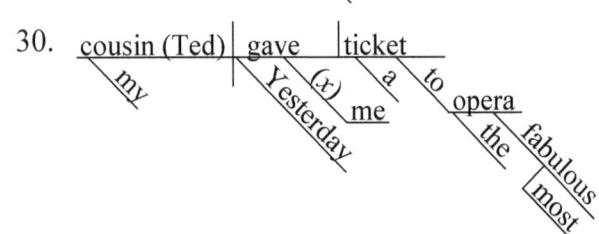

LESSON 111   Active or Passive Voice

Practice 111

a. passive
b. active
c. passive
d. active
e. elucidate
f. lucid

Review Set 111

1. Apathy
2. disagreement
3. hopeless
4. digression
5. imprudent
6. leads, really
7. surely, well
8. a
9. most
10. onto
11. Whose
12. I ("am" omitted)
13. saw
14. have
15. You're
16. fit well
17. <u>National Geographic</u>
18. We drove through Springfield, Illinois; Indianapolis, Indiana; and Columbus, Ohio.
19. My sister-in-law borrowed a six-foot ladder.

20. a. con- cise
    b. no division
21. a. they'll
    b. haven't
22. Please excuse the following students: Amy Ngo, Rod Vargas, and Rosa Green.
23. "Are you from Georgia?" asked Mark.
24. a. states'
    b. Amy's
    c. Avis's
25. adverb
26. Her second song was "Consider Yourself."
27. complex sentence
28. Later (when); more (how much)
29. *diagram:* you | Can elucidate | lesson — for me, after school, this, difficult, very
30. *diagram:* you | Have finished | diagram — finally, the, last, in book, very, this, grammar

LESSON 112 Interjections

Practice 112

a. Whoops
b. Hey
c. Bam
d. Yuck
e. Hurrah That | is \ news \ good

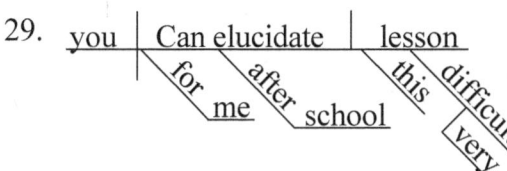

f. Shh people | are thinking
g. finale
h. finalize

Review Set 112

1. last
2. concern
3. finalize
4. clear
5. elucidate
6. has, really
7. surely, well
8. a
9. more
10. onto
11. Whose
12. I ("am" omitted)
13. saw
14. have
15. Your
16. cuts well
17. passive voice
18. This bus passes through Denver, Colorado; Cheyenne, Wyoming; and Helena, Montana.
19. My brother-in-law has an eight-foot python.
20. a. be- guile
    b. no division
21. a. you're
    b. they're
22. Please call the following people: James Lu, John García, and Rachel Cohen.
23. "Have you caught any fish?" asked Daisy.
24. a. countries'
    b. Kerry's
    c. Mr. Davis's
25. preposition

26. For the grand finale, the band played "America the Beautiful."

27. compound sentence

28. Then (when); most (how much)

29.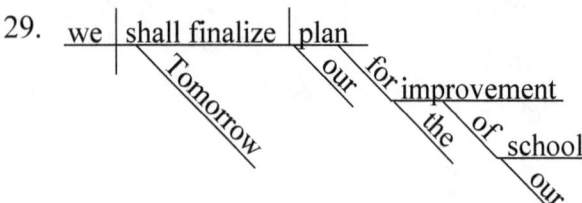

30.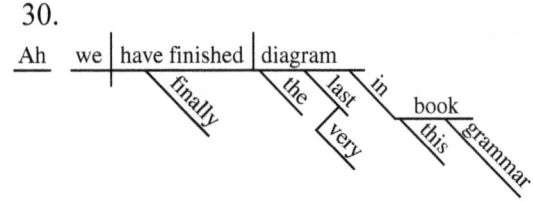

Test 1 READ CAREFULLY Name: _____

Give after Lesson 10.

Circle the correct word(s) to complete sentences 1–5.

1. A (subject, **sentence**) is a word group that expresses a complete thought.

2. The two essential parts of a sentence are the subject and the (predator, **predicate**).

3. The (**subject**, predicate) tells whom or what the sentence is about.

4. The (subject, **predicate**) tells what the subject does, is, or is like.

5. A complete sentence has (**two**, four) main parts.

6. For a–e, circle the correct definition. (1 point for each correct answer)

   (a) *Essential* means "(opposite, **necessary**, unnecessary)."

   (b) Antonyms are (dinosaurs, **opposites**, optimists).

   (c) *Abundant* means "(scarce, **plentiful**, essential)."

   (d) Pessimism is the belief that things are going to get (better, **worse**).

   (e) *Their* and *there* are (synonyms, antonyms, **homophones**).

For 7–10, write whether the sentence is declarative, interrogative, exclamatory, or imperative.

7. Rosa Parks refused to give up her seat in a bus. ____declarative____

8. How cold does it get in Alaska? ____interrogative____

9. Bring water on your hike through the desert. ____imperative____

10. It's a rattlesnake! ____exclamatory____

Circle the simple subject of sentences 11–13.

11. Some **people** in Arkansas listen to delightful kitchen bands.

12. Can **Jenny** play the fiddle?

13. **Archaeologists** have found dinosaur fossils in Colorado.

Circle the simple predicate of sentences 14–16.

14. Some people in Arkansas **listen** to delightful kitchen bands.

Grammar and Writing 5   113   Teacher Guide Test Answers

15. Jenny (can play) the fiddle.
(4)

16. Archaeologists (have found) dinosaur fossils in Colorado.
(4)

For 17–19, write whether the word group is a sentence fragment or a complete sentence.

17. Picking seeds from the watermelon. __sentence fragment__
(5)

18. Mount McKinley is the tallest mountain in North America. __complete sentence__
(5)

19. To catch a catfish in the pond. __sentence fragment__
(5)

20. Draw a vertical line between the subject and predicate parts of the sentence below.
(1)

Horseshoe crabs | have endured the changes of man.

Test 2 — READ CAREFULLY — Name: _____

Give after Lesson 15.

Circle the correct word(s) to complete sentences 1–5.

1. Yesterday Martin (fry, fries, (fried)) catfish for supper.
   (10)

2. An alligator (sleep, (sleeps)) in the Everglades.
   (9)

3. Leon (ski, (skis)) in Vail, Colorado.
   (9)

4. The sentence below is (declarative, interrogative, (exclamatory), imperative).
   (2)
   Look at all the ladybugs!

5. The sentence below is (declarative, interrogative, exclamatory, (imperative)).
   (2)
   Use sunscreen at the beach.

6. For a–e, circle the correct definition. (1 point for each correct answer)

   (a) ((Its), It's) is the possessive form of *it*.
   (6)

   (b) To disclose is to (hide, (uncover), sneeze).
   (7)

   (c) ((Geology), Archipelago, Flora) is Earth science.
   (8)

   (d) An archipelago is a chain of many (beads, (islands), events).
   (9)

   (e) Fauna is (plant, (animal)) life.
   (10)

7. On the lines below, make a complete sentence from the following sentence fragment:
   (6)
   After finishing this test, ___example: I shall relax and read a good book. (Answers will vary.)___

Circle the action verb in sentences 8 and 9.

8. Various space missions (launch) from Cape Canaveral.
   (7)

9. Groups (protect) endangered species such as whales.
   (7)

10. In the sentence below, circle each proper noun needing a capital letter.
    (8)
    (r)uth (h)andler created plastic dolls named (b)arbie in (d)enver, (c)olorado.

Grammar and Writing 5 — 115 — Teacher Guide Test Answers

Circle the simple subject of sentences 11–13.

11. (Skiers) flock to the snow-capped mountains of Colorado.
₍₃₎

12. Are (students) at the university working hard?
₍₃₎

13. Here is a famous seafood (restaurant.)
₍₃₎

Circle the simple predicate of sentences 14–16.

14. Skiers (flock) to the snow-capped mountains of Colorado.
₍₄₎

15. Students at the university (are working) hard.
₍₄₎

16. Here (is) a famous seafood restaurant.
₍₄₎

For 17–19, write whether the word group is a sentence fragment or a complete sentence.

17. Jimmy Carter, our thirty-ninth President ,was born in Georgia. __complete sentence__
₍₅₎

18. To begin selling peanut butter. __sentence fragment__
₍₅₎

19. Measuring the enormous span of the pelican's wings. __sentence fragment__
₍₅₎

20. Draw a vertical line between the subject and predicate parts of the sentence below.
₍₁₎

The 1858 Gold Rush | began in Colorado at Pike's Peak.

Test 3   **READ CAREFULLY**   Name: _____

Give after Lesson 20.

Circle the correct word(s) to complete sentences 1–5.

1. The two essential parts of a sentence are the (subordinate, **(subject)**) and the predicate.

2. The simple (**(subject)**, predicate) is the main word or words in a sentence that tell who or what is doing or being something.

3. Norma (carve, **(carves)**) ice sculptures in Minnesota.

4. The sentence below is (declarative, **(interrogative)**, exclamatory, imperative).

    Does Michigan have copper mines?

5. The sentence below is a (complete sentence, **(sentence fragment)**).

    Named for the Indian word meaning great lake.

6. For a–e, circle the correct definition. (1 point for each correct answer)

    (a) An isthmus is a narrow strip of (**(land)**, ocean, water) connecting two larger bodies of land.

    (b) A (lagoon, **(strait)**, peninsula) is a narrow waterway connecting two larger bodies of water.

    (c) A (delta, **(tributary)**, archipelago) is a river or stream that flows into a larger river or stream.

    (d) A (strait, lagoon, **(hemisphere)**) is one half of Earth.

    (e) (Meridian, Hemisphere, **(Latitude)**) is a distance north or south of the equator.

7. On the lines below, rewrite and correct the sentence fragment, making a complete sentence.

    Fur traders trapping wolverines.

    _____Example: Fur traders were trapping wolverines. (Answers will vary.)_____

    _____

8. Circle the action verb in the sentence below.

    People **(nicknamed)** Michigan the Wolverine State.

9. In the sentence below, replace the blank with the correct verb form.

    Chi (past of *shop*) ____shopped____ at the Mall of America in Bloomington, Minnesota.

10. In the sentence below, circle each proper noun needing a capital letter.

    (michigan's) **(windmill island municipal park)** has an authentic **(dutch)** windmill.

11. Circle the simple subject in the sentence below.
(3)

Along came (Melody) on a calico horse.

12. Circle the simple predicate in the sentence below.
(4)

Along (came) Melody on a calico horse.

13. Circle the abstract noun in the following list: horse, island, (pessimism), peninsula, wolverine
(11)

14. Circle the word from this list that could *not* be a helping verb: is, am, are, was, were, be, (and)
(12)

15. Circle the compound noun from this list: Washington, (afternoon), predicate, optimism
(13)

16. Circle the possessive noun in the sentence below.
(13)

(Minnesota's) prairie has a large gopher population.

Circle each letter that should be capitalized in 17–19.

17. (i) am always amazed at how little (i) know.
(15)

18. (a) famous medical center, (m)ayo (c)linic treats people from all over the world.
(15)

19.   (i) love my red rooster;
(15)   (m)y rooster loves me.
    (i) love my red rooster
    (u)nder the cottonwood tree.

20. Draw a vertical line between the subject and predicate parts of the sentence below.
(1)

A statue of Paul Bunyan | stands in Bemidji, Minnesota.

Test 4   READ CAREFULLY   Name: _____

Give after Lesson 25.

Circle the correct word(s) to complete sentences 1–5.

1. *John's* is a ((possessive), plural) noun.
   (13)

2. *Team* is a (compound, (collective)) noun.
   (11)

3. A diamond (scratch, (scratches)) granite.
   (9)

4. The sentence below is (declarative, interrogative, exclamatory, (imperative)).
   (2)

   Don't eat too many French fries.

5. The sentence below is a (complete sentence, (sentence fragment)).
   (5)

   To build and repair submarines.

6. For a–e, circle the correct definition. (1 point for each correct answer)

   (a) A (mesa, plateau, (chasm)) is a deep, wide crack in Earth's surface.
   (20)

   (b) (Arroyo, Atoll, (Tundra)) is a flat, frozen, treeless plain.
   (19)

   (c) Trees do not grow above the ((timber), date, twenty-yard) line.
   (18)

   (d) The Tropic of Cancer is an imaginary (friend, (line), atoll) parallel to the equator.
   (17)

   (e) A(n) (arroyo, (atoll), savanna) is a circular coral reef.
   (16)

7. On the lines below, write the four principal parts of the verb *plant*.
   (19)

plant	(is) planting	planted	(has) planted
(present tense)	(present participle)	(past tense)	(past participle)

8. Circle the two action verbs in the sentence below.
   (7)

   Today, people in New Hampshire's shipyards (build) and (repair) submarines.

9. In the sentence below, replace the blank with the correct verb form.
   (10)

   The sculptor (past of *chip*) ___chipped___ the granite.

10. Circle each preposition in the sentence below.
    (20)

    (Without) good sense, an explorer ventures (into) a dark cave.

11. Circle the simple subject in the sentence below.
    (3)

    On the eastern border of New Hampshire are (shipyards).

Grammar and Writing 5 — Teacher Guide Test Answers

12. Circle the simple predicate in the sentence below.

On the eastern border of New Hampshire (are) shipyards.

13. In the sentence below, replace the blank with the correct verb form.

New Hampshire (past of *be*) ____was____ the first to declare independence from Great Britain.

14. Circle the word from this list that is *not* a preposition: about, before, by, for, from, (drown)

15. For a–e, write the plural of each singular noun. (1 point for each correct answer)

(a) sky ____skies____

(b) Lewis ____Lewises____

(c) eggplant ____eggplants____

(d) loaf ____loaves____

(e) tooth ____teeth____

16. Circle the possessive noun in the sentence below.

Vines covered the (cave's) entrance.

Circle each letter that should be capitalized in 17 and 18.

17. (i) have never read (m)iss (p)ickerell (g)oes to (m)ars.

18. (a)lejandro will climb (m)ount (w)ashington to the highest point in (n)ew (e)ngland.

19. Circle the entire verb phrase in the sentence below.

People in Portsmouth (have been building) ships since 1630.

20. Draw a vertical line between the subject and predicate parts of the sentence below.

Eva's great-grandfather | planted potatoes in New Hampshire.

Test 5   READ CAREFULLY   Name: _____

Give after Lesson 30.

Circle the correct word(s) to complete sentences 1–11.

1. (Do, **Did**) Johnny Appleseed plant apple trees in Ohio?
(18)

2. We (will, **shall**) see Ohio's Rock and Roll Hall of Fame tomorrow.
(14)

3. Thomas Edison invented and (perfects, **perfected**) the lightbulb.
(10)

4. The sentence below is (**declarative**, interrogative, imperative, exclamatory).
(2)
                 The first cash register came from Dayton, Ohio.

5. The following is a (sentence fragment, run-on sentence, **complete sentence**):
(5)
                 An ancient dugout canoe was found in Ohio.

6. The word *around* is a (noun, verb, **preposition**).
(20)

7. The noun *lightbulb* is (abstract, **concrete**).
(11)

8. The noun *compass* is (**singular**, plural).
(13)

9. To *placate* means to "(disturb, anger, **calm**)."
(22)

10. To *ignite* is to (disclose, **burn**, freeze).
(25)

11. Jenny and Phil marry. Phil (marrys, **marries**) Jenny.
(9)

12. Write the plural form of a–d:
(16, 17)
     (a) tooth __teeth__   (b) cuff __cuffs__   (c) county __counties__   (d) ditch __ditches__

Circle each letter that should be capitalized in 13–15.

13. **O**ne sometimes reads of **J**ohnny **A**ppleseed. **H**is trees still grow around **O**hio.
(15)

14. **R**hett **B**utler remains a popular character from the novel ***G**one with the **W**ind*.
(25)

15. **L**ake **E**rie forms part of the northern border of **O**hio.
(8)

16. Circle each preposition that you find in this sentence:
(20)
         Two (**of**) the astronauts, Neil Armstrong and John Glenn, are (**from**) the state (**of**) Ohio.

17. Circle the two helping verbs in the following sentence:

Thomas Edison (had) (been) experimenting with electricity for many years.

18. For a–d, circle the correct irregular verb form.

(a) She (am, (is), are)   (b) They ((do), does)   (c) You (has, (have))   (d) He (do, (does))

19. Complete the four principal parts of the verb *wish*.

<u>   *wish*   </u>   <u> *(is)* wishing </u>   <u>   wished   </u>   <u> *(has)* wished </u>
(1) present tense   (2) present participle   (3) past tense   (4) past participle

20. Circle the simple subject of the sentence below.

Deep under the ground rested the oldest (watercraft).

21. Circle the simple predicate of the sentence below.

Deep under the ground (rested) the oldest watercraft.

22. Write the plural form of the singular noun *commander in chief*.   <u>commanders in chief</u>

23. Circle the action verb in the sentence below.

The state of Ohio (produces) many tires.

24. Rewrite the following sentence fragment, making a complete sentence.

To see a tire factory in Ohio.

<u>Example: I would like to see a tire factory in Ohio. (Answers will vary.)</u>

25. Rewrite and correct the run-on sentence below.

Annie Oakley was born in Ohio she was a famous sharpshooter.

<u>Annie Oakley was born in Ohio. She was a famous sharpshooter.</u>

Test 6   READ CAREFULLY   Name: _____

Give after Lesson 35.

Circle the correct word(s) to complete sentences 1–11.

1. (Have, **Has**) the museum opened yet?

2. We (will, **shall**) see the faces carved on Mount Rushmore.

3. Nancy went out and (talks, **talked**) to the horses.

4. The sentence below is (declarative, **interrogative**, imperative, exclamatory).

    Did Wild Bill Hickock die in South Dakota?

5. The following is a (sentence fragment, **run-on sentence**, complete sentence):

    We saw the Black Hills the trees there look almost black.

6. The word *through* is a (noun, verb, **preposition**).

7. The noun *peace* is (**abstract**, concrete).

8. The noun *cat's* is (plural, **possessive**).

9. A large meteorite might create a (mountain, **crater**, hill) on Earth's surface.

10. A(n) (meteorite, caldera, **etymology**) shows a word's original language and meaning.

11. Chickens scratch. A chicken (scratch, **scratches**).

12. Write the plural form of a–d:

    (a) knife __knives__   (b) monkey __monkeys__   (c) cupful __cupfuls__   (d) entry __entries__

Circle each letter that should be capitalized in 13–15.

13. (L)ilah said, "(T)hat (N)orth (D)akota blizzard was terrible."

14. (O)n (S)aturday we shall read (A)lice (I)n (W)onderland.

15. (L)ake (O)ntario forms part of the northern border of (N)ew (Y)ork.

16. Circle each preposition that you find in the sentence below.

    (Since) yesterday, the explorer has been (inside) the cave (by) himself, (without) a buddy.

Grammar and Writing 5 — 123 — Teacher Guide Test Answers

17. Circle the two helping verbs in the following sentence:

Clara Barton (had)(been) nursing the wounded for three years.

18. For a–d, circle the correct irregular verb form.

(a) They (am, is, (are)) (b) She (do, (does)) (c) He ((has), have) (d) You ((do), does)

19. Complete the four principal parts of the verb *try*.

try	*(is)* trying	tried	*(has)* tried
(1) present tense	(2) present participle	(3) past tense	(4) past participle

20. Circle the simple subject of the sentence below.

Out on the range roams a (herd) of buffalo.

21. Circle the simple predicate of the sentence below.

Out on the range (roams) a herd of buffalo.

22. Write the plural form of the singular noun *father-in-law*. _____fathers-in-law_____

23. Draw a vertical line between the subject and the predicate of the sentence below.

Wild Bill Hickok and Wyatt Earp | chased outlaws in the Wild West.

24. Circle each silent letter in the words below.

(a) (h)our   (b) ri(d)ge   (c) wa(l)k   (d) de(b)t

25. Rewrite and correct the run-on sentence below.

South Dakota is the Mount Rushmore State its capital is Pierre.

South Dakota is the Mount Rushmore State. Its capital is Pierre.

Test 7   **READ CAREFULLY**   Name: _____

Give after Lesson 40.

Circle the correct word(s) to complete sentences 1–10.

1. Etymologies are (antonyms, synonyms, **word histories**).

2. George Washington (**was**, were) born in Virginia.

3. Stephen stepped outside and (calls, **called**) his dog.

4. The sentence below is (declarative, interrogative, imperative, **exclamatory**).

    The musical was fabulous!

5. The following is a (**sentence fragment**, run-on sentence, complete sentence):

    Buried treasure in the Mojave Desert.

6. The word *at* is a (noun, verb, **preposition**).

7. The noun *backpack* is (abstract, **concrete**).

8. The noun *cats* is (**plural**, possessive).

9. The verb (**look**, laugh, smile) is a common linking verb.

10. Many people watch. One person (watch, **watches**).

11. For a–d, circle the correct definition. (1 point for each correct answer)

    (a) (**Kin**, Clamor, Panacea) refers to one's relatives.

    (b) A (kin, **clamor**, panacea) is a loud cry or uproar.

    (c) (Clamor, **Indispensable**, Dispensable) means "absolutely necessary."

    (d) The Greek root *pan* means "(fire, table, **all**)."

12. Write the plural form of a–d:

    (a) suffix __suffixes__ (b) inch __inches__ (c) dairy __dairies__ (d) deer __deer__

Circle each letter that should be capitalized in 13–15.

13. **m**rs. **n**g asked, "**h**ave you seen **m**eg's other shoe?"

14. **p**lease read me "**t**he **c**at in the **h**at."

Grammar and Writing 5   **125**   Teacher Guide / Test Answers

15. (the)(mississippi)(river) forms the eastern border of (arkansas).
₍₈₎

16. Circle each preposition that you find in the sentence below.
_(20, 21)

(Over) this hill and (across) the field lies a grove (of) apple trees (with) many blossoms.

17. For a–d, circle the word that is spelled correctly. (1 point for each correct answer)
₍₃₃₋₃₅₎

(a) (weigh), wiegh   (b) decieve, (deceive)   (c) forgeting, (forgetting)   (d) (countries), countrys

18. For a–d, circle the correct irregular verb form. (1 point for each correct answer)
₍₁₈₎

(a) He (am, (is), are)   (b) I ((am), is, are)   (c) She ((has), have)   (d) It (do, (does))

19. Complete the four principal parts of the verb *flap*.
₍₁₉₎

flap	*(is)* flapping	flapped	*(has)* flapped
(1) present tense	(2) present participle	(3) past tense	(4) past participle

20. Add suffixes. (2 points for each correct answer)
₍₃₃₎

(a) dry + est ___driest___   (b) say + ed ___said___

21. Add suffixes. (2 points for each correct answer)
₍₃₄₎

(a) glad + ly ___gladly___   (b) begin + ing ___beginning___

22. From the following list, circle the word that could *not* be a linking verb: is, am, are, (wash), were
₍₃₁₎

23. Circle each silent letter in the words below. (1 point for each correct answer)
_(28, 29)

(a) (w)ho   (b) rece(i)pt   (c) lam(b)   (d) clim(b)

On the lines provided, diagram the simple subject and simple predicate of sentences 24 and 25.

24. Across the desert gallops an Arabian horse.
₍₃₂₎

horse	gallops

25. Has the stallion seen the mare?
₍₃₂₎

stallion	Has seen

Test 8   READ CAREFULLY   Name: _____

Give after Lesson 45.

Circle the correct word(s) to complete sentences 1–10.

1. (**Etymologies**, Atolls, Peninsulas) are word histories.

2. (Do, **Does**) she like jazz music?

3. A muddy beagle (follows, **followed**) me home yesterday.

4. The word group below is a (**phrase**, clause).

    throughout the state of Washington

5. The following is a (sentence fragment, **run-on sentence**, complete sentence):

    Nevada gets very little rain it is mostly desert.

6. The word *across* is a (noun, verb, **preposition**).

7. The noun *miracle* is (**abstract**, concrete).

8. The noun *Jameses* is (**plural**, possessive).

9. The verb (wait, **seem**, stare) is a common linking verb.

10. Sodas fizz. A soda (fizzs, **fizzes**).

11. For a–d, circle the correct definition. (1 point for each correct answer)

    (a) A (**dogmatic**, timid, humble) person speaks with authority and sometimes arrogance.

    (b) To humiliate is to shame or (exalt, praise, **embarrass**).

    (c) A heavy load might (encourage, enable, **encumber**) a traveler.

    (d) Avarice is (generosity, **greed**, patience).

12. Write the plural form of a–d:

    (a) fax __faxes__   (b) dish __dishes__   (c) baby __babies__   (d) child __children__

Circle each letter that should be capitalized in 13–15.

13. **A**ddicus asked, "**D**id you find that book on **M**s. **B**lue's bookshelf?"

14. **M**ay **I** borrow your copy of **A**lice in **W**onderland?

15. (I) offered (m)s. (h)oo some hot (F)rench bread.
₍₃₈₎

16. Circle each preposition that you find in the sentence below.
_(20, 21)

(Without) your help, I could not have rescued my horse (from) the flood.

17. For a–d, circle the word that is spelled correctly. (1 point for each correct answer)
₍₃₃₋₃₅₎

(a) nieghbor (neighbor) (b) (priest), preist (c) runing (running) (d) librarys (libraries)

18. Circle each limiting adjective in the sentence below.
₍₄₀₎

(Fernando's) band has (a) drummer, (a) pianist, and (two) guitarists.

19. Complete the four principal parts of the verb *reply*.
₍₁₉₎

reply   *(is)* replying   replied   *(has)* replied

(1) present tense   (2) present participle   (3) past tense   (4) past participle

20. Add suffixes. (2 points for each correct answer)
_(33, 34)

(a) win + ing   winning   (b) pay + ed   paid

21. Circle each descriptive adjective in the sentence below.
₍₃₉₎

(Lush)(colorful) trees in (beautiful) Vermont attract (appreciative) spectators.

22. From the following list, circle the word that could *not* be a linking verb: seem, appear, (blow), stay
₍₃₁₎

23. Circle each silent letter in the words below. (1 point for each correct answer)
_(28, 29)

(a) si(g)n   (b) (h)onor   (c) lis(t)en   (d) lim(b)

On the lines provided, diagram each word of sentences 24 and 25.

24. My puppy has chewed my new shoes.
₍₃₂₎

     puppy | has chewed | shoes
     \My   \my \new

25. Has that puppy chewed your new shoes?
₍₃₂₎

     puppy | Has chewed | shoes
     \that   \your \new

Test 9   READ CAREFULLY   Name: _____

Give after Lesson 50.

Circle the correct word(s) to complete sentences 1–10.

1. (Field labels, **Etymologies**, Antonyms) are word histories showing the original language and meaning.
(30)

2. West Virginia (have, **has**) many coal mines.
(18)

3. Settlers followed the trail and (arrive, **arrived**) in West Virginia.
(10)

4. The word group below is a (phrase, **clause**).
(36)

   because it lies in the Appalachian Mountain system

5. The following is a (**sentence fragment**, run-on sentence, complete sentence):
(5)

   Jamestown, the first permanent English colony.

6. The word *the* is a(n) (noun, verb, **adjective**, preposition).
(40)

7. The noun *success* is (**abstract**, concrete).
(11)

8. The noun *James's* is (plural, **possessive**).
(13)

9. The verb (think, sing, **was**) is a common linking verb.
(31)

10. Bees buzz. A bee (buzzs, **buzzes**).
(9)

11. For a–d, circle the correct definition. *(1 point for each correct answer)*

    (a) (Frugal, **Cognizant**, Paternal) means "having knowledge; aware."
    (41)

    (b) An imprudent decision is (frugal, **unwise**, wise).
    (44)

    (c) (**Frugal**, Cognizant, Paternal) means "avoiding waste."
    (42)

    (d) (Frugal, Cognizant, **Paternal**) means "of or like a father."
    (43)

12. Write the plural form of a–d:
(16, 17)

    (a) loaf __loaves__   (b) cupful __cupfuls__   (c) man __men__   (d) piano __pianos__

Circle each letter that should be capitalized in 13–15.

13. **d**aniel explained, "**w**est **v**irginia was once a part of **v**irginia."
(26)

14. "**u**nfortunately, diseases such as measles, mumps, and chicken pox caused the deaths of many
(43) **n**ative **a**mericans," said **d**aniel.

15. ⓓear ⓖrandma,
(38, 41)
ⓗave you visited the ⓔast?
ⓛove,
ⓖenevie

16. Circle each preposition that you find in the sentence below.
(20, 21)
West Virginia sided ⓦith the North ⓓuring the Civil War.

17. Circle the misspelled word in the list below.
(33-35)
relieve, height, ⓦiegh, eight, deceive

18. Circle each adjective in the sentence below.
(39, 40)
ⓟrudent students will do ⓣhe homework.

19. Complete the four principal parts of the verb *drop*.
(19)

drop	*(is)* dropping	dropped	*(has)* dropped
(1) present tense	(2) present participle	(3) past tense	(4) past participle

20. Add suffixes. (2 points for each correct answer)
(33, 34)
(a) clap + ing ___clapping___   (b) pretty + er ___prettier___

21. In the sentence below, underline the prepositional phrase and circle the object of the preposition.
(44)
Did she tell you the secret <u>of her ⓢuccess</u>?

22. Circle the proper adjective in the sentence below.
(42)
Jamestown was the first permanent ⓔnglish colony.

23. Circle each silent letter in the words below. (1 point for each correct answer)
(28, 29)
(a) cu(p)board   (b) ta(l)k   (c) (g)uess   (d) com(b)

On the lines provided, diagram each word of sentences 24 and 25.

24. Do you eat a variety of healthful foods?
(40, 45)

25. A prudent student will do the homework.
(40)

Grammar and Writing 5   130   Teacher Guide
Test Answers

Test 10   READ CAREFULLY   Name: _____

Give after Lesson 55.

Circle the correct word(s) to complete sentences 1–10.

1. The boldfaced word that begins a dictionary entry gives the (etymology, part of speech, (spelling)).
(27)

2. Terry (do, (does)) the homework.
(18)

3. He unlocked the treasure chest and (looks, (looked)) inside.
(10)

4. The word group below is a ((phrase), clause).
(36)
   six feet long with mossy, leathery skin, the alligator

5. The following is a (sentence fragment, run-on sentence, (complete sentence)):
(5, 23)
   The man at the piano is Duke Ellington.

6. The word *an* is a(n) (noun, verb, (adjective), preposition).
(40)

7. The noun *alligator* is (abstract, (concrete)).
(11)

8. The noun *alligators* is ((plural), possessive).
(13)

9. The verb (*whisper*, *sneeze*, (*smell*)) is a common linking verb.
(31)

10. Birds fly. A bird (flys, (flies)).
(9)

11. For a–d, circle the correct definition. (1 point for each correct answer)

   (a) ((Illiterate), Frugal, Benevolent) means "unable to read or write."
   (46)

   (b) A (plausible, (momentous), intolerable) occasion is one of great importance.
   (47)

   (c) A believable story is (frugal, intolerable, (plausible)).
   (48)

   (d) *Benevolent* means "((kind), believable, unbearable)."
   (50)

12. Add periods as needed: **I.** Washington D(.) C(.)
(47, 50)
   A(.) The White House
   B(.) The Capitol Building

Circle each letter that should be capitalized in 13 and 14.

13. (N)olan asked, "(M)ay (I) borrow your book about (G)eorgia?"
(26)

14. (D)ear (G)avin,
(38, 41)
   (Y)our grandfather owned land in the (M)idwest and in the (S)outh.
         (L)ove,
         (A)unt (B)essie

Grammar and Writing 5   131   Teacher Guide
                                    Test Answers

15. Circle the linking verb in the sentence below.
(31)

That Georgia peach (smells) so sweet!

16. Circle each coordinating conjunction in the sentence below.
(48)

He toured the White House (and) the Capitol Building, (but) she went to the Smithsonian Museum.

17. Circle the misspelled word in the list below.
(33-35)

believe, (nieghbor), weigh, niece

18. Circle each adjective in the sentence below.
(39, 40)

(Two) (sleepy) alligators lie in (the) (hot) sun.

19. Complete the four principal parts of the verb *cry*.
(19)

cry	_(is)_ crying	cried	_(has)_ cried
(1) present tense	(2) present participle	(3) past tense	(4) past participle

20. Add suffixes. *(2 points for each correct answer)*
(33, 34)

(a) trap + ed ____trapped____   (b) cloudy + er ____cloudier____

21. In the sentence below, underline each prepositional phrase, circling the object of each preposition.
(44)

Lucas looks <u>down the basketball (court)</u> and sprints <u>to the (basket)</u>.

22. Circle the proper adjective in the sentence below.
(42)

Does Fido like (Swiss) cheese?

23. Circle the indirect object in the sentence below.
(46)

The benevolent couple gave stray (dogs) food and shelter.

On the lines provided, diagram each word of sentences 24 and 25.

24. Did the man at the piano play classical music?
(40, 45)

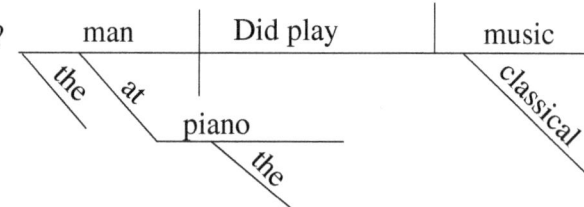

25. Joe and Moe repair and polish old bikes.
(40, 49)

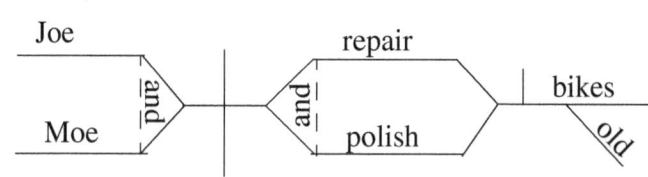

Test 11   READ CAREFULLY   Name: _____

Give after Lesson 60.

Circle the correct word(s) to complete sentences 1–10.

1. Of the two buildings, this one is (**taller**, tallest).
(55)

2. Terry (have, **has**) two brothers.
(18)

3. She closed the window and (locks, **locked**) the door.
(10)

4. The word group below is a (phrase, **clause**).
(36)
                if you see an alligator with an open mouth

5. The following is a (**sentence fragment**, run-on sentence, complete sentence):
(5)
                Duke Ellington, the man at the piano.

6. The word *the* is a(n) (noun, verb, **adjective**, preposition).
(40)

7. The noun *optimism* is (**abstract**, concrete).
(11)

8. The noun *alligator's* is (plural, **possessive**).
(13)

9. The verb (honk, clap, **sound**) is a common linking verb.
(31)

10. Students try hard. A student (trys, **tries**) hard.
(9)

11. For a–d, circle the correct definition. (1 point for each correct answer)

   (a) (Bovine, **Canine**, Feline) relates to dogs.
      (51)

   (b) (**Bovine**, Canine, Equine) relates to cows.
      (52)

   (c) Auditory relates to the sense of (smell, **hearing**, touch).
      (53)

   (d) Gentility is (malice, **courtesy**, greed).
      (55)

12. Add periods as needed in the sentence below.
(47, 50)
            Mr**.** Brite wrote, "The First Ave**.** market will be closed Tues**.** this week**.**"

Circle each letter that should be capitalized in 13 and 14.

13. (**m**)imi said, "(**s**)ome crops in the (**s**)outh are harvested in spring."
(26)

14. (**d**)ear (**a**)lsumana,
(38, 41)
      (**d**)o you have rollercoasters in (**p**)apua (**n**)ew (**g**)uinea? (**i**) like fast and twisty ones.
        (**y**)our friend,
        (**e**)lisa

15. Circle the predicate nominative in the sentence below.
(51)

Mrs. Cruz is a prudent (attorney).

16. Circle each coordinating conjunction in the sentence below.
(48)

Ian (and) Rosa are visiting North (or) South Carolina, (but) their home is in Florida.

17. Circle the misspelled word in the list below.
(33-35)

(beleive), neighbor, weigh, niece

18. Circle each adjective in the sentence below.
(39, 40)

(Four) (fuzzy) rabbits hide inside (a) (hollow) log.

19. Complete the four principal parts of the verb *trap*.
(19)

trap	*(is)* trapping	trapped	*(has)* trapped
(1) present tense	(2) present participle	(3) past tense	(4) past participle

20. Add suffixes. (2 points for each correct answer)
(33, 34)

(a) cry + ed ____cried____ (b) happy + est ____happiest____

21. In the sentence below, underline each prepositional phrase, circling the object of each
(44) preposition.

A dog <u>with a rhinestone (collar)</u> leaps <u>into the (car)</u>.

22. Circle the proper adjective in the sentence below.
(42)

Juicy (California) oranges make a good snack.

23. Circle the indirect object in the sentence below.
(46)

Hnin passed (Borden) the baton.

On the lines provided, diagram each word of sentences 24 and 25.

24. The man at the piano is my brother.
(45, 51)

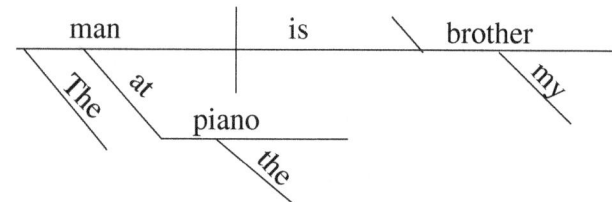

25. Joe and Moe wash and wax their car.
(40, 49)

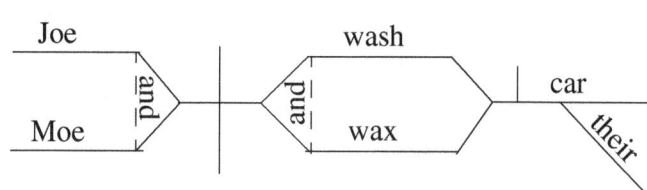

Test 12   **READ CAREFULLY**   Name: _____

Give after Lesson 65.

Circle the correct word(s) to complete sentences 1–10.

1. Of the two computers, this one is (**better**, best).
   (56)

2. We (was, **were**) friends.
   (18)

3. Yesterday he (fry, fries, **fried**) potatoes.
   (10)

4. The word group below is a (**phrase**, clause).
   (36)
             instead of the movie about pirates

5. The following is a (sentence fragment, **run-on sentence**, complete sentence):
   (23, 24)
             The truck swerved it hit a curb.

6. A(n) (declarative, **interrogative**, imperative, exclamatory) sentence asks a question.
   (2)

7. The noun *elephant* is (abstract, **concrete**).
   (11)

8. I have two (sister-in-laws, **sisters-in-law**).
   (13, 16)

9. The verb (touch, grab, **feel**) is a common linking verb.
   (31)

10. Bees buzz. A bee (buzzs, **buzzes**).
    (9)

11. For a–d, circle the correct definition. (1 point for each correct answer)

    (a) (Intangible, **Superfluous**, Malicious) means "more than needed or desired."
    (58)

    (b) (**Opportune**, Inopportune, Indolent) means "suitable; well-timed."
    (60)

    (c) *Indolent* means "(**lazy**, generous, hard-working)."
    (56)

    (d) To illuminate is to give (food, money, **light**) to.
    (59)

12. Add periods as needed in the sentence below.
    (47, 50)
              Mrs**.** Lynch's note reads, "Buy two lbs**.** of apples at the Main St**.** market**.**"

Circle each letter that should be capitalized in 13 and 14.

13. **M**s. **H**oo said, "**S**ome states in the **E**ast are humid in summer."
    (26)

14. **D**ear **R**afael,
    (38, 41)
           Are there alligators in **T**allahassee, **F**lorida? **I** hope not.
              Your friend,
              Josef

15. Add commas as needed in the sentence below.
(57, 59)

Aunt Sue**,** may I borrow your scissors**,** a pen**,** and some paper?

16. Circle each coordinating conjunction in the sentence below.
(48)

They offered soup (or) salad, (so) I chose soup.

17. Circle the misspelled word in the list below.
(33-35)

believe, neighbor, (wiegh) niece

18. Circle each adjective in the sentence below.
(39, 40)

(An) (industrious) student typed (sixteen) (long) pages of notes.

19. Complete the four principal parts of the verb *fry*.
(19)

<u>fry</u>	(is) <u>frying</u>	<u>fried</u>	(has) <u>fried</u>
(1) present tense	(2) present participle	(3) past tense	(4) past participle

20. Add suffixes. (2 points for each correct answer)
(33, 34)

(a) sad + est   <u>saddest</u>   (b) jolly + er   <u>jollier</u>

21. In the sentence below, underline each prepositional phrase, circling the object of each preposition.
(44)

A player <u>in left (field)</u> ducks <u>under the (ball)</u>.

22. Circle the proper adjective in the sentence below.
(42)

I sliced a shiny red (Washington) apple.

23. Circle the indirect object in the sentence below.
(46)

Onping bought (Kim) a lemonade.

On the lines provided, diagram each word of sentences 24 and 25.

24. The girl in the picture is my cousin.
(45, 51)

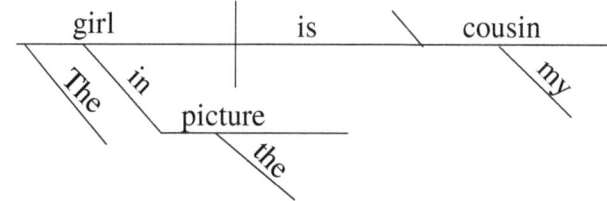

25. Joe and Moe wash and dry their dishes.
(40, 49)

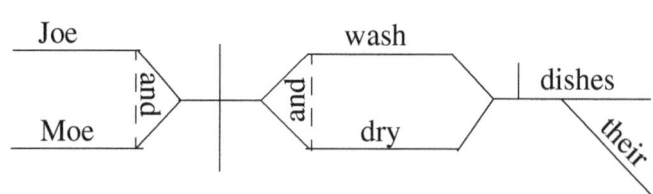

Test 13 READ CAREFULLY Name: _____

Give after Lesson 70.

Circle the correct word(s) to complete sentences 1–10.

1. You made (less, **fewer**) mistakes than I did.
(56)

2. After the test, we (was, **were**) elated.
(18)

3. The pronoun *he* is (first, second, **third**) person.
(64)

4. The word group below is a (phrase, **clause**).
(36)
        for they produce breakfast cereal

5. The following is a (**sentence fragment**, run-on sentence, complete sentence):
(5, 23)
        Raising hogs in both Indiana and Illinois.

6. The hardy tree (**grew**, grown) quickly.
(65)

7. The noun *tenacity* is (**abstract**, concrete).
(11)

8. She has two (brother-in-laws, **brothers-in-law**).
(13, 16)

9. The verb (sing, speak, **were**) is a common linking verb.
(31)

10. Julia has (wore, **worn**) out her socks.
(65)

11. For a–d, circle the correct definition. (1 point for each correct answer)

   (a) (Gentility, **Intuition**, Pessimism) is an instinctive feeling or knowledge.
   (61)

   (b) Cowardice is lack of (food, money, **courage**).
   (62)

   (c) One who is (**tenacious**, malicious, indolent) does not give up.
   (63)

   (d) (**Ethical**, Unethical, Intrepid) means "morally right."
   (64)

12. Add periods as needed in the sentence below.
(47, 50)
        Mr. Cross paid $1.99 (one dollar and ninety-nine cents) for four lbs. of bananas.

13. Circle each letter that should be capitalized in the sentence below.
(42, 43)
        a british musician played the **f**rench horn skillfully.

14. For a–d, write the plural of each noun.
(16, 22)
   (a) dish __dishes__   (b) monkey __monkeys__
   (c) baby __babies__   (d) spoonful __spoonfuls__

Grammar and Writing 5 | 137 | Teacher Guide Test Answers

15. Add commas as needed in the sentence below.
(59, 60)

Ms. Hoo**,** I would like you to meet my mother**,** Mrs. Loya.

16. Circle each coordinating conjunction in the sentence below.
(48)

I ordered soup (and) salad, (for) I was hungry.

17. Circle the misspelled word in the list below.
(33-35)

neighbor, weigh, view, (veiw)

18. Circle the antecedent of the italicized pronoun in the sentence below.
(62)

(Leo) left *his* skateboard outside.

19. Complete the four principal parts of the verb *wrap*.
(19)

<u>wrap</u>	<u>*(is)* wrapping</u>	<u>wrapped</u>	<u>*(has)* wrapped</u>
(1) present tense	(2) present participle	(3) past tense	(4) past participle

20. Add suffixes. (2 points for each correct answer)
(33, 34)

(a) give + ing <u>giving</u>   (b) pretty + er <u>prettier</u>

21. In the sentence below, underline each prepositional phrase, circling the object of each preposition.
(44)

The cheese <u>on the (table)</u> comes <u>from (Wisconsin)</u>

22. Circle the proper adjective in the sentence below.
(42)

Please slice some (Wisconsin) cheese for sandwiches.

23. Circle the indirect object in the sentence below.
(46)

He handed (me) an envelope.

On the lines provided, diagram each word of sentences 24 and 25.

24. The trip was expensive but worthwhile.
(49, 54)

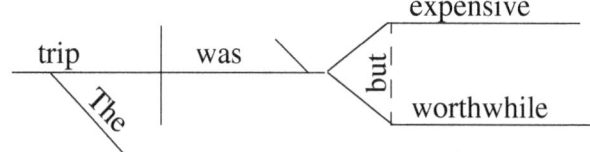

25. The little boat on the lake endured a big storm.
(40, 45)

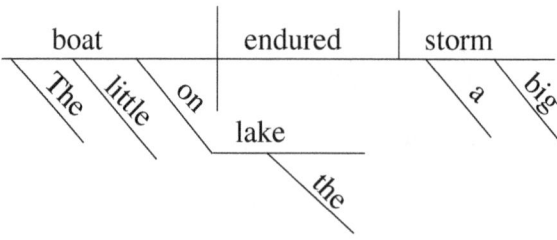

Test 14 READ CAREFULLY Name: _____

Give after Lesson 75.

Circle the correct word(s) to complete sentences 1–10.

1. I have eaten (less, **fewer**) tacos than she has.
(56)

2. Doreen went to Yosemite with Austin and (I, **me**).
(70)

3. The pronoun *you* is (first, **second**, third) person.
(64)

4. The word group below is a (**phrase**, clause).
(36)
    a locomotive and many passenger cars at the station

5. The following is a (**sentence fragment**, run-on sentence, complete sentence):
(23, 24)
    The long, lonesome whistle of the steam train.

6. Vintage Shay locomotives have (blow, blew, **blown**) their whistles for decades.
(65)

7. The comparative form of the adjective *bad* is (bad, **worse**, worst).
(55, 56)

8. The word *brother-in-law's* is a (plural, **possessive**) noun.
(13)

9. The verb (**seemed**, said, whispered) is a common linking verb.
(31)

10. Julia has (drank, **drunk**) eight glasses of water today.
(65)

11. For a–d, circle the correct definition. (1 point for each correct answer)

    (a) Ornithology is the study of (weather, rocks, **birds**).
    (68)

    (b) To feign is to (**pretend**, listen, travel).
    (69)

    (c) (Intrepid, Tenacious, **Contrite**) means "sorry."
    (66)

    (d) (Irrelevant, **Pertinent**, Contrite) means "relevant or applicable."
    (67)

12. Add periods as needed in the sentence below.
(47, 50)
    At two a.m., Ms. Overwork finally finished her essay.

13. Circle each letter that should be capitalized in the sentence below.
(42, 43)
    In the **E**ast, **I**talian **A**mericans settled to begin a new life.

14. For a–d, write the plural of each noun.
(16, 22)
    (a) bench **benches**   (b) donkey **donkeys**

    (c) cherry **cherries**   (d) cupful **cupfuls**

15. Add commas as needed to clarify the sentence below.

With Lucy**,** Thomas writes well.

16. Circle each coordinating conjunction in the sentence below.

I have no pen (or) pencil, (yet) I have plenty of paper.

17. Circle the misspelled word in the list below.

neighbor, weigh, (reciept), receipt

18. Circle the antecedent of the italicized pronoun in the sentence below.

(Sharon) carries *her* heavy backpack for miles.

19. Complete the four principal parts of the verb *grow*.

grow	*(is)* growing	grew	*(has)* grown
(1) present tense	(2) present participle	(3) past tense	(4) past participle

20. Add suffixes. (2 points for each correct answer)

(a) hope + ing   **hoping**   (b) sunny + est   **sunniest**

21. In the sentence below, underline each prepositional phrase, circling the object of each preposition.

The train at the (station) will soon leave for (Chicago).

22. Circle the proper adjective in the sentence below.

How many (Georgia) peaches are in this pie?

23. Circle the indirect object in the sentence below.

The ranger gave (us) a tour of the area.

On the lines provided, diagram each word of sentences 24 and 25.

24. Your brother seems tenacious and ethical.

25. The rabbit in the garden ate two ripe melons.

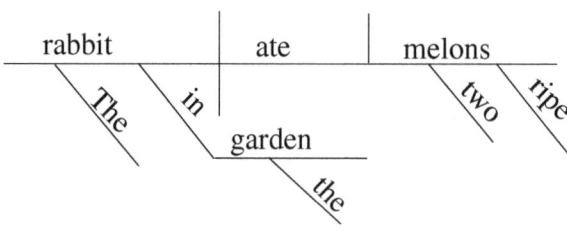

Test 15
Give after Lesson 80.

READ CAREFULLY   Name: _____

Circle the correct word(s) to complete sentences 1–10.

1. Anita is the (**better**, best) of the two guitarists.
 (56)

2. The geology experts were Rocky and (her, **she**).
 (66)

3. The pronoun *we* is (**first**, second, third) person.
 (64)

4. The clause below is (**dependent**, independent).
 (73)
 when minerals form around geyser vents

5. The following is a (sentence fragment, **run-on sentence**, complete sentence):
 (23, 24)
 The geyser is quiet it will erupt soon.

6. The ship (sink, **sank**, sunk) long ago.
 (65)

7. The superlative form of the adjective *bad* is (bad, worse, **worst**).
 (55, 56)

8. The sentence below is (simple, **compound**).
 (75)
 The geyser blew, and I ran for cover!

9. The verb (**looks**, says, sings) is a common linking verb.
 (31)

10. Norm has (break, broke, **broken**) his arm again.
 (65)

11. For a–d, circle the correct definition. (1 point for each correct answer)

 (a) (Serene, Ethical, **Ardent**) means "passionate and zealous."
  (71)

 (b) *Serene* means "(angry, troubled, **peaceful**)."
  (72)

 (c) Sagacity is (**wisdom**, sorrow, trouble).
  (73)

 (d) (**Redundancy**, Linguistics, Serenity) is needless repetition.
  (74)

12. Add periods as needed in the sentence below.
 (47, 50)
 Mrs. Starlyn saw the geyser's six p.m. eruption.

13. Circle each letter that should be capitalized in the sentence below.
 (42, 43)
 Can **i** buy **i**talian suasage in **n**ew **y**ork?

14. For a–d, write the plural of each noun.
 (16, 22)
 (a) lunch ___lunches___   (b) key ___keys___

 (c) berry ___berries___   (d) handful ___handfuls___

Grammar and Writing 5   **141**   Teacher Guide
                                        Test Answers

15. Add commas as needed in the sentence below.
(68)

When Old Faithful erupts**,** I shall take pictures of it.

16. Circle the coordinating conjunction in the compound sentence below.
(75)

We have been watching, (but) the geyser has not blown.

17. Circle the misspelled word in the list below.
(33-35)

neighbor, weigh, piece, (peice)

18. Circle the antecedent of the italicized pronoun in the sentence below.
(62)

Although *he* has studied geology, (Clark) cannot explain everything.

19. Complete the four principal parts of the verb *freeze*.
(65)

| *freeze* | *(is)* freezing | froze | *(has)* frozen |
| (1) present tense | (2) present participle | (3) past tense | (4) past participle |

20. Add suffixes. (2 points for each correct answer)
(33, 34)

(a) snap + ed   __snapped__   (b) argue + ment   __argument__

21. In the sentence below, underline each prepositional phrase, circling the object of each preposition.
(44)

A man <u>with an (umbrella)</u> stood <u>beside (me)</u>.

22. Circle the predicate nominative in the sentence below.
(51)

Old Faithful is a magnificent (geyser).

23. Circle the indirect object in the sentence below.
(46, 69)

Alberto handed (Quan) a photo.

On the lines provided, diagram each word of sentences 24 and 25.

24. The eruption was sudden and spectacular.
(49, 54)

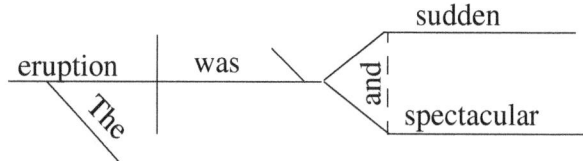

25. The man with the umbrella has two children.
(40, 45)

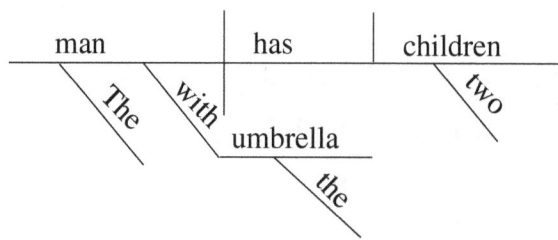

Test 16   READ CAREFULLY   Name: _____

Give after Lesson 85.

Circle the correct word(s) to complete sentences 1–10.

1. Of the two kittens, that one is ((fuzzier), fuzziest).

2. You know more than (me, (I)) about prairie dogs.

3. The pronoun *him* is (nominative, (objective), possessive) case.

4. The clause below is (dependent, (independent)).

   coyotes threaten the prairie dog colony

5. The following is a ((sentence fragment), run-on sentence, complete sentence):

   Burrowing to escape the golden eagle.

6. A prairie dog hides in (it's, (its)) burrow.

7. A coyote snarls at Rocky and (he, (him)).

8. The sentence below is ((simple), compound).

   The prairie dog stopped and looked at me.

9. The man ((who), which) counts prairie dogs rides a horse.

10. Norm has (tear, tore, (torn)) his shirt again.

11. For a–d, circle the correct definition. (1 point for each correct answer)

    (a) (Dauntless, (Quaint), Ardent) means "attractive in an old-fashioned way."

    (b) To ameliorate is to (destroy, (improve), harm).

    (c) *Dauntless* means "(afraid, (heroic), weak)".

    (d) (Redundancy, (Salinity), Serenity) is saltiness.

12. Add periods as needed in the sentence below. (4 periods)

    Cherries cost $2.99 (two dollars and ninety-nine cents) per lb., so I bought only eight oz. today.

13. Circle each letter that should be capitalized in the sentence below.

    (c)an (i) purchase (a)laskan crab in (m)aine?

14. For a–d, write the plural of each noun.

    (a) bunch ___bunches___   (b) toy ___toys___

    (c) colony ___colonies___   (d) mouthful ___mouthfuls___

Grammar and Writing 5   143   Teacher Guide
                                        Test Answers

15. Add commas and quotation marks as needed in the sentence below.
(76, 80)

"After lunch," said Ms. Hoo, "we shall discuss the Utah prairie dog."

16. Circle the coordinating conjunction in the compound sentence below.
(75)

Some prairie dogs are hiding, (for) hawks are circling above.

17. Circle the subordinating conjunction in the sentence below.
(73)

(Because) prairie dogs are social animals, they live together in large colonies.

18. Circle the antecedent of the italicized pronoun in the sentence below.
(62)

Mimi likes (prairie dogs) because *they* are cute.

19. Complete the four principal parts of the verb *steal*.
(65)

steal	*(is)* stealing	stole	*(has)* stolen
(1) present tense	(2) present participle	(3) past tense	(4) past participle

20. Add suffixes. (2 points for each correct answer)
(33, 34)

(a) win + er __winner__   (b) salty + ness __saltiness__

21. Circle the interrogative pronoun in the sentence below.
(79)

(Which) shall we study first?

22. Circle the predicate nominative in the sentence below.
(51)

The Utah prairie dog is an endangered (species).

23. Circle the indirect object in the sentence below.
(46, 69)

Elle made (Daisy) a taco.

On the lines provided, diagram each word of sentences 24 and 25.

24. Prairie dogs are rodents with short tails.
(45, 51)

Prairie dogs | are \ rodents
                     \ with
                       \ tails
                         \ short

25. Max is listening, but Perlina is napping.
(75)

Max | is listening
but
Perlina | is napping

Test 17   READ CAREFULLY   Name: _____

Give after Lesson 90.

Circle the correct word(s) to complete sentences 1–10.

1. That planet is the (**bigger**, biggest) of the two.
   (56)

2. I am shorter than (**he**, him).
   (78)

3. The pronoun *his* is (nominative, objective, **possessive**) case.
   (70, 72)

4. The clause below is (**dependent**, independent).
   (73)
   since the moon is full tonight

5. One of the students (give, **gives**) (their, **his or her**) report each morning.
   (83)

6. (**Your**, You're) car is fast, but (**ours**, our's) is faster.
   (72)

7. A bear watches Grace and (she, **her**).
   (69, 70)

8. The sentence below is (simple, **compound**).
   (75)
   The sky is cloudy, so I cannot see the stars.

9. The woman (**who**, which) owns the telescope can identify many stars.
   (77)

10. (Them, **Those**) photographs show the solar eclipse.
    (82)

11. For a–d, circle the correct definition. (1 point for each correct answer)

    (a) A (docent, curator, **culprit**) is a guilty one.
    (81)

    (b) Bliss is great (sorrow, **happiness**, pain).
    (82)

    (c) (**Subversion**, Rapport, Rapprochement) is destruction.
    (83)

    (d) (Subversion, **Rapport**, Quaintness) is harmony in a relationship.
    (84)

12. Add periods as needed in the sentence below. (4 periods)
    (47, 50)
    Mrs**.** Vega lives on S**.** First St**.** in Denver**.**

13. Circle each letter that should be capitalized in the sentence below.
    (42, 43)
    Will **I** find **W**ashington apples in **F**lorida?

14. For a–d, write the plural of each noun.
    (16, 22)
    (a) branch __branches__   (b) day __days__

    (c) company __companies__   (d) child __children__

Grammar and Writing 5   **145**   Teacher Guide
                                                   Test Answers

15. Add commas and quotation marks as needed in the sentence below.
(76, 80)

"Next week," said Ms. Hoo, "we shall view a solar eclipse."

16. Circle the coordinating conjunction in the compound sentence below.
(75)

The moon is a cold, rocky body, (and) it has no light of its own.

17. Circle the subordinating conjunction in the sentence below.
(73)

The moon appears luminous (because) sunlight reflects from the moon's surface.

18. Circle the antecedent of the italicized pronoun in the sentence below.
(62)

Tex gazed at the (moon) until clouds covered *it*.

19. Complete the four principal parts of the verb *catch*.
(85)

<u>catch</u>	<u>(is) catching</u>	<u>caught</u>	<u>(has) caught</u>
(1) present tense	(2) present participle	(3) past tense	(4) past participle

20. Add suffixes. *(2 points for each correct answer)*
(33, 34)

(a) begin + er <u> beginner </u>   (b) happy + ness <u> happiness </u>

21. Underline the words that should be italicized in the sentence below.
(84)

Someday I shall read Melville's novel, <u>Moby Dick</u>.

22. Circle the predicate nominative in the sentence below.
(51)

That solar eclipse was an awesome (spectacle).

23. Circle the indirect object in the sentence below.
(46, 69)

Did Fido leave (her) any dog food?

On the lines provided, diagram each word of sentences 24 and 25.

24. Is Saturn the planet with rings?
(45, 51)

Saturn | Is \ planet
                    the   with
                          rings

25. Cora and she sew their own clothes.
(40, 71)

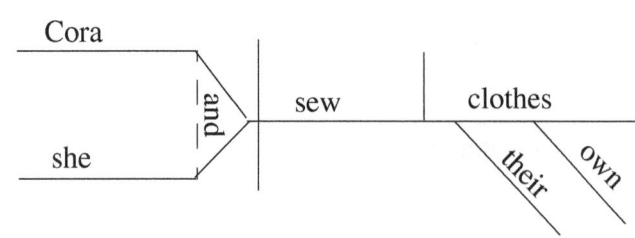

Test 18   READ CAREFULLY   Name: _____

Give after Lesson 95.

Circle the correct word(s) to complete sentences 1–10.

1. That cave is the (bigger, **biggest**) of all!
2. Are you as courageous as (me, **I**)?
3. The pronoun *she* is (**nominative**, objective, possessive) case.
4. The clause below is (dependent, **independent**).

    stalactites and stalagmites decorate the caverns

5. Each of the bats (flap, **flaps**) (their, **its**) wings.
6. (They're, **Their**, There) lawn is greener than (her's, **hers**).
7. This vase of flowers (need, **needs**) water.
8. The sentence below is (**simple**, compound).

    Inside the dark cave, bats sleep during the daytime.

9. The people (**who**, which) entered the cave have not come out!
10. Neither the flowers nor the lawn (have, **has**) been watered.

11. For a–d, circle the correct definition. (1 point for each correct answer)

    (a) *Colossal* means "extremely (small, skinny, **large**)."

    (b) To (languish, daunt, **coerce**) is to force.

    (c) (Colossal, **Complacent**, Languid) means "content; self-satisfied."

    (d) To (**languish**, daunt, coerce) is to grow weak.

12. Add periods as needed in the sentence below. (4 periods)

    That library in St. George opens at nine a.m. on Saturdays.

13. Circle each letter that should be capitalized in the sentence below.

    Can we buy **W**isconsin cheese in **n**ew **m**exico?

14. For a–d, write the plural of each noun.

    (a) bush __bushes__   (b) valley __valleys__

    (c) country __countries__   (d) loaf __loaves__

15. Add punctuation marks as needed in the sentence below.
(80, 88)

"In what state are the Carlsbad Caverns?" asked Ernesto.

16. Circle the coordinating conjunction in the compound sentence below.
(75)

The cave is dark, (but) I have a flashlight.

17. Circle the subordinating conjunction in the sentence below.
(73)

(Since) the underground chambers are accessible, many tourists visit Carlsbad Caverns.

18. Circle the antecedent of the italicized pronoun in the sentence below.
(62)

The (bat) hangs by *its* toes and thumbs from the cave's ceiling.

19. Complete the four principal parts of the verb *swim*.
(87)

swim	_(is)_ swimming	_swam_	_(has)_ swum
(1) present tense	(2) present participle	(3) past tense	(4) past participle

20. Add suffixes. (2 points for each correct answer)
(33, 34)

(a) scare + y ___scary___   (b) run + er ___runner___

21. Underline the word that should be italicized in the sentence below.
(84)

<u>Chiroptera</u> is the scientific name for bat.

22. Circle the predicate nominative in the sentence below.
(51)

The bat is a (mammal)

23. Circle the indirect object in the sentence below.
(46, 69)

I mailed (them) a postcard from New Mexico.

On the lines provided, diagram each word of sentences 24 and 25.

24. Is this cave a home for bats?
(45, 51)

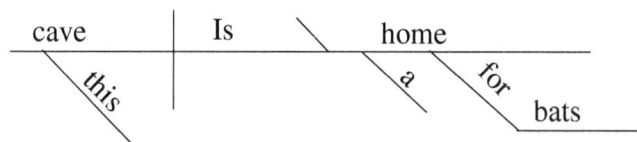

25. Huey and Lucy gave me a box of pencils.
(40, 71)

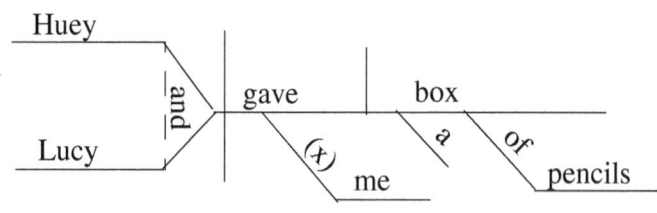

Test 19   READ CAREFULLY   Name: _____

Give after Lesson 100.

Circle the correct word(s) to complete sentences 1–10.

1. I don't have (no, **any**) homework today.

2. We have less homework than (**they**, them).

3. The pronoun *them* is (nominative, **objective**, possessive) case.

4. The clause below is (**dependent**, independent).

    while they were imprisoned on Alcatraz Island

5. One of the ships (**has**, have) sunk.

6. (**It's**, Its) hunting for (it's, **its**) prey.

7. This box of pencils (**is**, are) mine.

8. The sentence below is (simple, **compound**).

    The ship sank, so we took a helicopter.

9. (Them, **Those**) ruins must be the old prison.

10. Either the horses or the cow (eat, **eats**) that hay.

11. For a–d, circle the correct definition. (1 point for each correct answer)

    (a) *Paltry* means "(significant, **insignificant**, huge)."

    (b) To (**ostracize**, languish, coerce) is to exclude from a group.

    (c) *Concise* means "(long, wordy, **brief**)."

    (d) Obfuscation is (**confusion**, truth, force).

12. Add periods as needed in the sentence below. (5 periods)

    Dr. Parden, D.D.S., examined my teeth.

13. Circle each letter that should be capitalized in the sentence below.

    Alcatraz **I**sland lies in the middle of **S**an **F**rancisco **B**ay.

14. For a–d, write the plural of each noun.

    (a) ranch __ranches__   (b) bay __bays__

    (c) city __cities__   (d) leaf __leaves__

15. Add punctuation marks as needed in the sentence below.
(88, 94)

"How did thirty-four prisoners escape?" asked Amelia.

16. Circle the coordinating conjunction in the compound sentence below.
(75)

We must hurry,(for) the sun is setting.

17. Circle the subordinating conjunction in the sentence below.
(73)

(Although) the island is small, it held many dangerous prisoners.

18. Add quotation marks as needed in the sentence below.
(81)

When I was a child, I sang "London Bridge Is Falling Down."

19. Complete the four principal parts of the verb *write*.
(87)

write	*(is)* writing	wrote	*(has)* written
(1) present tense	(2) present participle	(3) past tense	(4) past participle

20. Add suffixes. (2 points for each correct answer)
(33, 34)

(a) beauty + ful __beautiful__   (b) smile + ing __smiling__

21. Underline the words that should be italicized in the sentence below.
(84)

The artist George Henry Broughton painted <u>Pilgrims Going to Church</u>.

22. Circle the adverb in the sentence below.
(95)

The painter worked (tirelessly).

23. Circle the interrogative pronoun in the sentence below.
(79)

(Who) lived on Alcatraz Island before the prison was built?

On the lines provided, diagram each word of sentences 24 and 25.

24. Is this island an attraction for tourists?
(45, 51)

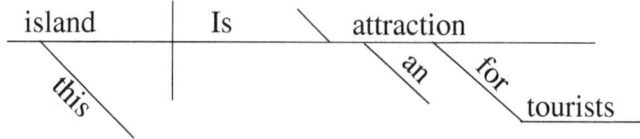

25. Can Joe or Moe pour me a cup of milk?
(40, 71)

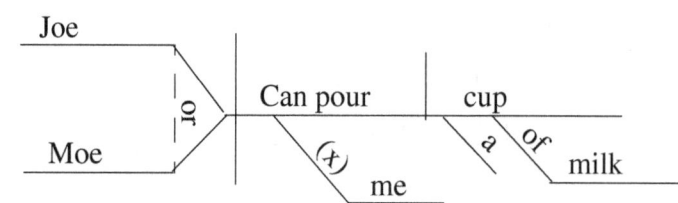

Test 20   READ CAREFULLY   Name: _____

Give after Lesson 105.

Circle the correct word(s) to complete sentences 1–10.

1. Polly doesn't want (no, **any**) crackers.

2. Kyle is as sagacious as (him, **he**).

3. Lucy skates (good, **well**).

4. The clause below is (dependent, **independent**).

   they live in the desert

5. One of the peacocks (**has**, have) flown away.

6. Ms. Hoo and (us, **we**) shall visit the art museum.

7. The lens on this camera (**is**, are) dirty.

8. The sentence below is (**simple**, compound).

   A peacock flew over the fence and landed on our car.

9. (Them, **Those**) canyons have rocky cliffs.

10. Neither the peacocks nor the goose (want, **wants**) my sandwich.

11. For a–d, circle the correct definition. (1 point for each correct answer)

    (a) (Profusion, **Perjury**, Propriety) is lying under oath.

    (b) (Profusion, Propriety, **Plagiarism**) is idea theft.

    (c) *Profuse* means "(scarce, **abundant**, insignificant)."

    (d) A prologue comes at the (**beginning**, middle, end).

12. Add periods as needed in the sentence below. (4 periods)

    Dr. Jacob B. Adan rushed to St. Vincent Hospital.

13. Circle each letter that should be capitalized in the sentence below.

    Catalina **I**sland lies off the coast of **S**outhern **C**alifornia.

14. For a–d, write the plural of each noun.

    (a) patch __patches__   (b) Tuesday __Tuesdays__

    (c) county __counties__   (d) knife __knives__

Grammar and Writing 5   151   Teacher Guide
                                             Test Answers

15. Add punctuation marks as needed in the sentence below.
(88, 94)

"Ms Hoo**,** have you read my essay?" asked Perlina.

16. Circle the coordinating conjunction in the compound sentence below.
(75)

The sun has set, ⟨yet⟩ the air remains warm.

17. Add a hyphen as needed in the sentence below.
(97)

We cyclists are looking forward to our fifty-mile ride.

18. Add quotation marks as needed in the sentence below.
(81)

Is the nursery rhyme "Humpty Dumpty" about an egg?

19. Complete the four principal parts of the verb *eat*.
(87)

eat	*(is)* eating	ate	*(has)* eaten
(1) present tense	(2) present participle	(3) past tense	(4) past participle

20. Circle the word below that is divided correctly.
(99)

⟨un-known⟩   unkno-wn   unkn-own

21. Underline the words that should be italicized in the sentence below.
(84)

<u>Crotalus atrox</u> and <u>Crotalus ruber</u> are types of rattlesnakes.

22. Circle the adverb in the sentence below.
(98)

Careless painters dripped blue and yellow paint ⟨everywhere⟩.

23. Circle the interrogative pronoun in the sentence below.
(79)

⟨What⟩ is your favorite sport?

On the lines provided, diagram each word of sentences 24 and 25.

24. Is Jill the girl with long hair?
(45, 51)

25. Joe politely offers Moe one of his mints.
(46, 71)

Test 21 READ CAREFULLY   Name: _____

Give after Lesson 110.

Circle the correct word(s) to complete sentences 1–10.

1. Polly doesn't want (nothing, **anything**) to eat.
(93)

2. Mr. Cuxil, (**who**, whom) teaches English, also coaches basketball.
(77)

3. Juan plays chess (good, **well**).
(96)

4. The clause below is (**dependent**, independent).
(73)
  until the cows come home

5. Each of the artists (have, **has**) (their, **his or her**) own style.
(91)

6. Please come with Daisy and (I, **me**).
(66, 69)

7. (Is, **Are**) your scissors sharp?
(92)

8. The sentence below is (simple, **compound**).
(75)
  The pianist played well, but the singer's voice was flat.

9. The Grand Canyon is (sure, **surely**) beautiful.
(104)

10. Of the two hikers, Jill climbs the hill (**faster**, fastest).
(102)

11. For a–d, circle the correct definition. (1 point for each correct answer)

  (a) An (anarchy, **enigma**, estuary) is a riddle or mystery.
  (101)

  (b) *Candid* means "(**honest**, dishonest, unethical)."
  (102)

  (c) *Parsimonious* means "(**stingy**, generous, extravagant)."
  (104)

  (d) To (consecrate, **desecrate**, ameliorate) is to destroy.
  (105)

12. Add periods as needed in the sentence below. (4 periods)
(47, 50)
  Ms. Hoo left at two p.m. on the last day of school.

13. Circle each letter that should be capitalized in the sentence below.
(42, 43)
  The **C**olorado **R**iver has carved the magnificent **G**rand **C**anyon in **A**rizona.

14. For a–d, write the plural of each noun.
(16, 22)
  (a) coach __coaches__ (b) library __libraries__

  (c) gallon of milk __gallons of milk__ (d) mouse __mice__

15. Add punctuation marks as needed in the sentence below.
(94, 97)

"Do the sweet-smelling flowers attract bees?" asks Andrew.

16. Add a semicolon as needed in the sentence below.
(103)

Adventuresome folk can stay at Phantom Ranch in Grand Canyon**;** however, it is only accessible by foot or mule.

17. Add a colon as needed in the sentence below.
(105)

The supply list includes these items**:** tent, sleeping bag, lantern, and canteen.

18. Add quotation marks as needed in the sentence below.
(81)

Luis wrote a poem titled **"**A Parsimonious Monarch.**"**

19. Complete the four principal parts of the verb *forgive*.
(87)

forgive	_(is) forgiving_	_forgave_	_(has) forgiven_
(1) present tense	(2) present participle	(3) past tense	(4) past participle

20. Circle the appositive phrase in the sentence below.
(58)

Amy baked a healthful snack, (whole-grain muffins with raisins.)

21. Underline the word that should be italicized in the sentence below.
(84)

I think that sentence contains a superfluous <u>and</u>.

22. Circle the adverb in the sentence below.
(100)

The forces of erosion are (constantly) changing the Grand Canyon's appearance.

23. Circle the subordinating conjunction in the sentence below.
(73, 74)

I shall hike up that mountain (even though) I am weary.

In the boxes provided, diagram each word of sentences 24 and 25.

24. Is the orca the whale with the triangular fin?
(45, 51)

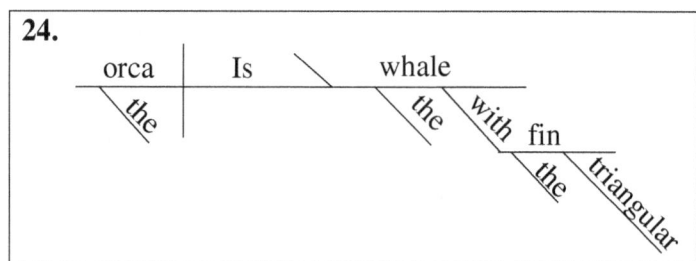

25. Has the whale swum away?
(98)

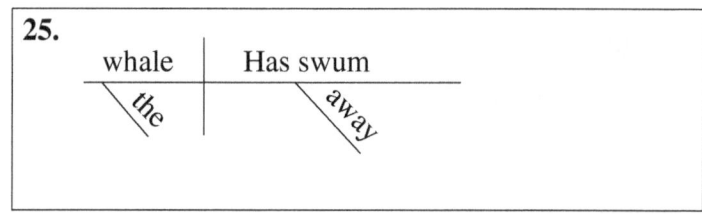

Test 22   READ CAREFULLY   Name: _____

Give after Lesson 112.

Circle the correct word(s) to complete sentences 1–10.

1. There wasn't (**anybody**, nobody) home.
   (93)

2. Mr. Cuxil, (who, **whom**) we chose as our leader, has taught me valuable lessons.
   (77)

3. Yesterday I was ill, but today I feel (good, **well**).
   (96)

4. The clause below is (dependent, **independent**).
   (73)
   armadillos usually live alone

5. Each of the hikers (carry, **carries**) (their, **his or her**) own food and water.
   (91)

6. Please tell Elle and (I, **me**) your secret.
   (66, 69)

7. Mumps (**is**, are) a miserable disease.
   (92)

8. The sentence below is (compound, complex, **compound-complex**).
   (75, 110)
   When my dog eats too much, his eyes bulge, and his stomach protrudes.

9. Josie was (real, **really**) frightened when she encountered a black bear.
   (104)

10. (Between, **Among**) the many icebergs swam penguins and polar bears.
    (107)

11. For a–d, circle the correct definition. (1 point for each correct answer)

    (a) To (consecrate, ameliorate, **beguile**) is to mislead or deceive.
    (106)

    (b) To (beguile, **digress**, consecrate) is to depart from the main subject.
    (107)

    (c) *Futile* means "(**hopeless**, effective, hopeful)."
    (108)

    (d) (Dissension, **Apathy**, Digression) is lack of interest or concern.
    (110)

12. Add periods as needed in the sentence below. (4 periods)
    (47, 50)
    Mr. Cabrera wakes at six a.m. to exercise.

13. Circle each letter that should be capitalized in the sentence below.
    (42, 43)
    (**C**)an you drive from (**O**)lympia, (**W**)ashington, to (**J**)uneau (**A**)laska?

14. For a–d, write the plural of each noun.
    (16, 22)
    (a) toothbrush __toothbrushes__   (b) dictionary __dictionaries__

    (c) class president __class presidents__   (d) tooth __teeth__

15. Add punctuation marks as needed in the sentence below.
(88)

"Are the grizzlies hibernating?" asks Amelia.

16. Add a semicolon and a comma as needed in the sentence below.
(103)

Most states have few grizzly bears; however, Alaska has many.

17. Add a colon as needed in the sentence below.
(105)

I remember one fact about grizzlies: they are dangerous.

18. Add apostrophes as needed in the sentence below.
(108, 109)

That plumber's license wasn't valid, for it dated back to the year '73.

19. Complete the four principal parts of the verb *weave*.
(87)

<u>weave</u>	(*is*) <u>weaving</u>	<u>wove</u>	(*has*) <u>woven</u>
(1) present tense	(2) present participle	(3) past tense	(4) past participle

20. Circle the indirect object in the sentence below.
(69)

Elle offered (us) a healthful snack of nuts and fruit.

21. Underline the word that should be italicized in the sentence below.
(84)

<u>Squash</u> can be either a noun or a verb.

22. Circle the adverb in the sentence below.
(95)

Two black bears are (happily) feasting on wild berries.

23. Circle the subordinating conjunction in the sentence below.
(73, 74)

My dog barks (whenever) she sees a bear.

In the boxes provided, diagram each word of sentences 24 and 25.

24. Is Fifi the poodle with the red collar?
(45, 51)

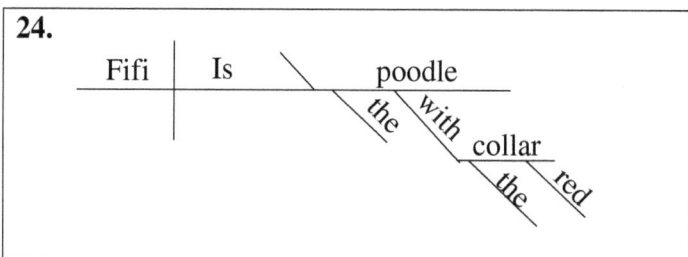

25. Grizzlies can run incredibly fast.
(40, 101)

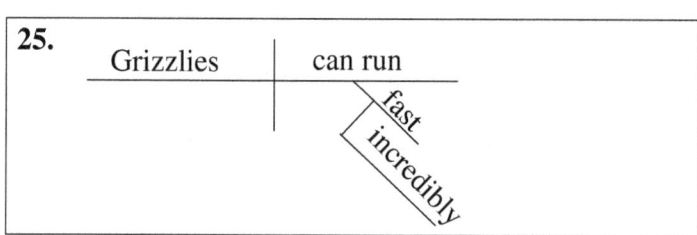

Student Workbook More Practice Answer Key

More Practice Lesson 4

Circle the simple subject and underline the simple predicate in each sentence.

1. The (Earth) turns.
2. The (Sun) shines all the time.
3. (We) see it during the daytime.
4. Does the (Sun) sleep at night?
5. Can (animals) live without sunlight?
6. Can (plants) live without sunlight?
7. (We) need the Sun's light and warmth.
8. Dark (clouds) were covering the city.
9. The (Sun) had disappeared.
10. Down came the (rain).
11. (Thunder) rumbled in the distance.
12. (Fido) splashed through the puddles.
13. Do (you) have an umbrella?
14. The (rain) has stopped.
15. Out came the (Sun).
16. My tomato (plants) are growing!
17. The (seeds) have sprouted.
18. Have (you) planted a garden?
19. Soon (we) shall pick some zucchini.
20. Does (Fido) like zucchini?

More Practice Lesson 8 Circle each letter that should be capitalized in the sentences below.

1. **M**y friend **K**elly crossed the famous **G**olden **G**ate **B**ridge in **S**an **F**rancisco, **C**alifornia. 8 capital letters

2. **T**he **P**anama **C**anal connects the **P**acific **O**cean and the **C**aribbean **S**ea. 7 capital letters

3. **T**he **A**mazon **R**iver in **S**outh **A**merica flows into the **A**tlantic **O**cean. 7 capital letters

4. **I** think **N**iagara **F**alls, between **L**ake **E**rie and **L**ake **O**ntario, is spectacular! 7 capital letters

5. **Y**ou will find the **A**ndes **M**ountains in **S**outh **A**merica. 5 capital letters

6. **I**n the center of **C**anada lies **L**ake **W**innipeg. 4 capital letters

7. **P**hil hopes to sing the famous hymn "**A**mazing **G**race" at **C**arnegie **H**all in **N**ew **Y**ork **C**ity next **A**pril. 9 capital letters

8. **L**ast **W**ednesday, **I** read the poem "**T**rees" by **J**oyce **K**ilmer. 6 capital letters

9. **M**r. **G**allup teaches at **P**asadena **C**ity **C**ollege in **C**alifornia. 6 capital letters

10. **I**s **C**oncord the capital of **N**ew **H**ampshire? 4 capital letters

11. **H**ave you ever swum in the **M**editerranean **S**ea? 3 capital letters

12. **M**onty and **A**llison surf in the **P**acific **O**cean. 4 capital letters

13. **Y**es, **B**oston is the capital of **M**assachusetts. 3 capital letters

14. **T**he ***T**itanic*, a luxury ship from **G**reat **B**ritain, hit an iceberg off the coast of **N**ewfoundland. 5 capital letters

15. **L**ast **J**uly the **R**ivas **F**amily camped near the **G**rand **C**anyon in **A**rizona. 7 capital letters

More Practice Lesson 12

Circle each helping verb in the following sentences.

1. Long ago, Alabama (was) called the Cotton State.
2. People (may) see moose, elk, caribou, and bears in Alaska.
3. Someday I (shall) visit the Grand Canyon in Arizona.
4. We (might) search for diamonds in Arkansas!
5. Gold (was) found in California in 1848.
6. Next winter Brent (will) (be) skiing in Colorado.
7. The Connecticut Colony (had) written a constitution more than a hundred years before the War of Independence.
8. (Do) people still live in Delaware's colonial homes?
9. In Florida's Everglades, a crocodile (is) sleeping peacefully.
10. Former President Jimmy Carter (was) born in Georgia.
11. (Did) this pineapple come from Hawaii?
12. (Do) all potatoes come from Idaho?
13. Our plane (will) land at O'Hare Airport in Chicago, Illinois, at 7:30 p.m.
14. (Does) Indiana manufacture baseball bats?
15. Nathan (has) (been) packing popcorn in Iowa for thirty years.
16. (Have) you driven through the wheat fields of Kansas?
17. Buffalo (were) wandering through the Kentucky mountains.
18. The Mississippi Delta (has) provided rich farmland in Louisiana.
19. People in Maine (have) built many ships.
20. (Did) your ship sail into the Chesapeake Bay in Maryland?

Corny Chronicle #1
Follows Lesson 13

The Fundraiser

Three clever friends, (1) _____, (2) _____,
                                    proper noun (person)   proper noun (person)

and (3) _____, wanted to raise money to purchase
        proper noun (person)

more (4) _____ for (5) _____. Their plan was to
         concrete plural noun   proper noun (place)

manufacture (6) _____ from (7) _____ and sell
                concrete plural noun   concrete plural noun

them to (8) _____, (9) _____, and others who
            proper noun (person) proper noun (person)

might be interested.

In preparation for the project, the three clever friends

(10) _____ and (11) _____ for many hours.
     past tense action verb   past tense action verb

United in their efforts, they were truly a (12) _____.
                                                collective noun

After working together for nearly (13) _____
                                       number

weeks, they finally had their first product to sell. It looked

like a (14) _____ but made them think of
            concrete singular noun

(15) _____ or (16) _____. Thrilled with their
     abstract singular noun   abstract singular noun

product, they felt sure that either (17) _____ or
                                         proper noun (person)

(18) _____ would buy it from them although
     proper noun (person)

(19) _____ doubted that it would sell.
     proper noun (person)

In the end the three clever friends were able to sell their

magnificent product for (20) _____ dollars to
                             number

(21) _____, who plans to rent a storage compartment
     proper noun (person)

for it in (22) _____.
               proper noun (place)

Teacher instructions:

(1) Have students number blank, lined papers from 1 to 22. Ask them to write an example of the part of speech indicated beside each number. Proceed slowly, making sure students have written correct examples.

(2) Give each student a copy of the story. Ask students to write each word from their list into the blank with the corresponding number.

(3) Ask some students to read their stories aloud.

(4) Student answers will vary. Accept all reasonable answers.

Grammar and Writing 5   Teacher Guide
More Practice Answers

More Practice Lesson 15

Circle each letter that should be capitalized in the following sentences, poems, and song lyrics (capitalized like poems).

1. (S)tephen (F)oster wrote some humorous songs during the 1800s. (M)y friends and (I) like to sing them around the campfire.   4 capital letters

2. (I) come from (A)labama
   (W)id my banjo on my knee,
   (I)'m gwan to (L)ouisiana
   (M)y true love for to see,
   (I)t rained all night the day (I) left,
   (T)he weather it was dry,
   (T)he sun so hot (I) froze to death,
   (S)usanna, don't you cry.
   —(S)tephen (F)oster   14 capital letters

3. (M)y teacher said that (I) should stop giggling, but (I) couldn't stop because (I) was reading poems by (O)gden (N)ash. (T)hey were so funny!   7 capital letters

4. (A) dog that is indoors
   (T)o be let out implores.
   (Y)ou let him out and what then?
   (H)e wants back in again.
   —(O)gden (N)ash   6 capital letters

5. (T)he ant has made himself illustrious
   (T)hrough constant industry industrious.
   (S)o what?
   (W)ould you be calm and placid
   (I)f you were full of acid?
   —(O)gden (N)ash   7 capital letters

6. (N)ow another day is breaking,
   (S)leep was sweet and so is waking.
   (D)ear Lord, (I) promised you last night
   (N)ever again to sulk or fight.
   (S)uch vows are easier to keep
   (W)hen a child is sound asleep.
   —(O)gden (N)ash   9 capital letters

More Practice Lesson 25

Circle each letter that should be capitalized in the following titles.

1. "**D**own in the **V**alley" 2 capital letters
2. "**A** **B**icycle **B**uilt for **T**wo" 4 capital letters
3. "**I**n the **G**ood **O**ld **S**ummertime" 4 capital letters
4. "**T**he **M**an on the **F**lying **T**rapeze" 4 capital letters
5. "**T**he **S**tars and **S**tripes **F**orever" 4 capital letters
6. **T**he **I**ndian in the **C**upboard 3 capital letters
7. **T**he **H**ouse at **P**ooh **C**orner 4 capital letters
8. **T**he **V**oyages of **D**r. **D**oolittle 4 capital letters
9. **T**he **L**ion, the **W**itch, and the **W**ardrobe 4 capital letters
10. **T**he **O**nly **G**ame in **T**own 4 capital letters
11. **W**here the **R**ed **F**ern **G**rows 4 capital letters
12. **T**he **W**ind in the **W**illows 3 capital letters
13. **O**ld **Y**eller 2 capital letters
14. **T**he **P**hantom **T**ollbooth 3 capital letters
15. **T**he **S**ign of the **B**eaver 3 capital letters
16. **E**mil and the **D**etectives 2 capital letters
17. **T**he **T**rumpet of the **S**wan 3 capital letters
18. **T**he **M**ouse and the **M**otorcycle 3 capital letters
19. **M**y **S**ide of the **M**ountain 3 capital letters
20. **L**ittle **H**ouse on the **P**rairie 3 capital letters

More Practice Lesson 26

Circle each letter that should be capitalized in the following sentences and outlines.

1. ⓒonfucius said, "ⓥirtue is not left to stand alone. ⓗe who practices it will have neighbors." 3 capital letters

2. ⓗave you read ⓐlice's ⓐdventures in ⓦonderland by ⓛewis ⓒarroll? 6 capital letters

3. ⓨesterday ⓘ read a story called "ⓐladdin and the ⓦonderful ⓛamp." 5 capital letters

4. ⓣonight ⓘ shall read "ⓐli ⓑaba and the ⓕorty ⓣhieves." 6 capital letters

5. ⓐs ⓐnabel drove toward ⓑoston, she sang her favorite song, "ⓜy ⓞld ⓚentucky ⓗome." 7 capital letters

6. I. ⓣhe orchestra
   A. ⓟercussion and strings
   B. ⓣhe brass family
   C. ⓣhe woodwind family   4 capital letters

7. II. ⓣypes of musical compositions
   A. ⓣhe waltz
   B. ⓣhe march
   C. ⓣhe symphony   4 capital letters

8. ⓑenjamin ⓕranklin said, "ⓞne today is worth two tomorrows." 3 capital letters

9. ⓗe also said, "ⓐ lie stands on one leg, truth on two." 2 capital letters

10. "ⓣhe ⓑallad of the ⓑoll ⓦeevil" is an ⓐmerican folk song. 5 capital letters

11. ⓘn 1892, ⓙohn ⓜuir, an ⓐmerican naturalist, wrote to the editor of a magazine, "ⓛet us do something to make the mountains glad." 5 capital letters

12. ⓙohn ⓜuir wrote about the beauty of nature in a book called ⓣhe ⓜountains of ⓒalifornia. 5 capital letters

13. ⓟearl ⓢ. ⓑuck's most popular novel, ⓣhe ⓖood ⓔarth, won the ⓟulitzer ⓟrize. 8 capital letters

14. ⓙames ⓣhurber, an ⓐmerican humorist, wrote a story called "ⓣhe ⓢecret ⓛife of ⓦalter ⓜitty." 8 capital letters

More Practice Lesson 38 Circle each letter that should be capitalized in the following sentences.

1. **I**f **G**randpa **Z**amora grew up in **N**icaragua, why doesn't he speak **E**nglish with an accent?   5 capital letters

2. Yes, **C**aptain **C**heung met **M**s. **P**han aboard the ship to **I**ndia.   5 capital letters

3. **N**ext year **I** shall take classes such as **S**panish, art, geography, mathematics, and **E**nglish.   4 capital letters

4. **A**lthough **D**r. **A**dan has taught history, he has never taught **A**merican government.   4 capital letters

5. **B**efore **A**unt **C**atherine traveled to **J**apan, she studied **J**apanese.   5 capital letters

6. **Y**es, **I** believe **M**om and **D**ad invited **M**r. and **M**rs. **F**ernando **C**abrera to their anniversary party in **J**une.   9 capital letters

7. **W**hile in **E**urope, **M**om took classes in art history and **F**rench.   4 capital letters

8. **Y**esterday **S**ergeant **M**undy told **M**iss **L**u that he could do nothing about the flock of **C**anadian geese in her yard.   6 capital letters

9. **D**uring our two-hour social studies class, **I** noticed that even the teacher, **D**r. **D**reamer, was yawning.   4 capital letters

10. **I** promised **M**other that **I** would clean the garage on **S**aturday.   4 capital letters

11. **I** assured **F**ather that **I** would find a safe place to store his fishing pole.   3 capital letters

12. **W**hen **A**unt **T**anisha took chemistry, there were fewer than a hundred known elements.   3 capital letters

13. **D**oes **D**eputy **C**ruz always comb her hair like that?   3 capital letters

14. **N**o, **U**ncle **W**assim, **I** cannot go fishing, for **I** have to do a homework assignment for language arts.   5 capital letters

Corny Chronicle #2
Follows Lesson 39

A Parade

(1) _____ and (2) _____ are organizing a
   proper noun (person)   proper noun (person)

parade to honor their (3) _____. Floats decorated with
                              collective noun

(4) _____ and (5) _____ to portray the parade's
  concrete plural noun   concrete plural noun

theme of (6) _____ will follow (7) _____, the
         abstract singular noun   proper noun (person)

grand marshall, through the streets of the city.

People from (8) _____ and as far away as
                proper noun (place)

(9) _____ will gather to watch the parade. They will
  proper noun (place)

see horses (10) _____ (11) _____ and
                present participle   preposition
                form of action verb

(12) _____ the street. Balloons will fly
   preposition

(13) _____ and (14) _____ the spectators as
   preposition   preposition

marching bands (15) _____, (16) _____, and
                    present tense   present tense
                    action verb   action verb

(17) _____ to the beat of (18) _____ drums and
   present tense   descriptive adjective
   action verb

the clash of (19) _____ cymbals.
                  descriptive adjective

The most (20) _____ part of the parade will be
              descriptive adjective

(21) _____ bicycle (22) _____, which will
   proper possessive   collective noun
   noun (person)

feature (23) _____ cyclists (24) _____
             adjective (number)   present participle
                                         form of action verb

(25) _____ banners advertising (26) _____.
   preposition   abstract noun

Teacher instructions:

(1) Have students number blank, lined papers from 1 to 26. Ask them to write an example of the part of speech indicated beside each number. Proceed slowly, making sure students have written correct examples.

(2) Give each student a copy of the story. Ask students to write each word from their list into the blank with the corresponding number.

(3) Ask some students to read their stories aloud.

(4) Student answers will vary. Accept all reasonable answers.

Grammar and Writing 5

165

Teacher Guide
More Practice Answers

More Practice Lesson 40

Limiting adjectives include the following:
Articles (*a, an, the*)
Demonstrative adjectives (*this, that, these, those*)
Numbers (*one, two, three,* etc.)
Possessive adjectives (*my, his, her, Bob's, Meg's,* etc.)
Indefinites (*some, many, few,* etc.)

Circle each limiting adjective that you find in the following sentences.

1. (Delaware's) capital is Dover.
2. In (the) north, (Delaware's) width narrows to (ten) miles.
3. (Jeff's) aunt works at (a) shipyard in (that) state.
4. (Her) son left (his) gloves in (my) car.
5. (Many) people live in (the) city of Wilmington.
6. Delaware has (much) industry.
7. From (the) shore I could see (several) ships in (the) bay.
8. Have (those) sailors lost (their) way?
9. (This) state wants to protect (its) beaches from pollution.
10. Have you seen (any) gulls in (your) area?

Complete the following sentence diagrams.

1. Maine's mills produce much paper.

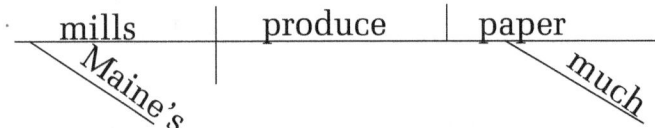

2. That business makes many computer components.

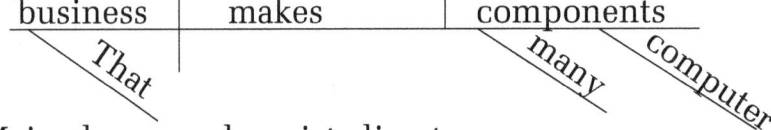

3. Maine has a cool, moist climate.

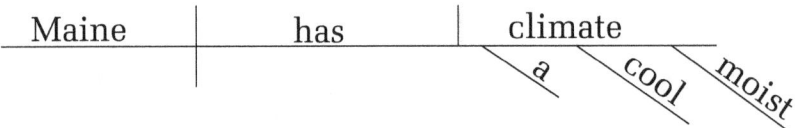

4. Two chickadees eat some seeds.

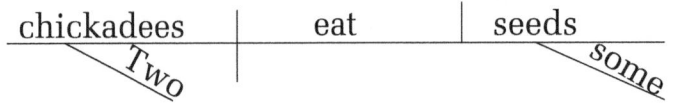

More Practice Lesson 43

Circle each letter that should be capitalized in the following sentences.

1. ⓜy grandfather worked in a ⓚentucky coal mine for forty years.   2 capital letters

2. ⓔvery fall ⓘ play football with my cousins.   2 capital letters

3. ⓤncle ⓣhurgood wants to tour an ⓐlabama auto assembly plant.   3 capital letters

4. ⓣhe ⓛouisiana cotton fields stretch as far as ⓘ can see.   3 capital letters

5. ⓛast summer ⓘ helped ⓖrandpa husk the ⓘowa corn for our meal.   4 capital letters

6. ⓦhen ⓖeorgia peaches ripen, ⓐunt ⓡosa will pick a bushel.   4 capital letters

7. ⓗave you smelled the blossoms on ⓕlorida orange trees?   2 capital letters

8. ⓜy brother likes peanut butter, but my sister prefers ⓦisconsin cheese.   2 capital letters

9. ⓐ ⓕrench chef served ⓜother and me a plate of steaming ⓒalifornia vegetables.   4 capital letters

10. ⓦould you rather have ⓑoston baked beans or ⓘdaho potatoes tonight?   3 capital letters

11. ⓜusicians on xylophones, tambourines, and ⓐfrican drums created rhythms to accompany the chorus.   2 capital letters

12. ⓓuring spring vacation we shall play afternoon baseball games and evening ⓒhinese checkers tournaments.   2 capital letters

13. ⓜario's grandfather played a ⓢteinway piano in the town's largest concert hall.   2 capital letters

14. ⓘ think ⓒousin ⓕoster's dog is a ⓦelsh terrier.   4 capital letters

15. ⓐ calico cat rode the muscular ⓖerman shepherd with a beagle named ⓣux right behind.   3 capital letters

16. ⓤncle ⓑob planted petunias and marigolds beneath his ⓐustralian willow trees.   3 capital letters

More Practice Lesson 47

Add periods as needed in each sentence or outline below. Then circle each period.

1. I. The state of Kansas
    A. Industry
    B. Agriculture

2. Herbert C. Hoover was the thirty-first President of the United States.

3. J. Edgar Hoover, who served as director of the Federal Bureau of Investigation, worked hard to stop organized crime.

4. Make the most of today.

5. General Robert E. Lee surrendered to General Ulysses S. Grant on April 9, 1865, in Virginia.

6. We shall read C. S. Lewis's *Chronicles of Narnia* before we see the movie.

7. I. The Southwest
    A. Arizona
    B. New Mexico
    C. Oklahoma
    D. Texas

8. Study the fifty states and their capitals.

9. Isabel M. Angles taught algebra at Francisco P. Cruz High School.

10. I. The state of Michigan
    A. History
    B. Government
    C. Economy

11. Officer U. B. Ware arrested Captain I. M. Loud for disturbing the peace.

12. Please turn down the volume.

More Practice Lesson 49

Diagram the simple subject and simple predicate of each sentence.

1. Florida and California produce citrus fruits.

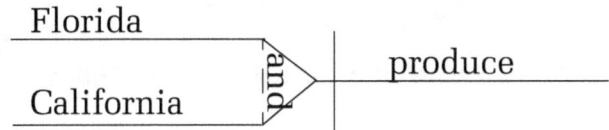

2. Mud-drenched frogs croak and leap around the pond.

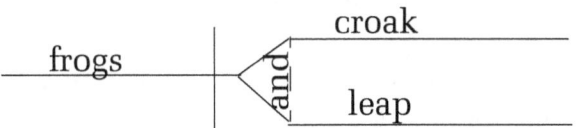

3. Elk, moose, and bison roam in Wyoming.

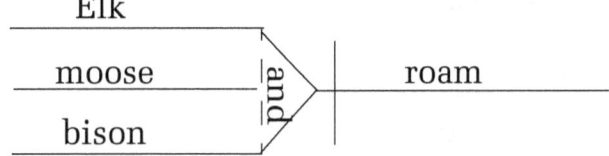

4. A coyote pauses and howls at the moon.

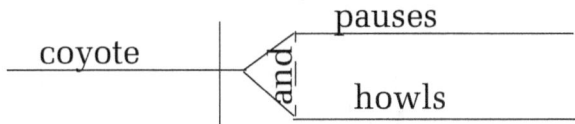

5. Maine, Vermont, and Massachusetts border New Hampshire.

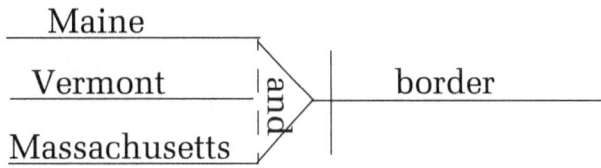

6. Amelia smiled and waved at Elle.

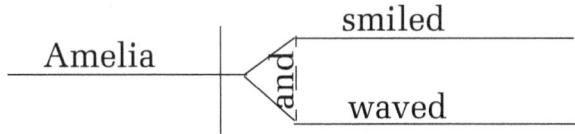

More Practice Lesson 50

Add periods as needed. Circle each period.

1. Mr. Yu took the 10:30 a.m. bus to Farmer's Market on S. Fifth Street.

2. There he purchased bananas, grapes, potatoes, etc. for his family.

3. Altogether he spent $30.42 (thirty dollars and forty-two cents) on misc. (miscellaneous) fruits and vegetables.

4. At 1:30 p.m., he boarded the bus on W. Spring Ave. to ride home.

5. Along the bus route, a sign read, "This road closed until Thurs., Feb. 3."

6. Mr. Yu's bus moved slowly through traffic on Mt. Carmel Rd., a detour.

7. Mrs. Yu feared that her husband would be late for his 4:20 p.m. appointment with Dr. Hatchet.

8. However, Mr. Yu reached the Hope Medical Bldg. on the S.E. corner of York Pl. just in time.

9. "The gerontology dept. has moved to the seventh floor," read a sign.

10. Breathing hard from climbing stairs, Mr. Yu paid his $68.50 (sixty-eight dollars and fifty cents) to the receptionist.

11. Then he sat down next to an Antz-Be-Gone, Inc. employee, who smelled like pesticide and reminded Mr. Yu of an old acquaintance, Capt. Cheesebreath.

12. After waiting over an hour, Mr. Yu heard the receptionist say that Dr. Hatchet was performing an emergency appendectomy and would not see any more patients until 9:15 a.m. the following day.

Corny Chronicle #3
Follows Lesson 51

A Field Trip

Teacher instructions:

(1) Have students number blank, lined papers from 1 to 22. Ask them to write an example of the part of speech indicated beside each number. Proceed slowly, making sure students have written correct examples.

(2) Give each student a copy of the story. Ask students to write each word from their list into the blank with the corresponding number.

(3) Ask some students to read their stories aloud.

(4) Student answers will vary. Accept all reasonable answers.

Three friends, (1)_____ , (2)_____ , and
          proper noun (person)   proper noun (person)

(3)_____ , were in charge of planning the annual class
 proper noun (person)

field trip. Their goal was to plan a (4)_____ trip that
                                    descriptive adjective

would give their classmates a sense of (5)_____ . This
                                       abstract singular noun

trip would be (6)_____ than last year's trip. In fact,
              comparative adjective

this would be their (7)_____ field trip ever. It would
                    superlative adjective

give each classmate an opportunity to (8)_____ ,
                                         present tense
                                         action verb

(9)_____ , and (10)_____ . The class would
   present tense   present tense
   action verb   action verb

travel (11)_____ mountains, (12)_____ tall
           preposition   preposition

buildings, (13)_____ historical monuments,
               preposition

(14)_____ (15)_____ rivers, and
    preposition   descriptive adjective

(16)_____ the (17)_____ oceans. Besides all
    preposition   descriptive adjective

this, they could photograph the many (18)_____ and
                                         concrete plural noun

(19)_____ along the way.
    concrete plural noun

Next the (20)_____ of classmates began working
             collective noun

on the trip schedule. This (21)_____ journey would
                               descriptive adjective

begin at nine a.m. on Friday. When their teacher said that the

class would have to return by one p.m. that day for their

dictation test, the three classmates (22)_____ and
                                         past tense
                                         action verb

frowned.

Grammar and Writing 5 — Teacher Guide More Practice Answers

More Practice Lesson 57

Add commas as needed to the following sentences.

1. Please come to my piano recital on May 10, 2006, at the auditorium.

2. On Wednesday, September 21, 2005, I moved from my childhood home in Denver, Colorado.

3. I moved to 517 Fox Lane, Blazer Township, New Jersey 07712.

4. Blanca and Cruz visit family in Boise, Idaho, every summer.

5. Kelly drove from Salem, Oregon, to Olympia, Washington, last week.

6. Luz's new address is 4750 Long Street, Arcadia, California 91006.

7. The Southwestern states include Arizona, New Mexico, Oklahoma, and Texas.

8. Illinois, Indiana, Iowa, and Kansas are some of the Midwest states.

9. States in the Northeast include Connecticut, Delaware, Maine, Maryland, Massachusetts, and others.

10. In Alaska you can walk on a glacier, paddle a kayak, and photograph wildlife.

11. Ms. Tidbit wore a red blouse, a green skirt, a purple vest, and pink cowboy boots.

12. She carried a bag of apples, a poodle with bows in its fur, and a half-eaten sandwich.

13. Please respond to my invitation by Monday, September 19, 2005.

14. I shall show you samples of igneous, metamorphic, and sedimentary rocks.

More Practice Lesson 59

Add commas as needed to the following sentences.

1. Try, my dear cousin, to remember which goal belongs to the other team.

2. Ask me, Wakefield, if you have any questions.

3. Grandma, where were you born?

4. Don't wake that sleeping tiger, Uncle Robert!

5. Aunt Waverly, have you ever seen an anteater?

6. Anteaters don't eat aunts, my silly nephew!

7. Marsha Mellow, Ph.D., has created new software for confection manufacturers.

8. Oscar Didit, D.D., teaches religion and philosophy at the university.

9. Jaime Chávez, M.B.A., became president of a large publishing company.

10. Did Duc Eng, R.N., bandage your wounded knees?

11. Come back soon, my friend, for I'll miss you.

12. Dad, have you seen my grammar book?

13. You left it out in the rain, sweetheart.

14. I'm sorry, Dad.

15. Mrs. Vega, you might want to take Cornflower to Luis P. Bensen, D.V.M., for her puppy shots.

16. Cornflower has already had her puppy shots, Mary.

17. Did Charles B. Heale, L.P.N., care for you at the hospital?

18. I've never met him, Wassim.

More Practice Lesson 60

Insert commas to offset the nonessential appositives in the sentences below.

1. Ogden Nash, a famous poet, wrote some hilarious limericks.

2. High-tech industries prosper in Raleigh, the capital of North Carolina.

3. I asked my best friend, Terrance, if he knew my sister's best friend, Wilda.

4. The oboe, a woodwind instrument, can sound sad.

5. *Pianissimo,* an Italian word, means "very quiet."

6. The French horn, a brass instrument, is shaped like a circle.

7. Tom plays the tuba, the largest horn in the brass family.

8. Peter Tchaikovsky, a Russian composer, wrote *The Nutcracker* and many other ballets.

9. Richmond, the capital of Virginia, has some wonderful museums and theaters.

10. The capital of Kansas, Topeka, lies west of Kansas City.

11. Gutzon Borglum, an amazing sculptor, carved four Presidents in the Mount Rushmore National Memorial in South Dakota.

12. Wisconsin, America's Dairyland, is famous for its milk and cheese.

13. Abraham Lincoln, our sixteenth President, lived in Illinois for many years.

14. Have you seen Penelope, my miniature rabbit?

15. She hasn't eaten her dinner, two juicy carrots and some alfalfa.

More Practice Lesson 67

Add commas to offset introductory and interrupting elements and afterthoughts.

1. Without a doubt, that was the funniest story I've ever heard.

2. Max attended a ballet for the first time, I believe, last Friday night.

3. He had never seen people dance on their toes, it seems.

4. The dancers, of course, were extremely athletic.

5. Their talent, I thought, was superb!

6. Max doesn't appreciate ballet, I guess.

7. In my opinion, his comment revealed his ignorance.

8. No, he was not trying to be silly.

9. He said that they should have hired taller dancers, of all things.

10. Yes, I laughed out loud.

More Practice Lesson 73

Underline the dependent clause in each sentence, and circle the subordinating conjunction.

1. (Although) he does not dance well, he has many other talents.

2. I have heard (that) he plays the oboe.

3. (When) she was six, she learned to swim.

4. (If) you turn left, you will come to the state Capitol building.

5. I shall not accept your money (because) bribery is unethical.

6. (While) John was elated at first, his elation did not last long.

7. An ornithologist might know (where) those eagles sleep.

8. Perhaps the meteorologist can tell us (when) the storm will hit.

9. (Though) he feigns bravery, he is frightened.

10. (If) the facts are pertinent, you may use them in your essay.

11. (Since) Eli was contrite, Ms. Hoo forgave him.

12. They call Raj a linguist (because) he speaks several languages.

More Practice Lesson 74

Place commas where they are needed in these sentences.

1. David is a genteel, industrious landscape artist.

2. When the boss arrived, she found indolent, disrespectful employees sitting around and sipping lemonade.

3. Lulu's superfluous, bulky baggage slows her on the trip.

4. Because we had a helpful, intuitive guide, we made it safely through the dark, dangerous jungle.

5. Before you were born, an elderly, benevolent man donated land for the park.

6. As soon as you finish, we shall take a long, pleasant drive through the countryside.

7. His wild, ridiculous story was implausible.

8. If you can tolerate hot, humid weather, then you will enjoy Florida in the summer.

9. My sensible, frugal aunt washed her paper plate and cup.

10. Her wealthy, extravagant uncle threw away his fancy, costly mug because it was dirty.

11. He gave me the valuable, intangible gift of his time.

12. I had the momentary, worrisome thought that it might rain on our parade.

More Practice Lesson 76

Place commas where they are needed in these sentences.

1. Mom told me, "Your great-grandparents' home was quaint and serene."

2. "I especially liked the potbellied stove," she said.

3. Wally shouted, "Watch out for the poison ivy!"

4. She tripped and fell, for the trail was steep and rocky.

5. Sue helped her up, and I carried her backpack.

6. That sentence goes on and on, but it is not redundant.

7. My sagacious friend studied hard, yet she forgot the capital of Alaska.

8. Molly moaned, "How could I have forgotten Juneau?"

9. Elle asked, "What is the capital of Wyoming?"

10. "I think it's Cheyenne," said Kurt.

11. Elle was not sure, so she looked at a map.

12. Elle said, "I cannot find Shy Ann on the map."

More Practice Lesson 80

Place quotation marks where they are needed in these sentences.

1. "An ice pack might meliorate the swelling," said Dr. Lacy.

2. Juan asked, "Is the melioration of swelling important?"

3. "Swelling," said Dr. Lacy, "can cause discomfort."

4. Ms. Hoo said, "Do not let prepositions daunt you."

5. "Prepositions don't daunt me. It's the diagramming!" cried Liz.

6. "Keep trying," said Ms. Hoo, "and you will learn."

7. "I once knew a dauntless explorer," she said, "who failed again and again."

8. "Did he or she ever succeed?" asked Liz.

9. "Of course," said Ms. Hoo, "but it took a long time."

10. Liz said, "Long and complicated sentences confuse me."

11. "Besides," she added, "diagramming taxes my brain cells."

12. "Diagramming," said Ms. Hoo, "will strengthen those brain cells."

More Practice Lesson 81

In the following sentences, enclose titles of songs and short literary works in quotation marks.

1. Ivy wrote a poem called "Oh, to Be a Bird!"

2. I titled my short story "In the Nick of Time."

3. Josh Billings's essay, "The Bumblebee," made people laugh.

4. A newspaper article called "Paper Sculpture" caught my eye.

5. All the way to Des Moines, they sang "She'll be Comin' Round the Mountain."

6. Can you play "Jingle Bells" on the clarinet?

7. Professor Cruz gave a lecture titled "How to Develop Good Study Habits."

8. "Backpacking in the High Sierras" is the magazine article that sparked my interest.

9. My friend titled her expository essay "Safety Tips for Kayaking."

10. People began tapping their feet to the song "Grandma's Feather Bed."

11. Please do not sing "Found a Peanut" again!

12. Max's poem, "The Banana Slug," won first prize.

More Practice Lesson 84

Underline all words that should be italicized in print.

1. Dad's favorite movie is <u>The Music Man</u>.

2. Quan reads <u>The Rocky Mountain News</u> every morning.

3. Have you seen the big musical production <u>Pilgrim</u>?

4. Caleb listens to a music CD called <u>White Noise</u>.

5. Someday I shall read Herman Melville's novel <u>Moby Dick</u>.

6. The aircraft carrier U.S.S. <u>Constitution</u> just left the harbor.

7. Karen named her sailboat the <u>Pelican</u>.

8. Have you seen Thomas Gainsborough's painting <u>Blue Boy</u>?

9. Max does not appreciate ballet, but he went to see <u>The Nutcracker</u> anyway.

10. Please use the word <u>subvert</u> in a sentence.

11. Its scientific name is <u>Columba fasciata</u>, but we call it a pigeon.

12. What does the Spanish word <u>demasiado</u> mean?

More Practice Lesson 85 Complete this irregular verb chart by writing the past and past participle forms of each verb.

	VERB	PAST	PAST PARTICIPLE
1.	beat	beat	(has) beaten
2.	bite	bit	(has) bitten
3.	bring	brought	(has) brought
4.	build	built	(has) built
5.	burst	burst	(has) burst
6.	buy	bought	(has) bought
7.	catch	caught	(has) caught
8.	come	came	(has) come
9.	cost	cost	(has) cost
10.	dive	dove or dived	(has) dived
11.	drag	dragged	(has) dragged
12.	draw	drew	(has) drawn
13.	drown	drowned	(has) drowned
14.	drive	drove	(has) driven
15.	eat	ate	(has) eaten
16.	fall	fell	(has) fallen
17.	feel	felt	(has) felt
18.	fight	fought	(has) fought
19.	find	found	(has) found
20.	flee	fled	(has) fled
21.	fly	flew	(has) flown
22.	forget	forgot	(has) forgotten
23.	forgive	forgave	(has) forgiven

More Practice Lesson 85 continued

Circle the correct verb form for each sentence.

1. Yesterday the Jays (beated, **beat**) the Doves in soccer.
2. The Jays have (beat, **beaten**) them in every tournament.
3. For yesterday's picnic, I (brang, **brought**) watermelon.
4. I have always (brung, **brought**) watermelon.
5. Last summer we (builded, **built**) a treehouse.
6. We have (builded, **built**) two treehouses.
7. Rob (buyed, **bought**) a plum tree.
8. He has (buyed, **bought**) three trees this week.
9. Len (catched, **caught**) a cold.
10. He has (catched, **caught**) a bad one.
11. Rachel (comed, **came**) home early.
12. She has (came, **come**) home to rest.
13. Last week, apples (costed, **cost**) 99¢ a pound.
14. They have (**cost**, costed) less in the past.
15. Melody (**dove**, dive) into the pool.
16. She has (dove, **dived**) in before.
17. I (drawed, **drew**) a happy face.
18. I have (drawed, **drawn**) several.
19. Leroy (drived, **drove**) to Kansas City.
20. He had (drove, **driven**) forty miles.
21. A limb (falled, **fell**) from the tree.
22. Limbs have (falled, fell, **fallen**) every year.
23. Tomcats (fighted, **fought**) last night.
24. They have (fighted, **fought**) every night this week.
25. A goose (flied, **flew**) by.
26. The geese have (flew, **flown**) south.

More Practice Lesson 86 Complete this irregular verb chart by writing the past and past participle forms of each verb.

VERB	PAST	PAST PARTICIPLE
1. get	got	(has) gotten
2. give	gave	(has) given
3. go	went	(has) gone
4. hang (execute)	hanged	(has) hanged
5. hang (suspend)	hung	(has) hung
6. hide	hid	(has) hidden or hid
7. hold	held	(has) held
8. keep	kept	(has) kept
9. lay (place)	laid	(has) laid
10. lead	led	(has) led
11. lend	lent	(has) lent
12. lie (recline)	lay	(has) lain
13. lie (deceive)	lied	(has) lied
14. lose	lost	(has) lost
15. make	made	(has) made
16. mistake	mistook	(has) mistaken
17. put	put	(has) put
18. ride	rode	(has) ridden
19. rise	rose	(has) risen
20. run	ran	(has) run
21. see	saw	(has) seen
22. sell	sold	(has) sold

More Practice Lesson 86 continued

Circle the correct verb form for each sentence.

1. The docent (gived, **gave**) a tour of the Capitol.
2. He has (gived, gave, **given**) several tours today.
3. Ana (goed, **went**) to Scotland.
4. She has (went, **gone**) once before.
5. We (hanged, **hung**) a painting on the wall.
6. We have (hanged, **hung**) paintings and photos.
7. She (hided, **hid**) the pie from me!
8. He (holded, **held**) a fluffy kitten.
9. Tom has (keeped, **kept**) the secret.
10. Pam (layed, **laid**) her pen on the table.
11. She has (layed, **laid**) two books on the table.
12. She was tired, so she (laid, **lay**) on the sofa.
13. She has (laid, **lain**) there all afternoon!
14. George (losed, **lost**) his keys again.
15. He has (losed, **lost**) them twice before.
16. I (maked, **made**) a friend yesterday.
17. I have (maked, **made**) many friends.
18. Last night, I (putted, **put**) hand lotion on my toothbrush!
19. I have never before (putted, **put**) hand lotion on anything but my hands.
20. The sun (rised, **rose**) at 6 a.m.
21. It has (**risen**, rosen) earlier each morning.
22. I (seen, **saw**) him earlier.
23. I have (**seen**, saw) him every day.
24. She (selled, **sold**) her skates.
25. She has (selled, **sold**) two pairs of skates.

More Practice Lesson 87 Complete this irregular verb chart by writing the past and past participle forms of each verb.

VERB	PAST	PAST PARTICIPLE
1. set	set	(has) set
2. shake	shook	(has) shaken
3. shine (light)	shone	(has) shone
4. shine (polish)	shined	(has) shined
5. shut	shut	(has) shut
6. sit	sat	(has) sat
7. slay	slew	(has) slain
8. sleep	slept	(has) slept
9. spring	sprang, sprung	(has) sprung
10. stand	stood	(has) stood
11. strive	strove	(has) striven
12. swim	swam	(has) swum
13. swing	swung	(has) swung
14. take	took	(has) taken
15. teach	taught	(has) taught
16. tell	told	(has) told
17. think	thought	(has) thought
18. wake	woke	(has) woken
19. weave	wove	(has) woven
20. wring	wrung	(has) wrung
21. write	wrote	(has) written

More Practice Lesson 87 continued

Circle the correct verb form for each sentence.

1. Lulu (setted, **set**) the alarm.
2. She has (setted, **set**) it every night.
3. He (**shook**, shaked) her hand.
4. She has (shaked, **shaken**) many hands.
5. A light (shined, **shone**) through the window.
6. The light has (shined, **shone**) each evening.
7. Josh (**shined**, shone) his black shoes.
8. He has (**shined**, shone) several pairs of shoes.
9. Jan (shutted, **shut**) the window.
10. She has (shutted, **shut**) all the windows.
11. He (sitted, **sat**) on the bench.
12. He has (sitted, **sat**) there for two innings.
13. I (**slept**, sleeped) twelve hours.
14. Have you ever (**slept**, sleeped) that long?
15. She (standed, **stood**) in line.
16. She has (standed, **stood**) there before.
17. We (**swam**, swum) in the pool.
18. We have (swam, **swum**) many laps.
19. He (taked, **took**) his boa to the vet.
20. He has (took, **taken**) it to the vet twice this week.
21. Ilbea (teached, **taught**) me to sew.
22. She has (teached, **taught**) me many new skills.
23. Grace (telled, **told**) me a joke.
24. Has she (telled, **told**) you the joke?
25. I (thinked, **thought**) you were sagacious.
26. I have always (thinked, **thought**) that.

More Practice Lesson 101 Circle each adverb in these sentences.

1. (Yesterday) the wind blew (hard).

2. I felt (somewhat) grumpy, for it (rudely) destroyed my hairdo.

3. I have (never) heard a noise (so) loud.

4. It swept (away) my homework.

5. (Then) it stopped.

6. I had (not)(quite) finished my math.

7. I (desperately) gathered the papers (together).

8. Will the wind blow (again)(tomorrow)?

9. (Now) it has calmed (nicely).

10. Will I (ever) find all those papers?

11. I shall smooth my hair (later).

12. I (really) think my homework has disappeared (forever).

More Practice Lesson 103

Replace commas with semicolons where they are needed in these sentences.

1. We shall pass through Denver, Colorado; Austin, Texas; and Memphis, Tennessee.

2. He plays the piano; she plays the drums, the flute, and the trumpet.

3. Carrots, celery, and peas are vegetables; apples, oranges, and bananas are fruits.

4. They have ants in their kitchen; moreover, termites are eating the door frame.

5. George washed the car, cleaned the house, and mowed the lawn; consequently, he fell asleep during the movie.

6. It snowed; therefore, I wore a jacket.

7. Gia and Allison will be there; also, Cecilia will come if she can.

8. Mae enjoys planting trees; for example, she planted two pines and an oak today.

9. Rita cleaned the garage; furthermore, she organized all the tools and boxes.

10. The sky was cloudy; nevertheless, we went to the park.

11. Ms. Hoo wore high heels; as a result, her feet hurt.

12. Would you rather visit Richmond, Virginia; Juneau, Alaska; or Phoenix, Arizona?

More Practice Lesson 109

Insert apostrophes where they are needed in these sentences.

1. She couldn't remember whether she'd been in Mexico in '88 or '89.

2. Mr. Collins yelled, "Good mornin'!" to his neighbor.

3. "Oh my," exclaimed Mabel, "they were just walkin' and talkin', and they never saw the bus leavin'!"

4. Can't you see that I haven't time to waste?

5. Didn't Mom graduate from high school with the class of '80?

6. Isn't her frugality obvious?

7. We're going to the library. Aren't you?

8. They're going to the library also.

9. Wouldn't you like to join us?

10. She'll come if she can.

11. We'll forgive her if she doesn't come.

12. We couldn't see through the foggy window.

Test 1   **READ CAREFULLY**   Name: _____

Give after Lesson 10.

Circle the correct word(s) to complete sentences 1–5.

1. A (subject, sentence) is a word group that expresses a complete thought.

2. The two essential parts of a sentence are the subject and the (predator, predicate).

3. The (subject, predicate) tells whom or what the sentence is about.

4. The (subject, predicate) tells what the subject does, is, or is like.

5. A complete sentence has (two, four) main parts.

6. For a–e, circle the correct definition. (1 point for each correct answer)

    (a) *Essential* means "(opposite, necessary, unnecessary)."

    (b) Antonyms are (dinosaurs, opposites, optimists).

    (c) *Abundant* means "(scarce, plentiful, essential)."

    (d) Pessimism is the belief that things are going to get (better, worse).

    (e) *Their* and *there* are (synonyms, antonyms, homophones).

For 7–10, write whether the sentence is declarative, interrogative, exclamatory, or imperative.

7. Rosa Parks refused to give up her seat in a bus. _____

8. How cold does it get in Alaska? _____

9. Bring water on your hike through the desert. _____

10. It's a rattlesnake! _____

Circle the simple subject of sentences 11–13.

11. Some people in Arkansas listen to delightful kitchen bands.

12. Can Jenny play the fiddle?

13. Archaeologists have found dinosaur fossils in Colorado.

Circle the simple predicate of sentences 14–16.

14. Some people in Arkansas listen to delightful kitchen bands.

15. Jenny can play the fiddle.
(4)

16. Archaeologists have found dinosaur fossils in Colorado.
(4)

For 17–19, write whether the word group is a sentence fragment or a complete sentence.

17. Picking seeds from the watermelon. _____
(5)

18. Mount McKinley is the tallest mountain in North America. _____
(5)

19. To catch a catfish in the pond. _____
(5)

20. Draw a vertical line between the subject and predicate parts of the sentence below.
(1)

Horseshoe crabs have endured the changes of man.

Test 2   **READ CAREFULLY**   Name: _____

Give after Lesson 15.

Circle the correct word(s) to complete sentences 1–5.

1. (10) Yesterday Martin (fry, fries, fried) catfish for supper.

2. (9) An alligator (sleep, sleeps) in the Everglades.

3. (9) Leon (ski, skis) in Vail, Colorado.

4. (2) The sentence below is (declarative, interrogative, exclamatory, imperative).

                   Look at all the ladybugs!

5. (2) The sentence below is (declarative, interrogative, exclamatory, imperative).

                   Use sunscreen at the beach.

6. For a–e, circle the correct definition. *(1 point for each correct answer)*

   (a) (6) (Its, It's) is the possessive form of *it*.

   (b) (7) To disclose is to (hide, uncover, sneeze).

   (c) (8) (Geology, Archipelago, Flora) is Earth science.

   (d) (9) An archipelago is a chain of many (beads, islands, events).

   (e) (10) Fauna is (plant, animal) life.

7. (6) On the lines below, make a complete sentence from the following sentence fragment:

   After finishing this test, _____

   _____

Circle the action verb in sentences 8 and 9.

8. (7) Various space missions launch from Cape Canaveral.

9. (7) Groups protect endangered species such as whales.

10. (8) In the sentence below, circle each proper noun needing a capital letter.

             ruth handler created plastic dolls named barbie in denver, colorado.

Circle the simple subject of sentences 11–13.

11. Skiers flock to the snow-capped mountains of Colorado.
(3)

12. Are students at the university working hard?
(3)

13. Here is a famous seafood restaurant.
(3)

Circle the simple predicate of sentences 14–16.

14. Skiers flock to the snow-capped mountains of Colorado.
(4)

15. Students at the university are working hard.
(4)

16. Here is a famous seafood restaurant.
(4)

For 17–19, write whether the word group is a sentence fragment or a complete sentence.

17. Jimmy Carter, our thirty-ninth President, was born in Georgia. _____
(5)

18. To begin selling peanut butter. _____
(5)

19. Measuring the enormous span of the pelican's wings. _____
(5)

20. Draw a vertical line between the subject and predicate parts of the sentence below.
(1)

The 1858 Gold Rush began in Colorado at Pike's Peak.

Test 3 READ CAREFULLY Name: _____

Give after Lesson 20.

Circle the correct word(s) to complete sentences 1–5.

1. The two essential parts of a sentence are the (subordinate, subject) and the predicate.
   (1)

2. The simple (subject, predicate) is the main word or words in a sentence that tell who or what is doing or being something.
   (3)

3. Norma (carve, carves) ice sculptures in Minnesota.
   (9)

4. The sentence below is (declarative, interrogative, exclamatory, imperative).
   (2)

   Does Michigan have copper mines?

5. The sentence below is a (complete sentence, sentence fragment).
   (5)

   Named for the Indian word meaning great lake.

6. For a–e, circle the correct definition. (1 point for each correct answer)

   (a) An isthmus is a narrow strip of (land, ocean, water) connecting two larger bodies of land.
   (11)

   (b) A (lagoon, strait, peninsula) is a narrow waterway connecting two larger bodies of water.
   (12)

   (c) A (delta, tributary, archipelago) is a river or stream that flows into a larger river or stream.
   (13)

   (d) A (strait, lagoon, hemisphere) is one half of Earth.
   (14)

   (e) (Meridian, Hemisphere, Latitude) is a distance north or south of the equator.
   (15)

7. On the lines below, rewrite and correct the sentence fragment, making a complete sentence.
   (6)

   Fur traders trapping wolverines.

   _____

   _____

8. Circle the action verb in the sentence below.
   (7)

   People nicknamed Michigan the Wolverine State.

9. In the sentence below, replace the blank with the correct verb form.
   (10)

   Chi (past of *shop*) _____ at the Mall of America in Bloomington, Minnesota.

10. In the sentence below, circle each proper noun needing a capital letter.
    (8)

    michigan's windmill island municipal park has an authentic dutch windmill.

Grammar and Writing 5   Teacher Guide
Tests

11. Circle the simple subject in the sentence below.
(3)

                    Along came Melody on a calico horse.

12. Circle the simple predicate in the sentence below.
(4)

                    Along came Melody on a calico horse.

13. Circle the abstract noun in the following list: horse, island, pessimism, peninsula, wolverine
(11)

14. Circle the word from this list that could *not* be a helping verb: is, am, are, was, were, be, and
(12)

15. Circle the compound noun from this list: Washington, afternoon, predicate, optimism
(13)

16. Circle the possessive noun in the sentence below.
(13)

                    Minnesota's prairie has a large gopher population.

Circle each letter that should be capitalized in 17–19.

17. i am always amazed at how little i know.
(15)

18. a famous medical center, mayo clinic treats people from all over the world.
(15)

19.
(15)
        i love my red rooster;
        my rooster loves me.
        i love my red rooster
        under the cottonwood tree.

20. Draw a vertical line between the subject and predicate parts of the sentence below.
(1)

                  A statue of Paul Bunyan stands in Bemidji, Minnesota.

Test 4 READ CAREFULLY Name: _____

Give after Lesson 25.

Circle the correct word(s) to complete sentences 1–5.

1. *John's* is a (possessive, plural) noun.
(13)

2. *Team* is a (compound, collective) noun.
(11)

3. A diamond (scratch, scratches) granite.
(9)

4. The sentence below is (declarative, interrogative, exclamatory, imperative).
(2)

Don't eat too many French fries.

5. The sentence below is a (complete sentence, sentence fragment).
(5)

To build and repair submarines.

6. For a–e, circle the correct definition. (1 point for each correct answer)

(a) A (mesa, plateau, chasm) is a deep, wide crack in Earth's surface.
(20)

(b) (Arroyo, Atoll, Tundra) is a flat, frozen, treeless plain.
(19)

(c) Trees do not grow above the (timber, date, twenty-yard) line.
(18)

(d) The Tropic of Cancer is an imaginary (friend, line, atoll) parallel to the equator.
(17)

(e) A(n) (arroyo, atoll, savanna) is a circular coral reef.
(16)

7. On the lines below, write the four principal parts of the verb *plant*.
(19)

_____   (is)_____   _____   (has)_____
(present tense)   (present participle)   (past tense)   (past participle)

8. Circle the two action verbs in the sentence below.
(7)

Today, people in New Hampshire's shipyards build and repair submarines.

9. In the sentence below, replace the blank with the correct verb form.
(10)

The sculptor (past of *chip*) _____ the granite.

10. Circle each preposition in the sentence below.
(20)

Without good sense, an explorer ventures into a dark cave.

11. Circle the simple subject in the sentence below.
(3)

On the eastern border of New Hampshire are shipyards.

Grammar and Writing 5   Teacher Guide
                                        Tests

12. Circle the simple predicate in the sentence below.
(4)

On the eastern border of New Hampshire are shipyards.

13. In the sentence below, replace the blank with the correct verb form.
(18)

New Hampshire (past of *be*) _____ the first to declare independence from Great Britain.

14. Circle the word from this list that is *not* a preposition: about, before, by, for, from, drown
(20)

15. For a–e, write the plural of each singular noun. (1 point for each correct answer)
(16, 17)

(a) sky _____

(b) Lewis _____

(c) eggplant _____

(d) loaf _____

(e) tooth _____

16. Circle the possessive noun in the sentence below.
(13)

Vines covered the cave's entrance.

Circle each letter that should be capitalized in 17 and 18.

17. i have never read *miss pickerell goes to mars*.
(15)

18. alejandro will climb mount washington to the highest point in new england.
(15)

19. Circle the entire verb phrase in the sentence below.
(12)

People in Portsmouth have been building ships since 1630.

20. Draw a vertical line between the subject and predicate parts of the sentence below.
(1)

Eva's great-grandfather planted potatoes in New Hampshire.

Test 5 　　　　READ CAREFULLY 　　　Name: _____

Give after Lesson 30.

Circle the correct word(s) to complete sentences 1–11.

1. (Do, Did) Johnny Appleseed plant apple trees in Ohio?
(18)

2. We (will, shall) see Ohio's Rock and Roll Hall of Fame tomorrow.
(14)

3. Thomas Edison invented and (perfects, perfected) the lightbulb.
(10)

4. The sentence below is (declarative, interrogative, imperative, exclamatory).
(2)

　　　　The first cash register came from Dayton, Ohio.

5. The following is a (sentence fragment, run-on sentence, complete sentence):
(5)

　　　　An ancient dugout canoe was found in Ohio.

6. The word *around* is a (noun, verb, preposition).
(20)

7. The noun *lightbulb* is (abstract, concrete).
(11)

8. The noun *compass* is (singular, plural).
(13)

9. To *placate* means to "(disturb, anger, calm)."
(22)

10. To *ignite* is to (disclose, burn, freeze).
(25)

11. Jenny and Phil marry. Phil (marrys, marries) Jenny.
(9)

12. Write the plural form of a–d:
(16, 17)

　　(a) tooth _____　(b) cuff _____　(c) county _____　(d) ditch _____

Circle each letter that should be capitalized in 13–15.

13. one sometimes reads of johnny appleseed. his trees still grow around ohio.
(15)

14. rhett butler remains a popular character from the novel *gone with the wind.*
(25)

15. lake erie forms part of the northern border of ohio.
(8)

16. Circle each preposition that you find in this sentence:
(20)

　　　　Two of the astronauts, Neil Armstrong and John Glenn, are from the state of Ohio.

17. Circle the two helping verbs in the following sentence:
(12)

Thomas Edison had been experimenting with electricity for many years.

18. For a–d, circle the correct irregular verb form.
(18)

(a) She (am, is, are)   (b) They (do, does)   (c) You (has, have)   (d) He (do, does)

19. Complete the four principal parts of the verb *wish*.
(19)

      <u> *wish* </u>   <u>*(is)*   </u>   <u>   </u>   <u>*(has)*   </u>

    (1) present tense   (2) present participle   (3) past tense   (4) past participle

20. Circle the simple subject of the sentence below.
(4)

Deep under the ground rested the oldest watercraft.

21. Circle the simple predicate of the sentence below.
(4)

Deep under the ground rested the oldest watercraft.

22. Write the plural form of the singular noun *commander in chief*. _____
(22)

23. Circle the action verb in the sentence below.
(7)

The state of Ohio produces many tires.

24. Rewrite the following sentence fragment, making a complete sentence.
(6)

To see a tire factory in Ohio.

_____

25. Rewrite and correct the run-on sentence below.
(24)

Annie Oakley was born in Ohio she was a famous sharpshooter.

_____

Test 6 READ CAREFULLY Name: _____

Give after Lesson 35.

Circle the correct word(s) to complete sentences 1–11.

1. (Have, Has) the museum opened yet?
(18)

2. We (will, shall) see the faces carved on Mount Rushmore.
(14)

3. Nancy went out and (talks, talked) to the horses.
(10)

4. The sentence below is (declarative, interrogative, imperative, exclamatory).
(2)
        Did Wild Bill Hickock die in South Dakota?

5. The following is a (sentence fragment, run-on sentence, complete sentence):
(23)
        We saw the Black Hills the trees there look almost black.

6. The word *through* is a (noun, verb, preposition).
(21)

7. The noun *peace* is (abstract, concrete).
(11)

8. The noun *cat's* is (plural, possessive).
(13)

9. A large meteorite might create a (mountain, crater, hill) on Earth's surface.
(29)

10. A(n) (meteorite, caldera, etymology) shows a word's original language and meaning.
(30)

11. Chickens scratch. A chicken (scratch, scratches).
(9)

12. Write the plural form of a–d:
(16, 17)
    (a) knife _____ (b) monkey _____ (c) cupful _____ (d) entry _____

Circle each letter that should be capitalized in 13–15.

13. lilah said, "that north dakota blizzard was terrible."
(26)

14. on saturday we shall read *alice in wonderland*.
(25)

15. lake ontario forms part of the northern border of new york.
(8)

16. Circle each preposition that you find in the sentence below.
(20, 21)
        Since yesterday, the explorer has been inside the cave by himself, without a buddy.

17. Circle the two helping verbs in the following sentence:
(12)

        Clara Barton had been nursing the wounded for three years.

18. For a–d, circle the correct irregular verb form.
(18)

   (a) They (am, is, are)   (b) She (do, does)   (c) He (has, have)   (d) You (do, does)

19. Complete the four principal parts of the verb *try*.
(19)

    <u>try</u>   (is) _____   _____   (has) _____

   (1) present tense   (2) present participle   (3) past tense   (4) past participle

20. Circle the simple subject of the sentence below.
(4)

        Out on the range roams a herd of buffalo.

21. Circle the simple predicate of the sentence below.
(4)

        Out on the range roams a herd of buffalo.

22. Write the plural form of the singular noun *father-in-law*. _____
(22)

23. Draw a vertical line between the subject and the predicate of the sentence below.
(1)

        Wild Bill Hickok and Wyatt Earp chased outlaws in the Wild West.

24. Circle each silent letter in the words below.
(28, 29)

   (a) hour   (b) ridge   (c) walk   (d) debt

25. Rewrite and correct the run-on sentence below.
(24)

        South Dakota is the Mount Rushmore State its capital is Pierre.

_____

Test 7   **READ CAREFULLY**   Name: _____

Give after Lesson 40.

Circle the correct word(s) to complete sentences 1–10.

1. Etymologies are (antonyms, synonyms, word histories).

2. George Washington (was, were) born in Virginia.

3. Stephen stepped outside and (calls, called) his dog.

4. The sentence below is (declarative, interrogative, imperative, exclamatory).

   The musical was fabulous!

5. The following is a (sentence fragment, run-on sentence, complete sentence):

   Buried treasure in the Mojave Desert.

6. The word *at* is a (noun, verb, preposition).

7. The noun *backpack* is (abstract, concrete).

8. The noun *cats* is (plural, possessive).

9. The verb (*look, laugh, smile*) is a common linking verb.

10. Many people watch. One person (watch, watches).

11. For a–d, circle the correct definition. (1 point for each correct answer)

    (a) (Kin, Clamor, Panacea) refers to one's relatives.

    (b) A (kin, clamor, panacea) is a loud cry or uproar.

    (c) (*Clamor, Indispensable, Dispensable*) means "absolutely necessary."

    (d) The Greek root *pan* means "(fire, table, all)."

12. Write the plural form of a–d:

    (a) suffix _____ (b) inch _____ (c) dairy _____ (d) deer _____

Circle each letter that should be capitalized in 13–15.

13. mrs. ng asked, "have you seen meg's other shoe?"

14. please read me "the cat in the hat."

15. the mississippi river forms the eastern border of arkansas.
₍₈₎

16. Circle each preposition that you find in the sentence below.
_(20, 21)

    Over this hill and across the field lies a grove of apple trees with many blossoms.

17. For a–d, circle the word that is spelled correctly. (1 point for each correct answer)
₍₃₃₋₃₅₎

  (a) weigh, wiegh   (b) decieve, deceive   (c) forgeting, forgetting   (d) countries, countrys

18. For a–d, circle the correct irregular verb form. (1 point for each correct answer)
₍₁₈₎

  (a) He (am, is, are)   (b) I (am, is, are)   (c) She (has, have)   (d) It (do, does)

19. Complete the four principal parts of the verb *flap*.
₍₁₉₎

    flap   *(is)* _____   _____   *(has)* _____

    (1) present tense   (2) present participle   (3) past tense   (4) past participle

20. Add suffixes. (2 points for each correct answer)
₍₃₃₎

  (a) dry + est _____   (b) say + ed _____

21. Add suffixes. (2 points for each correct answer)
₍₃₄₎

  (a) glad + ly _____   (b) begin + ing _____

22. From the following list, circle the word that could *not* be a linking verb: is, am, are, wash, were
₍₃₁₎

23. Circle each silent letter in the words below. (1 point for each correct answer)
_(28, 29)

  (a) who   (b) receipt   (c) lamb   (d) climb

On the lines provided, diagram the simple subject and simple predicate of sentences 24 and 25.

24. Across the desert gallops an Arabian horse.
₍₃₂₎

25. Has the stallion seen the mare?
₍₃₂₎

Test 8 READ CAREFULLY Name: _____

Give after Lesson 45.

Circle the correct word(s) to complete sentences 1–10.

1. (Etymologies, Atolls, Peninsulas) are word histories.
(30)

2. (Do Does) she like jazz music?
(18)

3. A muddy beagle (follows, followed) me home yesterday.
(10)

4. The word group below is a (phrase, clause).
(36)

   throughout the state of Washington

5. The following is a (sentence fragment, run-on sentence, complete sentence).
(23)

   Nevada gets very little rain it is mostly desert.

6. The word *across* is a (noun, verb, preposition).
(20)

7. The noun *miracle* is (abstract, concrete).
(11)

8. The noun *Jameses* is (plural, possessive).
(13)

9. The verb (*wait, seem, stare*) is a common linking verb.
(31)

10. Sodas fizz. A soda (fizzs, fizzes).
(9)

11. For a–d, circle the correct definition. (1 point for each correct answer)

   (a) A (dogmatic, timid, humble) person speaks with authority and sometimes arrogance.
   (39)

   (b) To humiliate is to shame or (exalt, praise, embarrass).
   (38)

   (c) A heavy load might (encourage, enable, encumber) a traveler.
   (37)

   (d) Avarice is (generosity, greed, patience).
   (36)

12. Write the plural form of a–d:
(16, 17)

   (a) fax _____   (b) dish _____   (c) baby _____   (d) child _____

Circle each letter that should be capitalized in 13–15.

13. addicus asked, "did you find that book on ms. blue's bookshelf?"
(26)

14. may i borrow your copy of *alice in wonderland*?
(25)

15. i offered ms. hoo some hot french bread.
(38)

16. Circle each preposition that you find in the sentence below.
(20, 21)

        Without your help, I could not have rescued my horse from the flood.

17. For a–d, circle the word that is spelled correctly. (1 point for each correct answer)
(33-35)

    (a) nieghbor, neighbor   (b) priest, preist   (c) runing, running   (d) librarys, libraries

18. Circle each limiting adjective in the sentence below.
(40)

        Fernando's band has a drummer, a pianist, and two guitarists.

19. Complete the four principal parts of the verb *reply*.
(19)

        <u>*reply*</u>   *(is)*<u>   </u>   <u>   </u>   *(has)*<u>   </u>

        (1) present tense   (2) present participle   (3) past tense   (4) past participle

20. Add suffixes. (2 points for each correct answer)
(33, 34)

    (a) win + ing _____   (b) pay + ed _____

21. Circle each descriptive adjective in the sentence below.
(39)

        Lush, colorful trees in beautiful Vermont attract appreciative spectators.

22. From the following list, circle the word that could *not* be a linking verb: seem, appear, blow, stay
(31)

23. Circle each silent letter in the words below. (1 point for each correct answer)
(28, 29)

    (a) sign   (b) honor   (c) listen   (d) limb

On the lines provided, diagram each word of sentences 24 and 25.

24. My puppy has chewed my new shoes.
(32)

25. Has that puppy chewed your new shoes?
(32)

Test 9   READ CAREFULLY   Name: _____

Give after Lesson 50.

Circle the correct word(s) to complete sentences 1–10.

1. (Field labels, Etymologies, Antonyms) are word histories showing the original language and meaning.
(30)

2. West Virginia (have, has) many coal mines.
(18)

3. Settlers followed the trail and (arrive, arrived) in West Virginia.
(10)

4. The word group below is a (phrase, clause).
(36)
                 because it lies in the Appalachian Mountain system

5. The following is a (sentence fragment, run-on sentence, complete sentence):
(5)
                 Jamestown, the first permanent English colony.

6. The word *the* is a(n) (noun, verb, adjective, preposition).
(40)

7. The noun *success* is (abstract, concrete).
(11)

8. The noun *James's* is (plural, possessive).
(13)

9. The verb (*think, sing, was*) is a common linking verb.
(31)

10. Bees buzz. A bee (buzzs, buzzes).
(9)

11. For a–d, circle the correct definition. (1 point for each correct answer)

    (a) (*Frugal, Cognizant, Paternal*) means "having knowledge; aware."
    (41)

    (b) An imprudent decision is (frugal, unwise, wise).
    (44)

    (c) (*Frugal, Cognizant, Paternal*) means "avoiding waste."
    (42)

    (d) (*Frugal, Cognizant, Paternal*) means "of or like a father."
    (43)

12. Write the plural form of a–d:
(16, 17)

    (a) loaf _____   (b) cupful _____   (c) man _____   (d) piano _____

Circle each letter that should be capitalized in 13–15.

13. daniel explained, "west virginia was once a part of virginia."
(26)

14. "unfortunately, diseases such as measles, mumps, and chicken pox caused the deaths of many native americans," said daniel.
(43)

15. dear grandma,
   have you visited the east?
       love,
         genevie

16. Circle each preposition that you find in the sentence below.

West Virginia sided with the North during the Civil War.

17. Circle the misspelled word in the list below.

relieve, height, wiegh, eight, deceive

18. Circle each adjective in the sentence below.

Prudent students will do the homework.

19. Complete the four principal parts of the verb *drop*.

<u>drop</u>   <u>(is)   </u>   <u>   </u>   <u>(has)   </u>
(1) present tense   (2) present participle   (3) past tense   (4) past participle

20. Add suffixes. (2 points for each correct answer)

(a) clap + ing _____   (b) pretty + er _____

21. In the sentence below, underline the prepositional phrase and circle the object of the preposition.

Did she tell you the secret of her success?

22. Circle the proper adjective in the sentence below.

Jamestown was the first permanent English colony.

23. Circle each silent letter in the words below. (1 point for each correct answer)

(a) cupboard   (b) talk   (c) guess   (d) comb

On the lines provided, diagram each word of sentences 24 and 25.

24. Do you eat a variety of healthful foods?

25. A prudent student will do the homework.

Test 10 READ CAREFULLY Name: _____

Give after Lesson 55.

Circle the correct word(s) to complete sentences 1–10.

1. The boldfaced word that begins a dictionary entry gives the (etymology, part of speech, spelling).
(27)

2. Terry (do, does) the homework.
(18)

3. He unlocked the treasure chest and (looks, looked) inside.
(10)

4. The word group below is a (phrase, clause).
(36)
        six feet long with mossy, leathery skin, the alligator

5. The following is a (sentence fragment, run-on sentence, complete sentence):
(5, 23)
        The man at the piano is Duke Ellington.

6. The word *an* is a(n) (noun, verb, adjective, preposition).
(40)

7. The noun *alligator* is (abstract, concrete).
(11)

8. The noun *alligators* is (plural, possessive).
(13)

9. The verb (*whisper, sneeze, smell*) is a common linking verb.
(31)

10. Birds fly. A bird (flys, flies).
(9)

11. For a–d, circle the correct definition. (1 point for each correct answer)

    (a) (*Illiterate, Frugal, Benevolent*) means "unable to read or write."
    (46)

    (b) A (plausible, momentous, intolerable) occasion is one of great importance.
    (47)

    (c) A believable story is (frugal, intolerable, plausible).
    (48)

    (d) *Benevolent* means "(kind, believable, unbearable)."
    (50)

12. Add periods as needed: I Washington D C
(47, 50)   A The White House
                                          B The Capitol Building

Circle each letter that should be capitalized in 13 and 14.

13. nolan asked, "may i borrow your book about georgia?"
(26)

14. dear gavin,
(38, 41)
        your grandfather owned land in the midwest and in the south.
            love,
            aunt bessie

15. Circle the linking verb in the sentence below.
(31)

That Georgia peach smells so sweet!

16. Circle each coordinating conjunction in the sentence below.
(48)

He toured the White House and the Capitol Building, but she went to the Smithsonian Museum.

17. Circle the misspelled word in the list below.
(33-35)

believe, nieghbor, weigh, niece

18. Circle each adjective in the sentence below.
(39, 40)

Two sleepy alligators lie in the hot sun.

19. Complete the four principal parts of the verb *cry*.
(19)

<u>cry</u>   <u>(is)   </u>   <u>   </u>   <u>(has)   </u>
(1) present tense   (2) present participle   (3) past tense   (4) past participle

20. Add suffixes. (2 points for each correct answer)
(33, 34)

(a) trap + ed _____   (b) cloudy + er _____

21. In the sentence below, underline each prepositional phrase, circling the object of each preposition.
(44)

Lucas looks down the basketball court and sprints to the basket.

22. Circle the proper adjective in the sentence below.
(42)

Does Fido like Swiss cheese?

23. Circle the indirect object in the sentence below.
(46)

The benevolent couple gave stray dogs food and shelter.

On the lines provided, diagram each word of sentences 24 and 25.

24. Did the man at the piano play classical music?
(40, 45)

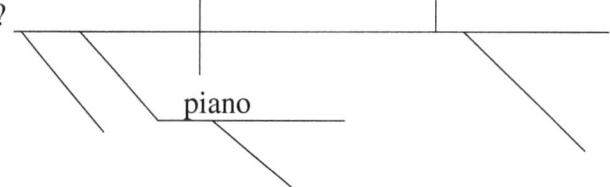

25. Joe and Moe repair and polish old bikes.
(40, 49)

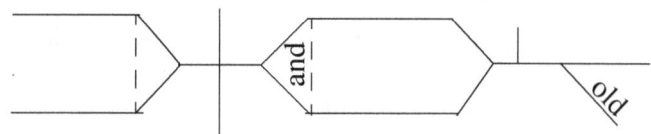

Test 11 READ CAREFULLY Name: _____

Give after Lesson 60.

Circle the correct word(s) to complete sentences 1–10.

1. Of the two buildings, this one is (taller, tallest).
(55)

2. Terry (have, has) two brothers.
(18)

3. She closed the window and (locks, locked) the door.
(10)

4. The word group below is a (phrase, clause).
(36)
                if you see an alligator with an open mouth

5. The following is a (sentence fragment, run-on sentence, complete sentence):
(5)
                Duke Ellington, the man at the piano.

6. The word *the* is a(n) (noun, verb, adjective, preposition).
(40)

7. The noun *optimism* is (abstract, concrete).
(11)

8. The noun *alligator's* is (plural, possessive).
(13)

9. The verb (*honk, clap, sound*) is a common linking verb.
(31)

10. Students try hard. A student (trys, tries) hard.
(9)

11. For a–d, circle the correct definition. (1 point for each correct answer)

    (a) (Bovine, Canine, Feline) relates to dogs.
    (51)

    (b) (Bovine, Canine, Equine) relates to cows.
    (52)

    (c) Auditory relates to the sense of (smell, hearing, touch).
    (53)

    (d) Gentility is (malice, courtesy, greed).
    (55)

12. Add periods as needed in the sentence below.
(47, 50)
                Mr Brite wrote, "The First Ave market will be closed Tues this week"

Circle each letter that should be capitalized in 13 and 14.

13. mimi said, "some crops in the south are harvested in spring."
(26)

14. dear alsumana,
(38, 41)
        do you have rollercoasters in papua, new guinea? i like fast and twisty ones.
            your friend,
            elisa

15. Circle the predicate nominative in the sentence below.
(51)

Mrs. Cruz is a prudent attorney.

16. Circle each coordinating conjunction in the sentence below.
(48)

Ian and Rosa are visiting North or South Carolina, but their home is in Florida.

17. Circle the misspelled word in the list below.
(33-35)

beleive, neighbor, weigh, niece

18. Circle each adjective in the sentence below.
(39, 40)

Four fuzzy rabbits hide inside a hollow log.

19. Complete the four principal parts of the verb *trap*.
(19)

trap	*(is)* _____	_____	*(has)* _____
(1) present tense	(2) present participle	(3) past tense	(4) past participle

20. Add suffixes. (2 points for each correct answer)
(33, 34)

(a) cry + ed _____   (b) happy + est _____

21. In the sentence below, underline each prepositional phrase, circling the object of each preposition.
(44)

A dog with a rhinestone collar leaps into the car.

22. Circle the proper adjective in the sentence below.
(42)

Juicy California oranges make a good snack.

23. Circle the indirect object in the sentence below.
(46)

Hnin passed Borden the baton.

On the lines provided, diagram each word of sentences 24 and 25.

24. The man at the piano is my brother.
(45, 51)

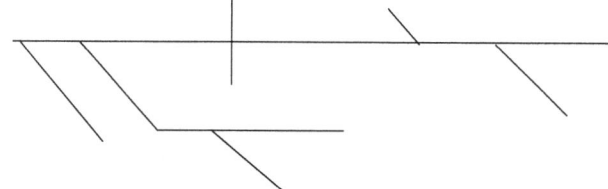

25. Joe and Moe wash and wax their car.
(40, 49)

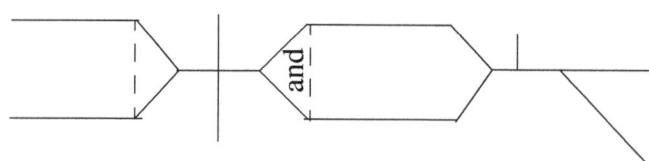

Test 12   READ CAREFULLY   Name: _____

Give after Lesson 65.

Circle the correct word(s) to complete sentences 1–10.

1. Of the two computers, this one is (better, best).
(56)

2. We (was, were) friends.
(18)

3. Yesterday he (fry, fries, fried) potatoes.
(10)

4. The word group below is a (phrase, clause).
(36)
                         instead of the movie about pirates

5. The following is a (sentence fragment, run-on sentence, complete sentence):
(23, 24)
                         The truck swerved it hit a curb.

6. A(n) (declarative, interrogative, imperative, exclamatory) sentence asks a question.
(2)

7. The noun *elephant* is (abstract, concrete).
(11)

8. I have two (sister-in-laws, sisters-in-law).
(13, 16)

9. The verb (*touch, grab, feel*) is a common linking verb.
(31)

10. Bees buzz. A bee (buzzs, buzzes).
(9)

11. For a–d, circle the correct definition. (1 point for each correct answer)

     (a) (*Intangible, Superfluous, Malicious*) means "more than needed or desired."
       (58)

     (b) (*Opportune, Inopportune, Indolent*) means "suitable; well-timed."
       (60)

     (c) *Indolent* means "(lazy, generous, hard-working)."
       (56)

     (d) To illuminate is to give (food, money, light) to.
       (59)

12. Add periods as needed in the sentence below.
(47, 50)
                         Mrs Lynch's note reads, "Buy two lbs of apples at the Main St market"

Circle each letter that should be capitalized in 13 and 14.

13. ms. hoo said, "some states in the east are humid in summer."
(26)

14. dear rafael,
(38, 41)
         are there alligators in tallahassee, florida? i hope not.
                 your friend,
                 josef

15. Add commas as needed in the sentence below.
(57, 59)

Aunt Sue may I borrow your scissors a pen and some paper?

16. Circle each coordinating conjunction in the sentence below.
(48)

They offered soup or salad, so I chose soup.

17. Circle the misspelled word in the list below.
(33-35)

believe, neighbor, wiegh, niece

18. Circle each adjective in the sentence below.
(39, 40)

An industrious student typed sixteen long pages of notes.

19. Complete the four principal parts of the verb *fry*.
(19)

<u>*fry*</u>   (*is*) _____   _____   (*has*) _____
(1) present tense   (2) present participle   (3) past tense   (4) past participle

20. Add suffixes. (2 points for each correct answer)
(33, 34)

(a) sad + est _____   (b) jolly + er _____

21. In the sentence below, underline each prepositional phrase, circling the object of each preposition.
(44)

A player in left field ducks under the ball.

22. Circle the proper adjective in the sentence below.
(42)

I sliced a shiny red Washington apple.

23. Circle the indirect object in the sentence below.
(46)

Onping bought Kim a lemonade.

On the lines provided, diagram each word of sentences 24 and 25.

24. The girl in the picture is my cousin.
(45, 51)

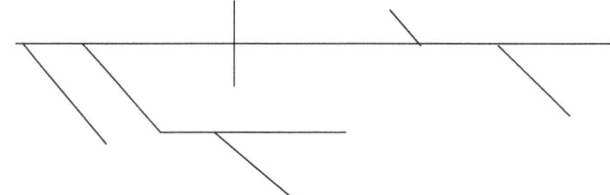

25. Joe and Moe wash and dry their dishes.
(40, 49)

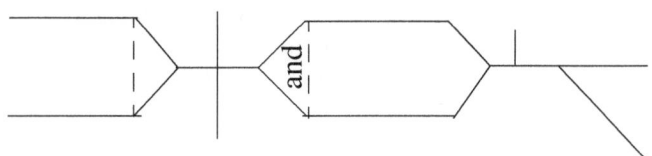

Test 13 READ CAREFULLY Name: _____

Give after Lesson 70.

Circle the correct word(s) to complete sentences 1–10.

1. You made (less, fewer) mistakes than I did.
(56)

2. After the test, we (was, were) elated.
(18)

3. The pronoun *he* is (first, second, third) person.
(64)

4. The word group below is a (phrase, clause).
(36)
                     for they produce breakfast cereal

5. The following is a (sentence fragment, run-on sentence, complete sentence):
(5, 23)
                     Raising hogs in both Indiana and Illinois.

6. The hardy tree (grew, grown) quickly.
(65)

7. The noun *tenacity* is (abstract, concrete).
(11)

8. She has two (brother-in-laws, brothers-in-law).
(13, 16)

9. The verb (*sing, speak, were*) is a common linking verb.
(31)

10. Julia has (wore, worn) out her socks.
(65)

11. For a–d, circle the correct definition. (1 point for each correct answer)

    (a) (Gentility, Intuition, Pessimism) is an instinctive feeling or knowledge.
    (61)

    (b) Cowardice is lack of (food, money, courage).
    (62)

    (c) One who is (tenacious, malicious, indolent) does not give up.
    (63)

    (d) (*Ethical, Unethical, Intrepid*) means "morally right."
    (64)

12. Add periods as needed in the sentence below.
(47, 50)
         Mr Cross paid $199 (one dollar and ninety-nine cents) for four lbs of bananas

13. Circle each letter that should be capitalized in the sentence below.
(42, 43)
         a british musician played the french horn skillfully.

14. For a–d, write the plural of each noun.
(16, 22)
    (a) dish _____   (b) monkey _____

    (c) baby _____   (d) spoonful _____

15. Add commas as needed in the sentence below.

Ms. Hoo I would like you to meet my mother Mrs. Loya.

16. Circle each coordinating conjunction in the sentence below.

I ordered soup and salad, for I was hungry.

17. Circle the misspelled word in the list below.

neighbor, weigh, view, veiw

18. Circle the antecedent of the italicized pronoun in the sentence below.

Leo left *his* skateboard outside.

19. Complete the four principal parts of the verb *wrap*.

wrap	*(is)* _____	_____	*(has)* _____
(1) present tense	(2) present participle	(3) past tense	(4) past participle

20. Add suffixes. (2 points for each correct answer)

(a) give + ing _____   (b) pretty + er _____

21. In the sentence below, underline each prepositional phrase, circling the object of each preposition.

The cheese on the table comes from Wisconsin.

22. Circle the proper adjective in the sentence below.

Please slice some Wisconsin cheese for sandwiches.

23. Circle the indirect object in the sentence below.

He handed me an envelope.

On the lines provided, diagram each word of sentences 24 and 25.

24. The trip was expensive but worthwhile.

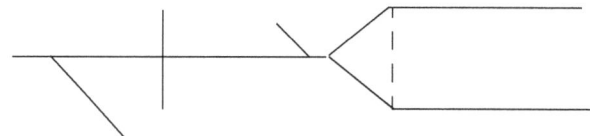

25. The little boat on the lake endured a big storm.

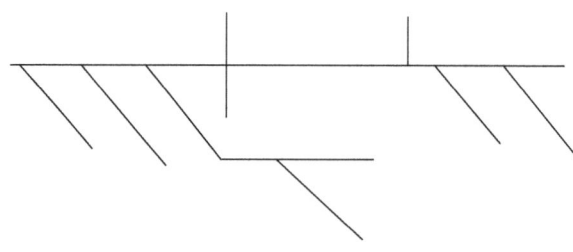

Test 14 READ CAREFULLY Name: _____

Give after Lesson 75.

Circle the correct word(s) to complete sentences 1–10.

1. I have eaten (less, fewer) tacos than she has.
(56)

2. Doreen went to Yosemite with Austin and (I, me).
(70)

3. The pronoun *you* is (first, second, third) person.
(64)

4. The word group below is a (phrase, clause).
(36)
      a locomotive and many passenger cars at the station

5. The following is a (sentence fragment, run-on sentence, complete sentence):
(5, 23)
      The long, lonesome whistle of the steam train.

6. Vintage Shay locomotives have (blow, blew, blown) their whistles for decades.
(65)

7. The comparative form of the adjective *bad* is (*bad, worse, worst*).
(55, 56)

8. The word *brother-in-law's* is a (plural, possessive) noun.
(13)

9. The verb (*seemed, said, whispered*) is a common linking verb.
(31)

10. Julia has (drank, drunk) eight glasses of water today.
(65)

11. For a–d, circle the correct definition. (1 point for each correct answer)

 (a) Ornithology is the study of (weather, rocks, birds).
 (68)

 (b) To feign is to (pretend, listen, travel).
 (69)

 (c) (*Intrepid, Tenacious, Contrite*) means "sorry."
 (66)

 (d) (*Irrelevant, Pertinent, Contrite*) means "relevant or applicable."
 (67)

12. Add periods as needed in the sentence below.
(47, 50)
      At two am Ms Overwork finally finished her essay

13. Circle each letter that should be capitalized in the sentence below.
(42, 43)
      in the east, italian americans settled to begin a new life

14. For a–d, write the plural of each noun.
(16, 22)
 (a) bench _____ (b) donkey _____

 (c) cherry _____ (d) cupful _____

15. Add commas as needed to clarify the sentence below.
₍₆₈₎

With Lucy, Thomas writes well.

16. Circle each coordinating conjunction in the sentence below.
₍₄₈₎

I have no pen or pencil, yet I have plenty of paper.

17. Circle the misspelled word in the list below.
₍₃₃₋₃₅₎

neighbor, weigh, reciept, receipt

18. Circle the antecedent of the italicized pronoun in the sentence below.
₍₆₂₎

Sharon carries *her* heavy backpack for miles.

19. Complete the four principal parts of the verb *grow*.
₍₁₉₎

<u>grow</u>   <u>(is)   </u>   <u>   </u>   <u>(has)   </u>

(1) present tense   (2) present participle   (3) past tense   (4) past participle

20. Add suffixes. (2 points for each correct answer)
_(33, 34)

(a) hope + ing _____ (b) sunny + est _____

21. In the sentence below, underline each prepositional phrase, circling the object of each preposition.
₍₄₄₎

The train at the station will soon leave for Chicago.

22. Circle the proper adjective in the sentence below.
₍₄₂₎

How many Georgia peaches are in this pie?

23. Circle the indirect object in the sentence below.
_(46, 69)

The ranger gave us a tour of the area.

On the lines provided, diagram each word of sentences 24 and 25.

24. Your brother seems tenacious and ethical.
_(49, 54)

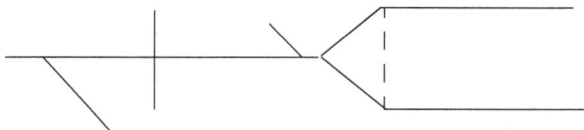

25. The rabbit in the garden ate two ripe melons.
_(40, 45)

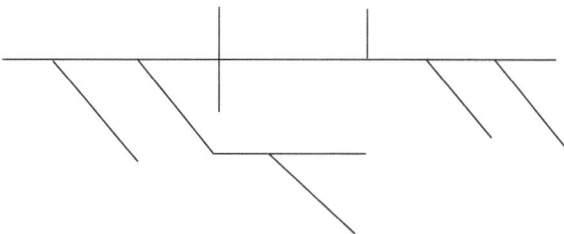

Test 15 NAME: _____
Give after Lesson 80. **READ CAREFULLY**

Circle the correct word(s) to complete sentences 1–10.

1. Anita is the (better, best) of the two guitarists.

2. The geology experts were Rocky and (her, she).

3. The pronoun *we* is (first, second, third) person.

4. The clause below is (dependent, independent).

    when minerals form around geyser vents

5. The following is a (sentence fragment, run-on sentence, complete sentence):

    The geyser is quiet it will erupt soon.

6. The ship (sink, sank, sunk) long ago.

7. The superlative form of the adjective *bad* is (*bad, worse, worst*).

8. The sentence below is (simple, compound).

    The geyser blew, and I ran for cover!

9. The verb (*looks, says, sings*) is a common linking verb.

10. Norm has (break, broke, broken) his arm again.

11. For a–d, circle the correct definition. (1 point for each correct answer)

    (a) (*Serene, Ethical, Ardent*) means "passionate and zealous."

    (b) *Serene* means "(angry, troubled, peaceful)."

    (c) Sagacity is (wisdom, sorrow, trouble).

    (d) (Redundancy, Linguistics, Serenity) is needless repetition.

12. Add periods as needed in the sentence below.

    Mrs Starlyn saw the geyser's six pm eruption

13. Circle each letter that should be capitalized in the sentence below.

    can i buy italian suasage in new york?

14. For a–d, write the plural of each noun.

    (a) lunch _____   (b) key _____

    (c) berry _____   (d) handful _____

15. Add commas as needed in the sentence below.

When Old Faithful erupts I shall take pictures of it.

16. Circle the coordinating conjunction in the compound sentence below.

We have been watching, but the geyser has not blown.

17. Circle the misspelled word in the list below.

neighbor, weigh, piece, peice

18. Circle the antecedent of the italicized pronoun in the sentence below.

Although *he* has studied geology, Clark cannot explain everything.

19. Complete the four principal parts of the verb *freeze*.

<u>freeze</u>   (is)_____   _____   (has)_____
(1) present tense   (2) present participle   (3) past tense   (4) past participle

20. Add suffixes. (2 points for each correct answer)

(a) snap + ed _____   (b) argue + ment _____

21. In the sentence below, underline each prepositional phrase, circling the object of each preposition.

A man with an umbrella stood beside me.

22. Circle the predicate nominative in the sentence below.

Old Faithful is a magnificent geyser!

23. Circle the indirect object in the sentence below.

Alberto handed Quan a photo.

On the lines provided, diagram each word of sentences 24 and 25.

24. The eruption was sudden and spectacular.

25. The man with the umbrella has two children.

Test 16 READ CAREFULLY Name: _____

Give after Lesson 85.

Circle the correct word(s) to complete sentences 1–10.

1. Of the two kittens, that one is (fuzzier, fuzziest).
(56)

2. You know more than (me, I) about prairie dogs.
(78)

3. The pronoun *him* is (nominative, objective, possessive) case.
(66, 69)

4. The clause below is (dependent, independent).
(73)
　　　　　　　　coyotes threaten the prairie dog colony

5. The following is a (sentence fragment, run-on sentence, complete sentence):
(5, 23)
　　　　　　　　Burrowing to escape the golden eagle.

6. A prairie dog hides in (it's, its) burrow.
(72)

7. A coyote snarls at Rocky and (he, him).
(69, 70)

8. The sentence below is (simple, compound).
(75)
　　　　　　　　The prairie dog stopped and looked at me.

9. The man (who, which) counts prairie dogs rides a horse.
(77)

10. Norm has (tear, tore, torn) his shirt again.
(65)

11. For a–d, circle the correct definition. (1 point for each correct answer)

　　(a) (*Dauntless, Quaint, Ardent*) means "attractive in an old-fashioned way."
　　(76)

　　(b) To ameliorate is to (destroy, improve, harm).
　　(77)

　　(c) *Dauntless* means "(afraid, heroic, weak)."
　　(79)

　　(d) (Redundancy, Salinity, Serenity) is saltiness.
　　(78)

12. Add periods as needed in the sentence below.
(47, 50)
　　　　Cherries cost $299 (two dollars and ninety-nine cents) per lb, so I bought only eight oz today

13. Circle each letter that should be capitalized in the sentence below.
(42, 43)
　　　　　　　　can i purchase alaskan crab in maine?

14. For a–d, write the plural of each noun.
(16, 22)
　　(a) bunch _____　　　　(b) toy _____

　　(c) colony _____　　　　(d) mouthful _____

Grammar and Writing 5　　　　　　　　　　　　　　　　　　　　　　　Teacher Guide
　　　　　　　　　　　　　　　　　　　　　　　　　　　　　　　　　　Tests

15. Add commas and quotation marks as needed in the sentence below.
(76, 80)

After lunch said Ms. Hoo we shall discuss the Utah prairie dog.

16. Circle the coordinating conjunction in the compound sentence below.
(75)

Some prairie dogs are hiding, for hawks are circling above.

17. Circle the subordinating conjunction in the sentence below.
(73)

Because prairie dogs are social animals, they live together in large colonies.

18. Circle the antecedent of the italicized pronoun in the sentence below.
(62)

Mimi likes prairie dogs because *they* are cute.

19. Complete the four principal parts of the verb *steal*.
(65)

<u>steal</u>	(is) _____	_____	(has) _____
(1) present tense	(2) present participle	(3) past tense	(4) past participle

20. Add suffixes. (2 points for each correct answer)
(33, 34)

(a) win + er _____ (b) salty + ness _____

21. Circle the interrogative pronoun in the sentence below.
(79)

Which shall we study first?

22. Circle the predicate nominative in the sentence below.
(51)

The Utah prairie dog is an endangered species.

23. Circle the indirect object in the sentence below.
(46, 69)

Elle made Daisy a taco.

On the lines provided, diagram each word of sentences 24 and 25.

24. Prairie dogs are rodents with short tails.
(45, 51)

25. Max is listening, but Perlina is napping.
(75)

Grammar and Writing 5   222   Teacher Guide
Tests

Test 17 READ CAREFULLY Name: _____

Give after Lesson 90.

Circle the correct word(s) to complete sentences 1–10.

1. That planet is the (bigger, biggest) of the two.
(56)

2. I am shorter than (he, him).
(78)

3. The pronoun *his* is (nominative, objective, possessive) case.
(70, 72)

4. The clause below is (dependent, independent).
(73)

   since the moon is full tonight

5. One of the students (give, gives) (their, his or her) report each morning.
(83)

6. (Your, You're) car is fast, but (ours, our's) is faster.
(72)

7. A bear watches Grace and (she, her).
(69, 70)

8. The sentence below is (simple, compound).
(75)

   The sky is cloudy, so I cannot see the stars.

9. The woman (who, which) owns the telescope can identify many stars.
(77)

10. (Them, Those) photographs show the solar eclipse.
(82)

11. For a–d, circle the correct definition. (1 point for each correct answer)

    (a) A (docent, curator, culprit) is a guilty one.
    (81)

    (b) Bliss is great (sorrow, happiness, pain).
    (82)

    (c) (Subversion, Rapport, Rapprochement) is destruction.
    (83)

    (d) (Subversion, Rapport, Quaintness) is harmony in a relationship.
    (84)

12. Add periods as needed in the sentence below.
(47, 50)

    Mrs Vega lives on S First St in Denver

13. Circle each letter that should be capitalized in the sentence below.
(42, 43)

    will i find washington apples in florida?

14. For a–d, write the plural of each noun.
(16, 22)

    (a) branch _____   (b) day _____

    (c) company _____   (d) child _____

15. Add commas and quotation marks as needed in the sentence below.
(76, 80)

        Next week said Ms. Hoo we shall view a solar eclipse.

16. Circle the coordinating conjunction in the compound sentence below.
(75)

        The moon is a cold, rocky body, and it has no light of its own.

17. Circle the subordinating conjunction in the sentence below.
(73)

        The moon appears luminous because sunlight reflects from the moon's surface.

18. Circle the antecedent of the italicized pronoun in the sentence below.
(62)

        Tex gazed at the moon until clouds covered *it*.

19. Complete the four principal parts of the verb *catch*.
(85)

    <u>catch</u>   <u>(is)   </u>   <u>   </u>   <u>(has)   </u>

    (1) present tense   (2) present participle   (3) past tense   (4) past participle

20. Add suffixes. (2 points for each correct answer)
(33, 34)

    (a) begin + er _____   (b) happy + ness _____

21. Underline the words that should be italicized in the sentence below.
(84)

        Someday I shall read Melville's novel, Moby Dick.

22. Circle the predicate nominative in the sentence below.
(51)

        That solar eclipse was an awesome spectacle.

23. Circle the indirect object in the sentence below.
(46, 69)

        Did Fido leave her any dog food?

On the lines provided, diagram each word of sentences 24 and 25.

24. Is Saturn the planet with rings?
(45, 51)

25. Cora and she sew their own clothes.
(40, 71)

Grammar and Writing 5   Teacher Guide
Tests

Test 18 READ CAREFULLY Name: _____

Give after Lesson 95.

Circle the correct word(s) to complete sentences 1–10.

1. That cave is the (bigger, biggest) of all!
(56)

2. Are you as courageous as (me, I)?
(78)

3. The pronoun *she* is (nominative, objective, possessive) case.
(70, 72)

4. The clause below is (dependent, independent).
(73)
        stalactites and stalagmites decorate the caverns

5. Each of the bats (flap, flaps) (their, its) wings.
(83)

6. (They're, Their, There) lawn is greener than (her's, hers).
(72)

7. This vase of flowers (need, needs) water.
(90)

8. The sentence below is (simple, compound).
(75)
        Inside the dark cave, bats sleep during the daytime.

9. The people (who, which) entered the cave have not come out!
(77)

10. Neither the flowers nor the lawn (have, has) been watered.
(89)

11. For a–d, circle the correct definition. (1 point for each correct answer)

    (a) *Colossal* means "extremely (small, skinny, large)."
    (86)

    (b) To (languish, daunt, coerce) is to force.
    (87)

    (c) (*Colossal, Complacent, Languid*) means "content; self-satisfied."
    (88)

    (d) To (languish, daunt, coerce) is to grow weak.
    (89)

12. Add periods as needed in the sentence below.
(47, 50)
        That library in St George opens at nine am on Saturdays

13. Circle each letter that should be capitalized in the sentence below.
(42, 43)
        can we buy wisconsin cheese in new mexico?

14. For a–d, write the plural of each noun.
(16, 22)

    (a) bush _____   (b) valley _____

    (c) country _____   (d) loaf _____

15. Add punctuation marks as needed in the sentence below.
(80, 88)

In what state are the Carlsbad Caverns asked Ernesto

16. Circle the coordinating conjunction in the compound sentence below.
(75)

The cave is dark, but I have a flashlight.

17. Circle the subordinating conjunction in the sentence below.
(73)

Since the underground chambers are accessible, many tourists visit Carlsbad Caverns.

18. Circle the antecedent of the italicized pronoun in the sentence below.
(62)

The bat hangs by *its* toes and thumbs from the cave's ceiling.

19. Complete the four principal parts of the verb *swim*.
(87)

<u>swim</u>   <u>(is)   </u>   <u>   </u>   <u>(has)   </u>

(1) present tense (2) present participle (3) past tense (4) past participle

20. Add suffixes. (2 points for each correct answer)
(33, 34)

(a) scare + y _____ (b) run + er _____

21. Underline the word that should be italicized in the sentence below.
(84)

Chiroptera is the scientific name for bat.

22. Circle the predicate nominative in the sentence below.
(51)

The bat is a mammal.

23. Circle the indirect object in the sentence below.
(46, 69)

I mailed them a postcard from New Mexico.

On the lines provided, diagram each word of sentences 24 and 25.

24. Is this cave a home for bats?
(45, 51)

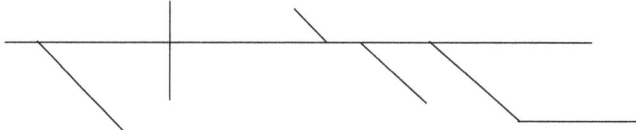

25. Huey and Lucy gave me a box of pencils.
(40, 71)

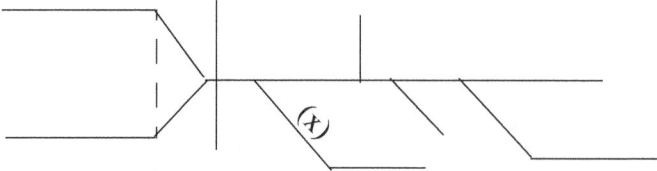

Test 19 READ CAREFULLY Name: _____

Give after Lesson 100.

Circle the correct word(s) to complete sentences 1–10.

1. I don't have (no, any) homework today.
(93)

2. We have less homework than (they, them).
(78)

3. The pronoun *them* is (nominative, objective, possessive) case.
(70, 72)

4. The clause below is (dependent, independent).
(73)

        while they were imprisoned on Alcatraz Island

5. One of the ships (has, have) sunk.
(91)

6. (It's, Its) hunting for (it's, its) prey.
(72)

7. This box of pencils (is, are) mine.
(90)

8. The sentence below is (simple, compound).
(75)

        The ship sank, so we took a helicopter.

9. (Them, Those) ruins must be the old prison.
(82)

10. Either the horses or the cow (eat, eats) that hay.
(89)

11. For a–d, circle the correct definition. (1 point for each correct answer)

    (a) *Paltry* means "(significant, insignificant, huge)."
(95)

    (b) To (ostracize, languish, coerce) is to exclude from a group.
(94)

    (c) *Concise* means "(long, wordy, brief)."
(92)

    (d) Obfuscation is (confusion, truth, force).
(91)

12. Add periods as needed in the sentence below.
(47, 50)

        Dr Parden, DDS, examined my teeth

13. Circle each letter that should be capitalized in the sentence below.
(42, 43)

        alcatraz island lies in the middle of san francisco bay.

14. For a–d, write the plural of each noun.
(16, 22)

    (a) ranch _____   (b) bay _____

    (c) city _____   (d) leaf _____

15. Add punctuation marks as needed in the sentence below.
(88, 94)

How did thirty four prisoners escape asked Amelia

16. Circle the coordinating conjunction in the compound sentence below.
(75)

We must hurry, for the sun is setting.

17. Circle the subordinating conjunction in the sentence below.
(73)

Although the island is small, it held many dangerous prisoners.

18. Add quotation marks as needed in the sentence below.
(81)

When I was a child, I sang London Bridge Is Falling Down.

19. Complete the four principal parts of the verb *write*.
(87)

write   *(is)* _____   _____   *(has)* _____

(1) present tense   (2) present participle   (3) past tense   (4) past participle

20. Add suffixes. (2 points for each correct answer)
(33, 34)

(a) beauty + ful _____   (b) smile + ing _____

21. Underline the words that should be italicized in the sentence below.
(84)

The artist George Henry Broughton painted Pilgrims Going to Church.

22. Circle the adverb in the sentence below.
(95)

The painter worked tirelessly.

23. Circle the interrogative pronoun in the sentence below.
(79)

Who lived on Alcatraz Island before the prison was built?

On the lines provided, diagram each word of sentences 24 and 25.

24. Is this island an attraction for tourists?
(45, 51)

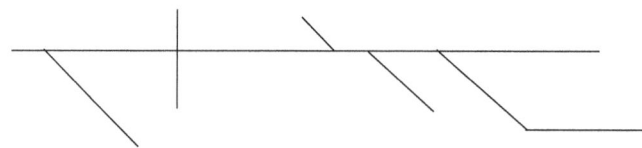

25. Can Joe or Moe pour me a cup of milk?
(40, 71)

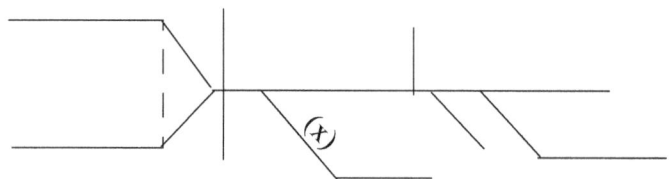

Test 20 READ CAREFULLY Name: _____

Give after Lesson 105.

Circle the correct word(s) to complete sentences 1–10.

1. Polly doesn't want (no, any) crackers.
(93)

2. Kyle is as sagacious as (him, he).
(78)

3. Lucy skates (good, well).
(96)

4. The clause below is (dependent, independent).
(73)

   they live in the desert

5. One of the peacocks (has, have) flown away.
(91)

6. Ms. Hoo and (us, we) shall visit the art museum.
(66)

7. The lens on this camera (is, are) dirty.
(92)

8. The sentence below is (simple, compound).
(75)

   A peacock flew over the fence and landed on our car.

9. (Them, Those) canyons have rocky cliffs.
(82)

10. Neither the peacocks nor the goose (want, wants) my sandwich.
(89)

11. For a–d, circle the correct definition. (1 point for each correct answer)

    (a) (Profusion, Perjury, Propriety) is lying under oath.
    (96)

    (b) (Profusion, Propriety, Plagiarism) is idea theft.
    (97)

    (c) *Profuse* means "(scarce, abundant, insignificant)."
    (98)

    (d) A prologue comes at the (beginning, middle, end).
    (99)

12. Add periods as needed in the sentence below.
(47, 50)

    Dr Jacob B Adan rushed to St Vincent Hospital

13. Circle each letter that should be capitalized in the sentence below.
(42, 43)

    catalina island lies off the coast of southern california.

14. For a–d, write the plural of each noun.
(16, 22)

    (a) patch _____   (b) Tuesday _____

    (c) county _____   (d) knife _____

15. Add punctuation marks as needed in the sentence below.
(88, 94)

        Ms Hoo have you read my essay asked Perlina

16. Circle the coordinating conjunction in the compound sentence below.
(75)

        The sun has set, yet the air remains warm.

17. Add a hyphen as needed in the sentence below.
(97)

        We cyclists are looking forward to our fifty mile ride.

18. Add quotation marks as needed in the sentence below.
(81)

        Is the nursery rhyme Humpty Dumpty about an egg?

19. Complete the four principal parts of the verb *eat*.
(87)

eat	(is) _____	_____	(has) _____
(1) present tense	(2) present participle	(3) past tense	(4) past participle

20. Circle the word below that is divided correctly.
(99)

        un-known   unkno-wn   unkn-own

21. Underline the words that should be italicized in the sentence below.
(84)

        Crotalus atrox and Crotalus ruber are types of rattlesnakes.

22. Circle the adverb in the sentence below.
(98)

        Careless painters dripped blue and yellow paint everywhere.

23. Circle the interrogative pronoun in the sentence below.
(79)

        What is your favorite sport?

On the lines provided, diagram each word of sentences 24 and 25.

24. Is Jill the girl with long hair?
(45, 51)

25. Joe politely offers Moe one of his mints.
(40, 71)

Test 21   READ CAREFULLY   Name: _____

Give after Lesson 110.

Circle the correct word(s) to complete sentences 1–10.

1. Polly doesn't want (nothing, anything) to eat.
(93)

2. Mr. Cuxil, (who, whom) teaches English, also coaches basketball.
(77)

3. Juan plays chess (good, well).
(96)

4. The clause below is (dependent, independent).
(73)

                until the cows come home

5. Each of the artists (have, has) (their, his or her) own style.
(91)

6. Please come with Daisy and (I, me).
(66, 69)

7. (Is, Are) your scissors sharp?
(92)

8. The sentence below is (simple, compound).
(75)

                The pianist played well, but the singer's voice was flat.

9. The Grand Canyon is (sure, surely) beautiful.
(104)

10. Of the two hikers, Jill climbs the hill (faster, fastest).
(102)

11. For a–d, circle the correct definition. (1 point for each correct answer)

    (a) An (anarchy, enigma, estuary) is a riddle or mystery.
    (101)

    (b) *Candid* means "(honest, dishonest, unethical)."
    (102)

    (c) *Parsimonious* means "(stingy, generous, extravagant)."
    (104)

    (d) To (consecrate, desecrate, ameliorate) is to destroy.
    (105)

12. Add periods as needed in the sentence below.
(47, 50)

                Ms Hoo left at two pm on the last day of school

13. Circle each letter that should be capitalized in the sentence below.
(42, 43)

                the colorado river has carved the magnificent grand canyon in arizona.

14. For a–d, write the plural of each noun.
(16, 22)

    (a) coach _____   (b) library _____

    (c) gallon of milk _____   (d) mouse _____

15. Add punctuation marks as needed in the sentence below.
(94, 97)

   Do the sweet smelling flowers attract bees asks Andrew

16. Add a semicolon as needed in the sentence below.
(103)

   Adventuresome folk can stay at Phantom Ranch in Grand Canyon however, it is only accessible by foot or mule.

17. Add a colon as needed in the sentence below.
(105)

   The supply list includes these items tent, sleeping bag, lantern, and canteen.

18. Add quotation marks as needed in the sentence below.
(81)

   Luis wrote a poem titled A Parsimonious Monarch.

19. Complete the four principal parts of the verb *forgive*.
(87)

   <u>forgive</u>   <u>(is)   </u>   <u>   </u>   <u>(has)   </u>
   (1) present tense   (2) present participle   (3) past tense   (4) past participle

20. Circle the appositive phrase in the sentence below.
(58)

   Amy baked a healthful snack, whole-grain muffins with raisins.

21. Underline the word that should be italicized in the sentence below.
(84)

   I think that sentence contains a superfluous and.

22. Circle the adverb in the sentence below.
(100)

   The forces of erosion are constantly changing the Grand Canyon's appearance.

23. Circle the subordinating conjunction in the sentence below.
(73, 74)

   I shall hike up that mountain even though I am weary.

In the boxes provided, diagram each word of sentences 24 and 25.

24. Is the orca the whale with the triangular fin?
(45, 51)

25. Has the whale swum away?
(98)

Test 22 　　　　　READ CAREFULLY　　　　　Name: _____

Give after Lesson 112.

Circle the correct word(s) to complete sentences 1–10.

1. There wasn't (anybody, nobody) home.
(93)

2. Mr. Cuxil, (who, whom) we chose as our leader, has taught me valuable lessons.
(77)

3. Yesterday I was ill, but today I feel (good, well).
(96)

4. The clause below is (dependent, independent).
(73)
　　　　　　　　armadillos usually live alone

5. Each of the hikers (carry, carries) (their, his or her) own food and water.
(91)

6. Please tell Elle and (I, me) your secret.
(66, 69)

7. Mumps (is, are) a miserable disease.
(92)

8. The sentence below is (compound, complex, compound-complex).
(75, 110)
　　　　　When my dog eats too much, his eyes bulge, and his stomach protrudes.

9. Josie was (real, really) frightened when she encountered a black bear.
(104)

10. (Between, Among) the many icebergs swam penguins and polar bears.
(107)

11. For a–d, circle the correct definition. (1 point for each correct answer)

　(a) To (consecrate, ameliorate, beguile) is to mislead or deceive.
　(106)

　(b) To (beguile, digress, consecrate) is to depart from the main subject.
　(107)

　(c) *Futile* means "(hopeless, effective, hopeful)."
　(108)

　(d) (Dissension, Apathy, Digression) is lack of interest or concern.
　(110)

12. Add periods as needed in the sentence below.
(47, 50)
　　　　　　　Mr Cabrera wakes at six am to exercise

13. Circle each letter that should be capitalized in the sentence below.
(42, 43)
　　　　　can you drive from olympia, washington, to juneau, alaska?

14. For a–d, write the plural of each noun.
(16, 22)
　(a) toothbrush _____　　(b) dictionary _____

　(c) class president _____　(d) tooth _____

15. Add punctuation marks as needed in the sentence below.

Are the grizzlies hibernating asks Amelia

16. Add a semicolon and a comma as needed in the sentence below.

Most states have few grizzly bears however Alaska has many.

17. Add a colon as needed in the sentence below.

I remember one fact about grizzlies they are dangerous.

18. Add apostrophes as needed in the sentence below.

That plumbers license wasnt valid, for it dated back to the year 73.

19. Complete the four principal parts of the verb *weave*.

<u>weave</u>	<u>(is)_____</u>	<u>_____</u>	<u>(has)_____</u>
(1) present tense	(2) present participle	(3) past tense	(4) past participle

20. Circle the indirect object in the sentence below.

Elle offered us a healthful snack of nuts and fruit.

21. Underline the word that should be italicized in the sentence below.

Squash can be either a noun or a verb.

22. Circle the adverb in the sentence below.

Two black bears are happily feasting on wild berries.

23. Circle the subordinating conjunction in the sentence below.

My dog barks whenever she sees a bear.

In the boxes provided, diagram each word of sentences 24 and 25.

24. Is Fifi the poodle with the red collar?

25. Grizzlies can run incredibly fast.

www.ingramcontent.com/pod-product-compliance
Lightning Source LLC
Chambersburg PA
CBHW060455300426
44113CB00016B/2597